THE EMERGENCE OF
CHRISTIANITY

"Cynthia White has written a concise, dynamic, and powerful introduction to early Christianity, bringing both experienced and inexperienced readers to new reflections and new questions about Christian origins. White addresses all the major questions of early Christian development in thoughtful ways. The book itself concludes boldly by opening the door to the future—glimpses of the meeting between Islam and Christianity, medieval Christianity, Reformation and Counter-Reformation, and the church in the modern world, all taking their context from Christianity's formative experience."

FRANK ROMER
Professor of Greek and Latin
East Carolina University

D1568360

THE EMERGENCE OF
CHRISTIANITY

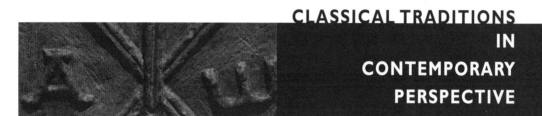

CLASSICAL TRADITIONS
IN
CONTEMPORARY
PERSPECTIVE

CYNTHIA WHITE

Fortress Press
Minneapolis

THE EMERGENCE OF CHRISTIANITY
Classical Traditions in Contemporary Perspective

Textbook adaptation and features copyright © 2011 Fortress Press. Published under license from Greenwood, an imprint of ABC-CLIO, LLC, Santa Barbara, Calif. Text copyright © 2007 by Cynthia White. All rights reserved. Except for brief quotations in critical articles or reviews, no part of this book may be reproduced in any manner without prior written permission from the publisher. Visit http://www.augsburgfortress.org/copyrights/contact.asp or write to Permissions, Augsburg Fortress, Box 1209, Minneapolis, MN 55440.

Cover image: Christ Pantocrator, from the Deesis mosaic, Byzantine, (12th century) / Haghia Sophia, Istanbul, Turkey / Bildarchiv Steffens / The Bridgeman Art Library
Cover design: Laurie Ingram
Book design: James Korsmo

Library of Congress Cataloging-in-Publication Data
White, Cynthia.
  The emergence of Christianity : classical traditions in contemporary perspective / Cynthia White.
      p. cm.
  Originally published: Westport, Conn. : Greenwood Press, 2007.
  Includes bibliographical references and index.
  ISBN 978-0-8006-9747-1 (alk. paper)
  1. Church history—Primitive and early church, ca. 30-600. I. Title.
  BR162.3.W487 2011
  270.1-—dc22
                        2010027463

The paper used in this publication meets the minimum requirements of American National Standard for Information Sciences—Permanence of Paper for Printed Library Materials, ANSI Z329.48-1984.

Manufactured in the U.S.A.

15   14   13   12   11   1   2   3   4   5   6   7   8   9   10

CONTENTS

Figures

Personalities in Christianity

From an Ancient Text

Tables

Every thing is full of God. Whatever men worship, it can be fairly called one and the same. We all look up to the same stars; the same heaven is above us all; the same universe surrounds every one of us. What does it matter by what system of knowledge each one of us seeks the truth? It is not by one single path that we attain to so great a secret.

—Symmachus, *Relationes* 3.5–10

The words of the Roman senator Quintus Aurelius Symmachus quoted above were written to represent the view of a group of Roman aristocrats at the removal of the altar of Victory from the *Curia*, the Roman senate house, in the late fourth century C.E. The altar had been in the *Curia* since Augustus's victory over Mark Antony and Cleopatra at the Battle of Actium in 31 B.C.E. Its religious significance grew over centuries: it was the senators' central altar of worship, where they vowed allegiance to the emperor and offered prayers for the state's prosperity; and it was a symbol of Rome's imperial glory and the gods who secured that glory. When it was removed from the *Curia* under the emperor Gratian in 382 C.E., a delegation from the senate appealed to him for its restoration. Gratian, however,

under the influence of Bishop Ambrose of Milan, refused even to receive the senatorial delegation.

Yet, the position of Symmachus and the Roman senators was one of an old, established, and revered religious polytheism. In the ancient Mediterranean world, religion was a panoply of creeds, gods, goddesses, cults, and rituals that served different worshippers on different occasions. Indeed, Symmachus and his fellow Roman aristocrats of the fourth century, along with most non-Christians and non-Jews, held that a wise man might follow any number of private devotions in addition to the worship of the gods of the state and the emperor himself. They were willing to accept the Christian God into that pantheon; but the Christians could not agree to worship the gods of the state and the Roman emperor. According to the pagan view, it was only when the entire community properly worshipped the gods that the state could expect divine favor, called the *pax deorum,* or "peace of the gods." Thus, Christians risked inciting the anger of the gods against the Roman state by their stubborn refusal to sacrifice. This was the position of the emperors in the first through the early fourth centuries who insisted upon general sacrifices to the gods by all citizens, and who called for the persecution of those who did not comply.

Early Christians believed exclusively in Jesus whom they considered the long-awaited Messiah, "anointed of God," a Hebrew word translated into Greek as *Christos* and into English as "Christ." For Christians, to participate in the public sacrifices demanded by emperor worship or by the state religion was apostasy. In his famous exchange of letters with the emperor Trajan, Pliny the Younger, the Roman governor of Bithynia, wondered whether he could punish the Christians for their pertinacity and inflexible obstinacy, apart from any crimes they had committed. This fundamentally different view of religion—the one, of tolerance for a multitude of deities, and the other, a monotheistic and singular view of salvation through the worship of Jesus—fairly sets out the conflict between Christians and non-Christians.

This book treats the evolution of that conflict in five essays from the perspective of a classicist with particular scholarly interests in the topography of Rome during its third- and fourth-century transformation from a classical into a Christian society. Thus, these chapters are not studies one would find in the work of a theologian or a New Testament scholar, but of someone with a literary (Greek and Latin, but not Hebrew or Aramaic) and Roman bias. Chapter 1 is an historical overview of the Jewish background of Christianity as it expands from a mere footnote in the Roman writers of the first century C.E. to the widespread religion of the imperial court by the fourth century C.E.

Chapter 2 details Jewish-Christian encounters under the Herods, the dynasty of kings who ruled the Jewish state of Judea and the larger surrounding area of Palestine at the discretion of the Roman emperors. This essay includes a short history of the life and ministry of Jesus of Nazareth, the Galilean Jew who led the splinter sect of Judaism that inspired the Christian movement. Chapter 3 examines Diocletian's reforms, his persecution of Christians, and the Christian monotheism adopted by Constantine at the battle of the Milvian Bridge in 312 C.E. Chapters 4 and 5 treat the church after Constantine's "conversion," when Christian emperors, popes, and pagan Roman senators debated the place of traditional religious practices in Rome. By the time the emperor Theodosius gave legal sanction to Christianity in 391 C.E., Rome was no longer the seat of the ancient imperial empire but the primate see of a new Christian empire.

Features and Illustrations

Throughout the book, the reader will find several features and illustrations that enrich the presentation of the origins of Christianity. These features include: a chronology of significant events which immediately follows this preface; illustrations and maps detailing significant locations and important sculpture, paintings, and other images in the early story of the tradition; textboxes titled *Personalities in Christianity* that provide brief descriptions of a number of important historical figures in the Christian tradition, as well as boxes titled *From an Ancient Text* that excerpt foundational primary sources dealing with the early period of the religion. Additionally, a glossary of selected terms and an extensive bibliography, together with an index for easy reference to specific topics in the text, may be found at the conclusion of the book.

Online resources
www.fortresspress.com/white

Online resources offered to support the use of this book, providing additional resources for both instructors and students. These materials will assist teachers in planning and enhancing their courses, and students will find helpful materials to improve their study and comprehension of the subject.

Acknowledgments

Many colleagues and students in the Department of Classics at the University of Arizona and in its study abroad program in Orvieto, the *Istituto Internazionale di Studi Classici di Orvieto*, have contributed to the completion of this book. Among these, I would especially like to thank the Program Administrator of the *Studi Classici di Orvieto*, Alba Frascarelli, who (magically) secured permissions to visit arcane sites and archives in Italy. Other friends and *collegae optimi*—David Christenson, Catherine Fruhan, Nicholas Horsfall, and Frank Romer—are owed many thanks for the daily exchanges that gratify our shared passion for antiquity, for Rome, for teaching, and for learning.

This study would have been impossible without the companionship of the many family members and colleagues who traveled to Jewish, Christian, and pagan holy places throughout Italy with me. I am especially grateful to my parents, Roy and Loretta Kahn, who explored Rome late in life, with the daring and curiosity of the ever young at heart; my nephews, Tony Kahn and Troy Kukorlo, and my niece, Julie Kahn, spirited traveling companions on our spring tours and during summers in Orvieto; fellow *Italophiles*, Carol Freundlich and Arthur Klein; and Melissa Conway and Mary Ellen O'Laughlin, dear friends and *comites optimae*. My deepest gratitude, however, is reserved for my husband John and our daughter Mary, who have shared with me all the inconsistent charms of *urbs Roma aurea*. My gratitude to them is as impossible to measure as my gratitude for them.

Finally, I acknowledge the debt I owe to my beloved niece, Laura Leigh Wilson, whose tragic death on July 3, 2005, left an emptiness that recast and deepened this study. This book is dedicated to her. *D. M. D. O. M.*

CHRONOLOGY OF SIGNIFICANT EVENTS
IN THE EMERGENCE OF CHRISTIANITY

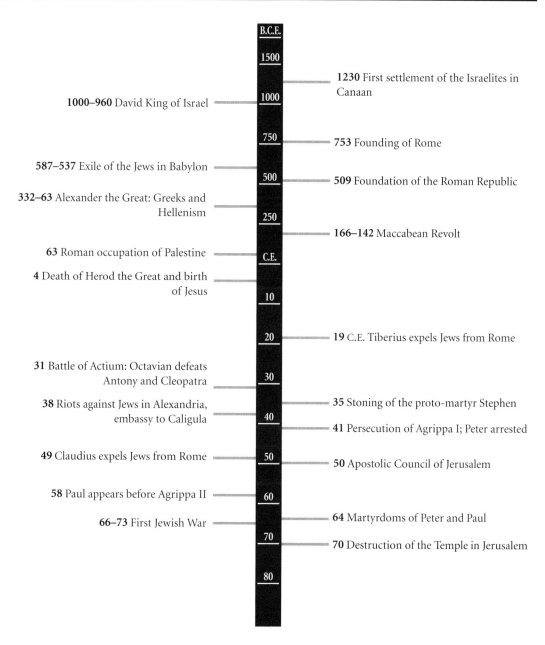

B.C.E.

1500

1000

750

500

250

C.E.

10

20

30

40

50

60

70

80

1000–960 David King of Israel

587–537 Exile of the Jews in Babylon

332–63 Alexander the Great: Greeks and Hellenism

63 Roman occupation of Palestine

4 Death of Herod the Great and birth of Jesus

31 Battle of Actium: Octavian defeats Antony and Cleopatra

38 Riots against Jews in Alexandria, embassy to Caligula

49 Claudius expels Jews from Rome

58 Paul appears before Agrippa II

66–73 First Jewish War

1230 First settlement of the Israelites in Canaan

753 Founding of Rome

509 Foundation of the Roman Republic

166–142 Maccabean Revolt

19 C.E. Tiberius expels Jews from Rome

35 Stoning of the proto-martyr Stephen

41 Persecution of Agrippa I; Peter arrested

50 Apostolic Council of Jerusalem

64 Martyrdoms of Peter and Paul

70 Destruction of the Temple in Jerusalem

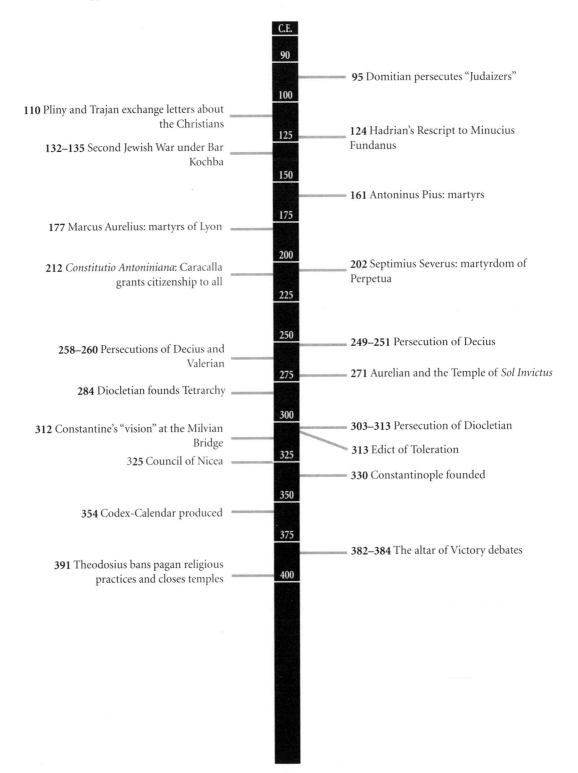

C.E.

90

95 Domitian persecutes "Judaizers"

100

110 Pliny and Trajan exchange letters about the Christians

124 Hadrian's Rescript to Minucius Fundanus

125

132–135 Second Jewish War under Bar Kochba

150

161 Antoninus Pius: martyrs

175

177 Marcus Aurelius: martyrs of Lyon

200

212 *Constitutio Antoniniana*: Caracalla grants citizenship to all

202 Septimius Severus: martyrdom of Perpetua

225

250

258–260 Persecutions of Decius and Valerian

249–251 Persecution of Decius

275

271 Aurelian and the Temple of *Sol Invictus*

284 Diocletian founds Tetrarchy

300

312 Constantine's "vision" at the Milvian Bridge

303–313 Persecution of Diocletian

313 Edict of Toleration

325 Council of Nicea

325

330 Constantinople founded

350

354 Codex-Calendar produced

375

382–384 The altar of Victory debates

391 Theodosius bans pagan religious practices and closes temples

400

Chapter I

HISTORICAL OVERVIEW

The emergence of Christianity—which quickly spread from a localized offshoot of Judaism, the religion of many Semitic nations in ancient Palestine, to the predominant religion of the vast Roman Empire with a major episcopal center in Rome—took place broadly in the time period between Alexander the Great and Constantine, from 330 B.C.E. to 330 C.E. The period from 330 to 31 B.C.E. is known as the Hellenistic period, one of the most important cultural intersections of the ancient Mediterranean. From 330 B.C.E. until 200 B.C.E. was its heyday, but after 200 B.C.E., Alexander's successors in Egypt, Palestine, Syria, and Asia reasserted their native cultures in a newly formed pan-Hellenic world. The Roman period extended from 163 B.C.E.

through the age of Constantine into the early fifth century, although Rome did not control the Mediterranean world until Octavian conquered Mark Antony and Cleopatra at the Battle of Actium in 31 B.C.E. Thus, when Jesus the Galilean taught and preached in the early first century C.E., it was in a Semitic world largely influenced by pan-Hellenic culture, education, and philosophy and ruled by Roman government and laws. At that time, the polytheistic Greco-Roman world contained innumerable gods and diverse religions, all implicated to some degree in the political and cultural structures of native populations: the Greek pantheon and Hellenism, the Roman pantheon and emperor worship, mystery religions and their various rituals and rites, Gnostic beliefs, and, most importantly, Judaism, which was uniquely characterized by monotheism, a strict moral code, and its body of sacred scripture. This chapter will discuss the essential historical background for the understanding of the events leading to the emergence of Christianity in first-century Palestine and its expansion to a fourth-century Rome that had been transformed from the capital of the ancient Roman Empire into a *new* Jerusalem.

Features of Ancient Mediterranean Religious Practices

Greek and Roman Deities

Ancient Greek religion included the polytheistic worship of twelve anthropomorphic, ageless, immortal deities on Mount Olympus, usually Zeus and his wife, Hera; Poseidon, god of the sea; Apollo, a sun god of music, healing, culture, and oracles; Artemis, the goddess of the moon and the hunt who oversaw the maturation of the young; Athena, goddess of wisdom and crafts, especially important as the patron goddess of Athens; Hermes, the messenger god who guided all travelers, including the dead whom he conducted into the realm of the god of the underworld, Hades; Ares, the god of war; Aphrodite, the goddess of love; Demeter, the goddess of grain, whose daughter Persephone was abducted by Hades and then became the queen of the underworld; Dionysus, the god of wine and religious ecstasy; and Hephaestus, the god of fire. Zeus was their leader and there were thousands of local gods. Religion was everywhere in the Greek world, and there was little distinction between religious and secular. The pan-Hellenic or national festivals of athletic and musical competitions were dedicated to the gods who presided over all community life. The pantheon of gods in the Roman world was modeled upon that of the Greek and similarly implicated with cultural and political life. By the end of the third century B.C.E., the Romans had imported and assimilated the Greek pantheon: Jupiter, like Zeus, was the father of the gods; Juno, the goddess of fertility and matrons, was similar to Hera; Neptune, like Poseidon, was the god of the seas and waters; Apollo remained unchanged; like Artemis, Diana was associated with the moon and hunting as the goddess of woods and nymphs, female divinities who live in mountains, trees, caves or other natural settings; Minerva, a city goddess like Athena, formed the Capitoline Triad with Jupiter and Juno, a trio of divinities brought to Rome by the Etruscans; Mercury corresponded to Hermes as the god of trade and travel; Mars was identified with Ares as the god of war; Venus was the Roman counterpart to the Greek goddess of love, Aphrodite; Ceres, the goddess of grain, was compared to Demeter, while Bacchus, the god of wine, was the Roman counterpart of Dionysus; and Vulcan, the god of fire and forges, had attributes similar to the Greek fire god Hephaestus.

Greek and Roman Religious Practices

To the ancient Romans, the core of religion was the cultic act or ritual sacrifice, which,

FIGURE 1.1. *Sculpture of Augustus as Pontifex Maximus. This first-century B.C.E. marble statue shows Augustus dressed as the Chief Priest of Rome.*

if correctly performed, ensured the correct contractual response (*quid pro quo*, "something in return for something") from the deity. Usually a living victim, a pig or sheep or ox, was offered to a god or goddess with a prayer for the continued prosperity of that deity, who then would grant the request of the worshipper. The ritual had to be performed with exacting precision: the size and color of the victim—for example, white for Jupiter and Juno, and black for the gods of the underworld—had to be just right; the dress of the priest, the music, the prayers, and all the ritual purifications were carefully prescribed. If there was an error, the entire ritual had to be repeated.

The *Pontifex Maximus*, "Chief Priest," oversaw all sacrifices and ceremonies essential to maintaining the *pax deorum*, "peace of the gods." His role paralleled that of the *pater-familias*, "head of the family," who served the gods as the primary guardian and representative of his family. As domestic religious sacrifices performed for births, marriages, funerals, and other rites of passage became community concerns the state began to oversee these sacrifices on behalf of larger communities. Corresponding priesthoods with specific functions developed: *pontifices*, "pontiffs," had jurisdiction over the religious calendar of holy days, called *feriae*, when religious rites were performed and no business was transacted; *flamines* were priests devoted to particular gods and their temple rites; *haruspices* were priests who read the entrails of sacrificial animals; and *augures* were the colleges of priests who interpreted various *auguria*, "omens," such as lightning or the flights of birds, to divine the will of the gods.

Roman Emperor Worship

From the time of Alexander the Great, eastern monarchs had become demigods whose native citizens worshipped them and performed sacrifices dedicated to them. As early as the second century B.C.E., rulers routinely adopted the title *epiphanes*, a term that means "the divine presence coming into light." Although Octavian, the first emperor of Rome, ostensibly refused to be worshipped as these eastern leaders, he did allow his name to be joined with the goddess *Roma* and his image to be placed in sacred places throughout the empire. Gradually the worship of his divinity took root in the Near East, especially after the Battle of Actium in 31 B.C.E., when he adopted

the title *Augustus* meaning "revered" or "honored." The province of Pergamum dedicated a temple to Augustus and *Roma* in 29 B.C.E. In the west, his stepson Drusus dedicated an altar to Augustus and *Roma* in 12 B.C.E. at Lugdunum, the modern Lyon, and by the end of his reign there was one in almost every province. It was not until after his death, however, that Augustus was proclaimed a god of the Roman state when a senator at his funeral attested to seeing him ascend into heaven.

This association of deification and death prevented other emperors from allowing themselves to become deified during their lifetimes. They did, however, allow their *genius* or "divinity," to be worshipped. Among the Julio-Claudians, Caligula (37–41 C.E.) built a temple and established a priesthood and ritual dedicated to his divinity in his own lifetime, and

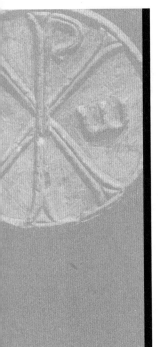

Personalities in Christianity 1.1
AUGUSTUS

Gaius Julius Caesar Octavianus (63 B.C.E.–14 C.E.) was the first emperor of Rome. Julius Caesar's great nephew (the son of his sister's daughter), he delivered the important funeral oration of his grandmother (Caesar's sister) in 51 B.C.E. and was adopted by Caesar in 45 B.C.E. When Caesar was murdered, his will named Octavian as his heir. He surprised many older statesmen and generals by his effective consolidation of power in a political alliance with Mark Antony and M. Aemilius Lepidus, called the Second Triumvirate. In several successive battles he first subdued Brutus and Cassius, the leaders of the conspiracy against Caesar, and then, in 31 B.C.E. at the Battle of Actium, he defeated Antony, his former fellow triumvir and brother-in-law (in 40 B.C.E. Antony had married Octavian's sister, Octavia) who had allied himself with Cleopatra. This was a great turning point in his political career and in the history of Rome, for the wealth and power and resources of the east now belonged to the Rome. Octavian received the quasi-divine title *Augustus*, which means "revered" or "honored," and with his two close supporters, M. Vipsanius Agrippa and C. Maecenas, he instituted a new governmental structure, an empire ruled by a monarch, that lasted until 410 C.E. His reign inaugurated a period of widespread peace and prosperity. The literary circle patronized by Maecenas that promoted this peace after so many years of civil wars produced a literary corpus that has been called the *Golden Age* of Latin literature. His building program also emphasized the peace and prosperity of his reign: he beautified Rome with temples and restored shrines, he built libraries and theatres, and he associated his domestic building with the god Apollo on the Palatine Hill. The biblical account (Luke 2:1) of the taxation system implemented in the Roman provinces associates the birth of Jesus with the *pax Romana* of Augustus. In subsequent centuries, ecclesiastical historians regarded the peace and territorial expansions of the reign of Augustus as a divinely ordained preparation for the entire world to receive the teaching of Jesus.

In the matter of succession, Augustus was continually foiled. In 39 B.C.E., he divorced his first wife Scribonia, the mother of his only child, Julia, to marry Livia Drusilla, who was at that time pregnant with her second son. Livia's sons, Drusus and Tiberius, several of Julia's children from a series of politically expedient marriages, and other relations (even Mark Antony's son) were all in the mix of candidates to succeed Augustus. In the end, Livia's son Tiberius succeeded to the throne, but by then Augustus had reconstituted the patrician senate and the resulting government was a shared monarchial system.

Claudius (41–54 C.E.) officially inserted the worship of the imperial *genius* into the state religion; the Flavian emperor Domitian (81–96 C.E.) referred to himself as *dominus et deus*, "lord and god." By the second century C.E., the Roman emperor had melded into local religious rituals all over the empire and was worshipped as a god, although there was no strict imperial religion with priests and prescribed rituals. Beginning with Diocletian in the late third century, court ceremonial surrounding the person of the emperor became increasingly elaborate. The emperor wore a purple robe, the symbol of his absolute power, and all who entered his presence were required to kiss the hem of the purple robe in a ritual called the *adoratio purpurae*, "adoration of the purple," and to approach his presence on their knees. Christians, as all citizens, were required to swear an oath to the *genius* of Caesar or be charged with treason. It is in this period, when the worship of an emperor's "divinity" was becoming more widespread, that Christianity was viewed as a threat to the state and that we date most systematic attempts to eradicate it through persecution. As offensive as emperor worship was to Christians, it nonetheless continued even after Constantine had proclaimed Christianity a legal religion.

Mystery Religions

Like Christianity, the mystery religions of the Greco-Roman world promised a blessed life after death through an initiation, baptism, and communion with the deity. One of the most important of the mystery religions in the ancient world was the annual ceremony connected to the worship of Demeter and her daughter Kore/Persephone at Eleusis, near Athens. The story of Demeter and Persephone is a mythical explanation for the seasons and their agricultural cycles. During the Eleusinian mysteries, the abduction of Persephone by Hades was ritually reenacted in a procession from Athens to Eleusis. At Eleusis, the initiates entered a dark pathway (a metaphor for death) and experienced a mystical union with the divine that left them serenely reconciled to death and hopeful of a blessed afterlife (a metaphor for the burgeoning of life in the spring). The rites of Isis and Osiris in Egypt and of Attis and Cybele in the Near East have their roots in a similar agricultural cycle of death and rebirth. In the Hellenistic and Roman periods these exotic oriental and Egyptian deities appealed to initiates who wanted to experience a personal epiphany that promised a blessed afterlife. Non-Roman priests of Cybele were so carried away by the ecstatic otherworldliness of their worship that they castrated themselves in dedication to the goddess. In what has been interpreted according to tradition as a Christian version of this act, Origen, the third-century Christian ascetic leader of the catechetical school of Alexandria, allegedly castrated himself to "renounce marriage for the kingdom of God" (Matt 19:12). Romans, however, were legally prohibited from participating fully in the worship of Cybele, whose rites they considered wild and grotesque, and which they eventually suppressed.

Mithraism was perhaps the most widespread of the ancient mystery religions even though it was based primarily in military camps and was exclusively male. According to the scant literature and the somewhat more abundance archaeological remains, the congregants of the Roman sun-god Mithras experienced a kind of "rebirth" after an elaborate initiation ceremony centered upon the cult image of Mithras slaughtering a bull. After this secretive initiation, they enjoyed the benefits of an exclusive religious-social community as well as the promise of salvation after death.

Certain Christian rituals and teachings about the afterlife were similar to those of various mystery religions. Christ (from the Greek *Christos*, "anointed"), called the Messiah, "anointed of God" in Hebrew, was sent from heaven to bring his Father's kingdom into the present time. The gift he promised was God's heavenly kingdom in the afterlife, that is, a divine gift of salvation. After an initiation by baptism, Christians could expect the forgiveness of sins, a life of fellowship with a shared code of morality, and the hope of resurrection. In 1 Cor 15:51, Paul's language echoes that of the mystery religions when he writes, "Listen, I will tell you a mystery! We will not all die, but we will all be changed at the last trumpet. For the trumpet will sound, the dead will be raised incorruptible, and we shall be changed." Just as those of many mystery religions, Christian rituals and beliefs were influenced in many ways by the rituals and beliefs surrounding an age-old pagan agricultural god who died in the winter and was resurrected in the spring.

We learned much more about early Gnostic sects, along with their various teachings, with the discovery of twelve codices in the Nag Hammadi library of Coptic texts. Among these were some forty previously unknown Gnostic texts (along with a few we had previously known only by name). From these texts,

FIGURE 1.2. *The Mithraeum of San Clemente. Dedicated to the worship of Mithras, this second-century altar is located in a sanctuary beneath the fourth-century Basilica of San Clemente in Rome.*

we learn that strains of Gnostic belief predated Christianity and that there were many and various sects within the movement that drew upon the teachings of Plato, Judaism, and, later, Christianity. Like the mystery religions, Gnosticism, from the Greek *gnosis,* "knowledge," held that there were two worlds, that of matter and that of spirit. In the second century, one form of Gnostic Christianity promised an escape through knowledge from the world of matter into the world of spirit where *gnosis* was reserved for an elect few. Theirs was a complex cosmogony of emanations (called aeons) from a creator god who was derived from an unknowable supreme god. Only the elect, in whom there was some divine flicker of the supreme divinity, were receptive to *gnosis,* which was sent through Jesus by the supreme divinity. According to the Gnostics, god the creator was distinct from the supreme divine god; the creator god was imperfect and, therefore, so was the material world. This belief came to be considered heretical, this is, opposed to church doctrine, by the developing Christian church in the first and second centuries, along with another of the Gnostic doctrines, namely, that Jesus did not truly assume humanity but rather only appeared to be human.

Historical Background of Judaism

Short History of the Jews

Through its many stages of development from the Mosaic covenant through the early Christian period, the Jewish religion was variously characterized by monotheism, adherence to a body of written scriptures called the law, dietary and food restrictions, a deliberate separation from non-Jews, and fractious dissent within and among the different Jewish communities. Their long and complicated history encompasses several periods of domination by political overlords who, to some extent, seem always to have recognized Judaism as a *religio licita,* "tolerated religion": the Persian Empire from 539 to 333 B.C.E., the Greek Empire of Alexander the Great from 333 to 320 B.C.E., the Seleucid Empire from 320 to 140 B.C.E., and the Parthian period from 140 B.C.E. to 226 C.E. The Roman period overlapped with the Seleucid and the Parthian empires and extended from 163 B.C.E. to 135 C.E., when the Romans destroyed Jerusalem.

For centuries, Judaism and the Hellenism of Alexander the Great and his successors' kingdoms were assimilated and polarized in mutual exchanges. Hellenism, as it appeared in Israelite accounts, was a derogatory term and referred particularly to those customs that contravened Jewish law, especially the Hellenic athletic pursuits practiced at the gymnasium. In 2 Macc 4:14-15, the Jewish priests were criticized for neglecting the Temple sacrifices to participate in unlawful athletic exercises, like discus-throwing. This "craze for Hellenism" as it was called in Maccabees not only reflected

the Jews' resentment of their foreign domination but also the antagonism between traditional and reformed religious obligations. Jewish monotheism was not compatible with any polytheistic traditional religions and it forbade the worship of the Roman emperor. Nonetheless, in the Temple in Jerusalem the Jews willingly offered a daily sacrifice for the well-being of the emperor.

Despite their long resistance to foreign rulers, the different Semitic communities throughout Palestine did not form a homogeneous religious entity. There were many different groups who worshipped the god of Israel, and they variously resisted, accommodated, and mixed with their fellow Jews. In the early Christian period, there were three sects of Jews, each distinct to some degree in their social, political, cultural and religious practices; yet, each one claimed to represent the true Judaism. The Sadducees and Pharisees were priests and religious leaders, who differed acrimoniously in their interpretation of Mosaic Law. The Sadducees were aristocratic and elite; they insisted upon a literal and strict interpretation of the written scripture, called the Torah, and they were devoted to Temple ritual. The Pharisees, in addition to the Torah, also honored laws handed down by oral tradition (eventually codified in the Talmud), and they believed (unlike the Sadducees) in a bodily resurrection in a messianic age yet to come. The Essenes were an ascetic sect that seems to have preferred to live outside of the urban Judaism of Jerusalem, although the "Gate of the Essenes" identified in Josephus (*Jewish War* 5.4.2) is perhaps evidence in this period that they continued to visit the Temple in Jerusalem. They followed careful ceremonial rituals regarding purity and adhered to an esoteric set of doctrines. Another ascetic Jewish community in Qumran was perhaps related to the Essenes. This community is known from the Dead Sea Scrolls, a cache of Hebrew and Aramaic prayers, hymns, and biblical texts discovered in 1947 in the Qumran caves along the northern shore of the Dead Sea. This collection of texts considerably enhances our understanding of the range of Jewish sects in the milieu of Jesus and his followers.

In addition to these sects, there were class distinctions among the various Israelite communities. By and large the priestly class was wealthier, better educated, and more likely to collaborate with their Hellenized rulers. This kind of collusion ensured social mobility and financial security, and it was the primary riff in the separation between the Hellenizing Jews and the traditionalists in Jerusalem. Four families—the Oniads, Simonites, Tobiads, and Maccabees—contended through the Hellenistic period for the high priesthood and were (at different times depending upon who was in power) pro-Seleucid, pro-Ptolemaic, traditionalists, or Hellenizers (to different degrees).

Judean Priest-Kings

The Maccabees, called the Hasmoneans from their ancestor Hashmon, emerged to rule, first as high priests then as priest-kings, after leading a revolution against the Seleucid ruler Antiochus IV Epiphanes (175–163 B.C.E.) and the Hellenized high priests (Jason and Menelaus) whom he had appointed. In the bargain, the Maccabees had initiated an alliance or *amicitia* with Rome, which had established dominion in Greece and Asia in a series of wars with Philip V of Macedon and Antiochus III in Asia. The Hasmoneans ruled from 161 B.C.E. until internal wars among competing family members left Judea vulnerable to foreign domination. In 63 B.C.E., Pompey the Great conquered Judea and introduced Roman rule.

The dissolution of the Hasmonean-led Jewish nation, from 63–40 B.C.E., coincided with the escalating presence of Rome in the east. Just as Pompey was claiming Syria from the Seleucids, the Jews were embroiled in a civil war between the Hasmoneans Hyrcanus II and Aristobulus II. Antipater, the Idumean general of Hyrcanus I, backed Hyrcanus II while shoring up power for himself and his own son, Herod (known to history as "Herod the Great"). When Pompey's legate (or deputy) Scaurus arrived in Jerusalem in 63 B.C.E., delegations from both parties besieged him; Scaurus backed Aristobulus, but Pompey was less accommodating. Rather than back either claimant, he declared war on Jerusalem and after a three-month siege finally took the Temple. After his victory, Pompey entered the Temple and the Holy of Holies.

In the parade of spoils from his conquests, Pompey led Aristobulus II and his sons through Rome as prisoners. Hyrcanus II remained in Jerusalem as High Priest. Much of what had been part of the Jewish state was now annexed by Syria. The Greek city-states enjoyed a new revitalization under Pompey's reorganization, and they offered support in return; the Jews and other Semitic nations, however, resented the Roman presence and control. Reduced to a client state of Rome, the same outrage against a foreign ruler and the same desire for religious and national independence that characterized Judea in the Hellenistic period and that had long plagued its internal politics now set the stage for the Messiah king, Jesus Christ, to incite a revolution for the return of an independent Judea ruled by a High Priest/King of the Jews.

Dynasty of the Herods

As administrators, the Herods were effective, but many resented them as outsiders: not only had they not descended from any priestly family, but they were Idumeans, who became proselytes during the territorial expansions under the Maccabeans. Moreover, they had supplanted the legitimate dynasty of Maccabean priest-kings and they served the interests of the Roman overlords as their client kings.

The only substantial account of the Herods comes from the Jewish historian Flavius Josephus (37–100 C.E.) whose two principal works—the *Jewish War* (*Bellum Iudaicum*) and the *Jewish Antiquities* (*Antiquitates Iudaicae*)—cover the Maccabean period into the 70s C.E., the First Jewish War. (The *Antiquities* begins with the account of the world's creation.) Alternately described with praise and with hostility, the first of the Herods, Antipater, was a politically astute opportunist. He had been appointed as royal governor of Idumea under the Hasmonean Alexander Janneus, and he

had formed an independent alliance with the neighboring Nabateans by marrying the king's daughter, named Cyprus. During Rome's civil war between Pompey and Caesar, Antipater successfully aligned himself first with Pompey and then with Caesar, earning for himself Roman citizenship, immunity from taxation, and secular authority over Jerusalem. When Caesar recognized him as the official administrator of Judea in 47 B.C.E., Antipater immediately appointed his son Herod as the local governor of Galilee.

It was on the clear understanding that he would champion Rome against the Parthians that the triumvirs Antony and Octavian appointed Herod tetrarch and then, in 40 B.C.E., King of the Jews. At the death of Cleopatra just after the Battle of Actium in 31 B.C.E., Octavian confirmed Herod's throne and enlarged his kingdom considerably. He enjoyed great political favor as a client-king when Augustus became emperor, and, despite his family intrigues, rivalries, and murders, his three sons were formally recognized as his heirs at his death in 4 B.C.E. Of the three, Herod Antipas ruled longest, until 39 C.E.; Herod's grandsons, Agrippa I and Agrippa II, ruled until 44 C.E. and c. 100 C.E. respectively, but no one of his heirs achieved the broad territorial expansion and power of Herod the Great.

Jesus of Nazareth in Galilee was born into this Semitic milieu under Herod and in the reign of the emperor Augustus (31 B.C.E.–14 C.E.) probably in, or shortly before, 4 B.C.E. (The sixth-century Greek monk Dionysius Exiguus, which means "Denis the Small," was the first to calculate dates from the birth of Jesus labeling them accordingly A.D., which is the abbreviation for *Anno Domini*, "in the year of our Lord.") The ministry of Jesus, that is, the time between his baptism and his death, when he traveled and taught in the area of Jerusalem that is now called the Holy Land, spanned a two- to three-year period between 30 and 33 C.E. entirely in the reign of the emperor Tiberius (14–37 C.E.) and the tetrarch Herod Antipas (4 B.C.E.–39 C.E.). It ended with his crucifixion, the outcome of a sequence of controversial inquiries. After the Passover meal, Jesus led several disciples to the Garden of Gethsemane, at the foot of the Mount of Olives outside the Jerusalem city walls. It was here that he was arrested after being betrayed by Judas. Gospel accounts differ concerning the trial, but Jesus seems to have appeared before the Sanhedrin, or Jewish council, where he was charged with blasphemy for claiming to be the Son of God and the Messiah (Matt 26:63). But whether this was an *ad hoc* investigation, an informal inquiry, or a formal trial is a matter still contested by scholars. Whatever else the Sanhedrin determined, they agreed to deliver Jesus to the Roman procurator Pontius Pilate. Of the gospel accounts, Luke (23:6-11) alone records that Pilate did not want to pass judgment on what seemed to be a question of religion but preferred to send Jesus to Herod Antipas, as a Jewish authority. Rather than judge the case, however, Antipas and his retinue mocked Jesus and sent him back to Pilate. Ultimately, Pilate condemned Jesus to death for claiming to be "King of the Jews" (Matt 27:11; Mark 15:1; Luke 23:2; John 18:33),

a *crimen maiestatis*, or "crime against the emperor," who alone could be called "King."

Rise of Christianity

After the death of Jesus, Christian Judaism became divided. Following Acts 6:1, we may conveniently distinguish between the Christian Hebrews, who spoke Aramaic (and perhaps also Greek) and continued to hold the Temple and the sacrificial cult in Jerusalem at the center of their worship, and the Christian Hellenists, or "Greek speakers," who seem to have been Jews whose different ethnic communities met for prayer in synagogues throughout Jerusalem (Acts 6:9). It is vital to recall, however, that in this very early period, there is not a clear distinction between these groups, and that there must have been many groups who perceived themselves as Christian Jews but who were "Hellenized" to various degrees. Paul, the Greek-speaking Pharisee who later became a Christian missionary to the Dispersion Jews and to the gentiles (from the Latin *gens,* "people," which to the Jews meant anyone who was not a Jew), initially harassed those early Hellenized Christian Jews. He zealously persecuted these Christian Hellenists who were beginning to develop and expand the gospels in the wider Jewish community, and he was present at the stoning in 35 C.E. of the proto-martyr Stephen, a Christian Hellenist who spoke against the Temple (Acts 6:13). After a dramatic conversion on the road to Damascus (Acts 9:1-19), however, Paul traveled through the cities of Syria, Asia Minor, and

FIGURE 1.3. *The Conversion of Saint Paul. Paul's conversion on the road to Damascus is shown in Caravaggio's (1571–1610) dramatic painting, now in the Basilica of Santa Maria del Populo in Rome.*

Greece to preach the message of Jesus to Jews and gentiles. According to Acts 11:26, it was in Antioch, one of the most important urban centers of the church outside of Palestine, that the term *Christianoi* was first used to refer to Christians. Scholars agree, however, that the term may have been in use earlier than the reference in Acts suggests, either by Christians to self-designate, or by non-Christians when referring to these "followers of Christ."

From the accounts in Acts, we can trace the growth of the church from Jerusalem to Judea, Samaria, Galilee and the coasts, to Antioch, to wide areas around the Aegean, and, finally, to Rome. In the expansion, as had happened within Jerusalem, the sects of Christian Jews as well as Jews and gentiles disagreed on several practical and theological issues, and all the while the Jews more generally were at odds with the Romans. Several events mark this transition of the mission of the church from Jews to gentiles: shared fellowship between Jews and gentiles (Acts 10:28); remission of sins for all who believe in Jesus (Acts 10:43); and baptism for all in the name of Jesus (Acts 10:47). Arguments about circumcision were settled, according to Acts 15, at the Apostolic Council in Jerusalem where it was decided that gentiles who converted to Christian Judaism no longer had to be circumcised. In his *Epistle to the Romans* (1:16-18), Paul insists that faith in God, morality, and ethical conduct, if not circumcision, bound Jews and converts alike to the Torah. But the only way to salvation was by repentance and baptism (Acts 2:38) through Jesus.

To many Jews such new directives, for example, repentance and baptism in Jesus Christ as the only means to salvation, were offensive. Moreover, the Jewish priests and scribes resented the popularity of Peter and Paul and the other missionaries, and they questioned their right to preach in this way (Acts 4:7). Fearing that the missionaries sought to replace Moses and the scriptures with faith in Jesus, a power struggle erupted among the various sects of Jews and Christian Jews. These examples from within the Jerusalem religious communities as well as from the tumultuous missionary experiences of Paul illustrate the growing conflict. Herod Agrippa I, who ruled in Jerusalem from 41–44 C.E., persecuted Christians in an effort to appease the traditional Jews who were not followers of Jesus and who were suffering under the increasing hostility and religious intolerance of local Roman governors. Often when Paul preached, local Jews rioted and stoned him, to force him to leave their synagogues and their cities. Both at Philippi in Greece and in Judea, Roman officials had to step in when the rioting became too serious. In Judea, fellow Christians feared for Paul's life and he was spirited away and brought before the Roman governor in Caesarea. There he was kept under house arrest for over two years. At that time he appealed his case to the emperor, a privilege reserved for Roman citizens, rather than stand trial against his accusers in Jerusalem. In 58 C.E., just before leaving Caesarea to go to Rome, Paul had an audience with Agrippa II, King of the Jews, and his sister Berenice at which Agrippa is reputed to have interrupted Paul's discourse to concede that he would soon make a Christian of him if he kept up his preaching. En route to Rome, where his case had been transferred, Paul was shipwrecked on Malta. Upon arriving in Rome, he was under house arrest but seems to have continued preaching until at least 64 C.E. Although Christian tradition provides several vivid accounts of Paul's death by martyrdom in Rome, perhaps under Nero, one of our most ancient documents (apart from the New Testament) is more vague. In the *First Epistle to the Corinthians*, the apostolic father Clement of Rome reports

FIGURE 1.4. *The Arch of Titus. The treasures from the destruction of the Jewish Temple (70 C.E.) are displayed in this triumphal procession on the Arch of Titus in Rome.*

only that Paul departed from the world and was taken up to a holy place (*1 Clement* 5.6).

The impact of Paul's organized ministries in synagogues throughout the Diaspora was strengthened by the destruction of the Jewish Temple in 70 C.E. under the Flavian emperors Vespasian and his son Titus. This war is considered by many to be the clear break between Judaism and Christianity: while the destruction of the Temple profoundly altered the nature of Judaism, Paul's message that salvation was possible without the law simultaneously hastened Christianity's transformation from a reform movement within Judaism into an *adversus Judaeos*, "against the Jews," religion. Christianity was a challenge to Judaism. For example, Christians conceived of Jesus as God and they believed that the prophecies of scripture were fulfilled in him, but this was something no Jew could accept; and although Jews and Christians both awaited the Messiah,

the Christians considered Jesus the Messiah and expected his return. By the early second century, Ignatius, Bishop of Antioch, had written a series of letters while traveling to his martyrdom in Rome in which he drew a clear line of separation between Christians and Jews, claiming that it was monstrous to talk of Jesus Christ and to practice Judaism.

Christianity and the Roman Empire

First to Second Centuries

For Romans, the distinction was not so clear. In the early second-century accounts of imperial reactions to Christians, Jews and Christians often seemed to be conflated, as the testimony of classical writers attests.

The historian Gaius Suetonius Tranquillus (75–140 C.E.) wrote his *Lives of the Caesars* while serving in the court of Hadrian (117–138

FROM AN ANCIENT TEXT ❖ I.I

Tacitus on the Expulsion of Jews from Rome

Although not extant in their entirety, the Annals, *written by the Roman historian Cornelius Tacitus (58–116 C.E.) treat the period from the death of Augustus to the death of Nero (14–68 C.E.). Annals 2.85 includes the account quoted below of Tiberius' expulsion of the Jews from Rome in 19 C.E.*

Another debate dealt with the proscription of the Egyptian and Jewish rites, and a senatorial edict directed that four thousand descendants of freedmen, tainted with that superstition and of a suitable age, were to be shipped to the island of Sardinia to catch pirates and he said that if they were to die in the oppressive climate, it would be a cheap loss. The rest were to leave Italy unless they had renounced their profane rights by a certain day.

Source: Tacitus, *Annals* 2.85 in *Tacitus*, tr. John Jackson, Loeb Classical Library, 5 vols. (Cambridge, Mass.: Harvard University Press, 1937), vol. 3, *Annals I–III*, p. 517.

FROM AN ANCIENT TEXT ❖ 1.2

Suetonius on the Expulsion of Jews from Rome

Tiberius

Suetonius twice mentions the expulsion of Jews from Rome: the first is under the emperor Tiberius in 19 C.E.

He abolished foreign cults, especially the Egyptian and the Jewish rites, compelling all who were addicted to such superstitions to burn their religious vestments and all their paraphernalia. Those of the Jews who were of military age he assigned to provinces of less healthy climate, ostensibly to serve in the army; the others of that same race or of similar beliefs he banished from the city, on pain of slavery for life if they did not obey.

   Source: Suetonius, *Life of Tiberius* 36 in *Suetonius*, tr. J. C. Rolfe, Loeb Classical Library, 2 vols. (Cambridge, Mass.: Harvard University Press, 1939), vol. 1, *The Lives of the Caesars*, p. 324.

Claudius

In the second instance, Jews are expelled from Rome by the emperor Claudius in 49 C.E. Here, "the Jews" may have been Christians since they are charged with causing dissension at the instigation of a certain Chrestos, which may be a corruption of Christus ("Christ").

Since the Jews constantly made disturbances at the instigation of Chrestus, he [Claudius] expelled them from Rome.

   Source: Suetonius, *Life of Claudius* 25.3 in Suetonius, tr. J. C. Rolfe, Loeb Classical Library, 2 vols. (Cambridge, Mass.: Harvard University Press, 1939), vol. 2, *The Lives of the Caesars*, p. 53.

C.E.). The *Lives of the Caesars* was published in 120 C.E. and includes biographies of the twelve Caesars from Julius Caesar to Domitian.

According to both Tacitus and Suetonius, the emperors expelled the Jews in fear that their proselytizing would result in larger close-knit religious communities that refused to participate in the religious practices, such as sacrifices and emperor worship, of the wider Roman state.

The emperor Nero (*Lives of the Caesars, Nero*, 16.2) called Christianity a "new and depraved superstition" (*superstitio nova ac malefica*), and Tacitus (*Annals* 5.44.1-8), who served under Trajan as a provincial governor, tells us that Nero blamed the Christians for

FROM AN ANCIENT TEXT ❖ 1.3

Tacitus and Suetonius on Nero and the Christians

Both the Roman historians Cornelius Tacitus (58-116 C.E.) and Gaius Suetonius Tranquillus (75–140 C.E.) corroborate Nero's conflict with the Christians. Christians are identified as troublemakers and Christianity as a new and malicious superstition that Nero attempted to check.

Tacitus on Nero

But these were only the precautions of human wisdom. Soon a way of propitiating the gods was sought, and the Sibylline Books were consulted and, according to the directions given there, prayers were offered to Vulcan, Ceres, and Proserpina. Juno was entreated by matrons, first in the Capitol, then on the nearest part of the coast, from where they drew water to sprinkle the temple and image of the goddess. And there were sacred banquets and all-night vigils celebrated by women with living husbands. But all human efforts, all the lavish gifts of the emperor and the propitiations of the gods, could not dispel belief that the fire had been ordered. Consequently, to get rid of the rumor, Nero provided scapegoats and inflicted the most exquisite tortures on those hated for their abominations and popularly called Christians. Christus, the founder of the sect, was executed during the reign of Tiberius at the hands of the procurator, Pontius Pilatus. For the moment this pernicious superstition was checked, but it broke out again not only in Judea, the origin of the evil, but even in Rome, where all horrible and shameful things from every part of the world come together and gain a following. Accordingly, the first to be arrested were those who confessed; then, on their evidence, a huge multitude was convicted, not so much for the crime of arson in the city, as for their hatred of mankind. Mockery of every sort was heaped on them as they died: wrapped in the skins of wild beasts, they were torn by dogs and perished, or they were nailed to crosses, or prepared to be torched, so they could be burned as torches in the night. Nero gave his own gardens for this spectacle and performed a Circus game, in the habit of a charioteer mixing with the plebs or driving about the race-course. Even though they were clearly guilty and merited being made the most recent example of the consequences of crime, people began to pity these sufferers, because they were consumed not for the public good but on account of the fierceness of one man.

    Source: Tacitus, *Annals* 15.44.1–8 in *Tacitus*, tr. John Jackson, Loeb Classical Library, 5 vols. (Cambridge, Mass.: Harvard University Press, 1937, repr. 1991), vol. 5, *The Annals Books XIII–XVI*, pp. 283–285.

Suetonius on Nero

Punishments were inflicted on the Christians, a class of men given to a new and depraved superstition.

    Source: Suetonius, "Life of Nero" 16.2 in *Suetonius*, tr. J. C. Rolfe, Loeb Classical Library 2 vols. (Cambridge, Mass.: Harvard University Press, 1939), vol. 1, *The Lives of the Caesars*, p. 111.

FIGURE I.5. *Story of the fiery furnace. The story of the redemption of three young men in the "fiery furnace" from the Old Testament (Daniel 3) is depicted in an early Christian setting. This late third-century painting is in the Catacombs of Priscilla in Rome.*

the great fire of 64 C.E. in Rome, in order to deflect the charge that he had started it himself so that he could build his famed *Domus Aurea* ("Golden House"). Tacitus's account of the fire reveals the reason that Christians were despised enough to become Nero's scapegoats: they were misanthropes who rejected civic intercourse. For this, Tacitus tells us, the Christians were covered with the skins of beasts and torn apart by dogs, or they were nailed to crosses and set on fire, then used as human torches to light the night. Suetonius also wrote of the antipathy Nero held for Christianity.

Pliny the Younger, who also served Trajan as a provincial governor, corresponded with him about the Christians. In his letter (*Epistula* 10.96) to Trajan, Pliny called Christianity a depraved and excessive superstition (*superstitio prava et immodica*) and described the Christian practices of worship and communion. He was unsure of whether he should punish those denounced to him as Christians, or how; whether he should allow them to recant; or whether they were genuinely conspiratorial and therefore subverting the interests of the state. For Trajan, as for his successor

FROM AN ANCIENT TEXT ❖ I.4

Pliny and Trajan on the Trials of the Christians

Pliny, friend of the emperor Trajan (98–117 C.E.), was sent to Asia Minor in 112 C.E. to the province of Pontus-Bithynia on the Black Sea. He wrote ten books of letters concerning his administration, among which are two letters on the Christians and their practices, the earliest by any Roman writer. In this exchange from his letters (10.96-97), Pliny seems to make a genuine attempt to deal fairly with the Christians, who are accused of impeding temple sacrifices.

Pliny to Trajan

It is my regular custom, my lord, to refer to you all questions which cause me doubt, for who can better guide my hesitant steps or instruct my ignorance? I have never attended hearings concerning Christians, so I am unaware what is usually punished or investigated, and to what extent. I am more than a little in doubt whether there is to be a distinction between ages, and to what extent the young should be treated no differently from the more hardened; whether pardon should be granted to repentance; whether the person who has been a Christian in some sense should not benefit by having renounced it; whether it is the name Christian, itself untainted with crimes, or the crimes which cling to the name which should be punished.

In the meantime, this is the procedure I have followed in the cases of those brought before me as Christians. I asked them whether they were Christians. If they admitted it, I asked them a second and a third time, threatening them with execution. Those who remained obdurate I ordered to be executed, for I was in no doubt, whatever it was which they were confessing, that their obstinacy and their inflexible stubbornness should at any rate be punished. Others similarly lunatic were Roman citizens, so I registered them as due to be sent back to Rome.

Later in the course of the hearings, as usually happens, the charge rippled outwards, and more examples appeared. An anonymous document was published containing the names of many. Those who denied that they were or had been Christians and called upon the gods after me, and with incense and wine made obeisance to your statue, which I had ordered to be brought in together with images of the gods for this very purpose, and who moreover cursed Christ (those who are truly Christian cannot, it is said, be forced to do any of these things), I ordered to be acquitted.

Others who were named by an informer stated that they were Christians and then denied it. They said that in fact they had been, but had abandoned their allegiance, some three years previously, some more years earlier, and one or two as many as twenty years before. All these as well worshipped your statue and images of the gods, and blasphemed Christ. They maintained, however, that all that their guilt or error involved was that they were accustomed to assemble at dawn on a fixed day, to sing a hymn antiphonally to Christ as God, and to bind themselves by an oath, not for the commission of some crime, but to avoid acts of theft, brigandage, and adultery, not to break their word, and not to withhold money deposited with them when asked for it. When these rites were completed, it was their custom to depart, and then to assemble again to take food, which was however common and harmless. They had ceased, they said, to do this following my edict, by which in accordance with your instructions I had outlawed the existence of secret brotherhoods. So I thought it all the more necessary to ascertain the truth from two maidservants, who were called deaconesses, even by employing torture. I found nothing other than a debased and boundless superstition.

I therefore postponed the inquiry, and hastened to consult you, since this issue seemed to me to merit consultation, especially because of the number indicted, for there are many of all ages, every rank, and both sexes who are summoned and will be summoned to confront danger. The infection of this superstition has extended not merely through the cities, but also through the villages and country areas, but it seems likely that it can be halted and corrected. It is at any rate certain that temples, which were almost abandoned, have begun to be crowded, and the solemn rites which for long had been suspended are being restored. The flesh of the victims, for which up to now only a very occasional buyer was found, is now on sale in many places. This leads me readily to believe that if opportunity of repentance is offered, a large crowd of people can be set right.

Trajan to Pliny

You have followed the appropriate procedure, my Secundus, in examining the cases of those brought before you as Christians, for no general rule can be laid down which would establish a definite routine. Christians are not to be sought out. If brought before you and found guilty, they must be punished, but in such a way that a person who denies that he is a Christian and demonstrates this by his action, that is, by worshipping our gods, may obtain pardon for repentance, even if his previous record is suspect. Documents published anonymously must play no role in any accusation, for they give the worst example, and are foreign to our age.

Source: Pliny the Younger, *Letters* 10.96–97 in *Pliny the Younger Complete Letters*, tr. P. G. Walsh (New York: Oxford University Press, 2006), pp. 278–279.

FROM AN ANCIENT TEXT ❖ 1.5

Rescript of Hadrian on the Christians

Like Trajan, Hadrian emphasizes the point that only public (not anonymous) accusations will be heard in Roman courts, and that false charges will be severely punished.

I have received a letter written to me by His Excellency Serennius Granianus, your predecessor. It is not my intention to leave the matter uninvestigated, for fear of causing the men embarrassment and abetting the informers in their mischief. If then the provincials can so clearly establish their case against the Christians that they can sustain it in a court of law, let them resort to this procedure only, and not rely on petitions or mere clamor. Much the most satisfactory course, if anyone should wish to prosecute, is for you to decide the matter. So if someone prosecutes them and proves them guilty of any illegality, you must pronounce sentence according to the seriousness of the offense. But if anyone starts such proceedings in the hope of financial reward, then for goodness sake arrest him for his shabby trick, and see that he gets his deserts.

Source: Eusebius, *Ecclesiastical History* 4.9 in *Eusebius: The History of the Church from Christ to Constantine*, tr. G. A. Williamson, rev. and ed. Andrew Louth (London: Penguin, 1965), p. 112.

Hadrian, Christianity was no crime as long as Christians participated in the worship of the state gods. Both of these emperors advised their local governors not to accept anonymous denunciations of Christians and to pursue a practice of leniency where possible.

In his letter to the proconsul of Asia, Minucius Fundanus, in 124–125 C.E., the emperor Hadrian (117–138 C.E.) makes clear that a Christian must be accused of definite crimes under due process of law before being condemned, and if the charge is false, the accuser may be cross-charged.

Among the Flavians, Domitian accused Christians of atheism for refusing to worship him as a god. He also prosecuted members of his family in the imperial court for Judaizing, that is, worshipping and living like Jews but refusing to pay the *fiscus Iudaicus*, the tax for the Temple in Jerusalem. Many scholars interpret this to mean that those who refused to pay the tax were not *really* Jews, but seemed to be to those who could not distinguish between Christians and Jews. So while the target of Domitian's wrath seems to have been Jews or their sympathizers, in fact, "Judaizing" may refer to non-Jews (including Christians) who seem (still) very similar to Jews in their personal conduct and worship.

The second century saw the greatest geographical expansion of the Roman Empire—approximately 2.5 million square miles—under the famous widespread peace called the *pax Romana*, "Roman peace." Some fifty to eighty million inhabitants stretching between Spain and the Rhine, Danube, and

Euphrates rivers, and from the Sudan northwest to Scotland lived under Roman rule. This perception of widespread peace inspired many Christian writers to consider the *pax Romana* as God's plan to ensure that Jesus' word could spread as efficiently as possible to the largest audience. In Rome alone there were estimated to be 1,000,000 people, who were governed by a broadly homogeneous imperial aristocracy. The economic structure of the empire was largely agrarian; there was a uniform currency and cheap labor. The *lingua franca*, "common language," in the west was Latin and in the east, Greek. Roman citizenship alone was enough to guarantee safe travel, and the general economic prosperity and peace promoted trade all over the empire. In this century, emperor worship was unchecked. Like a god on earth, the emperor governed all provinces, led the army, dispensed justice, and acted as the mediator between the gods and his citizens.

At the same time, the reverence the emperor demanded caused the Christian communities to erupt into open conflict with the state. To ensure the *pax deorum*, "peace of the gods," which, in turn, sustained the *pax Romana*, the emperor's *virtus*, "noble excellence," and *pietas*, "piety," had to be properly acknowledged through ritual rites performed by professional priests. Christians refused to do this. They were attacked as atheists who had apostasized from the old religion, the *mos maiorum*, "customs of the elders," and abandoned the mysteries, the sacrifices, and the initiations; they were said to practice Thyestean feasts (so called from the mythical banquet where Atreus killed his brother Thyestes's children and served them

to him) in taking the Eucharist, which they interpreted as the flesh and blood of Jesus; and to indulge in Oedipean intercourse (from the legend of Oedipus who unwittingly killed his father and married his mother) in kissing each other during their worship and referring to each other as "brother" or "sister" or "father." In the first two centuries, Christian apologists (from the Greek *apologia*, "speech in defense") wrote to counter the charges of cannibalism and incest against their faith.

At times, the Christians seem just as unsure as the pagans and Jews about the details of their religious practices. In many instances these are clarified as orthodox (from the Greek *orthodoxia*, "right thinking") after long theological and doctrinal clashes against the opposition, called heresy (from the Greek *hairesis*, "choice"). We have seen above that Gnosticism, the belief that certain elite people had special knowledge that ensured their salvation, in its varied forms was deemed a Christian heresy almost from its inception. We have also seen mentioned above the idea that God only appeared to be human but that he never really assumed a mortal incarnate existence, a heresy called Docetism (from the Greek *dokesis*, "disguise").

Third to Fourth Centuries

The third century, in sharp contrast to the widespread peace and prosperity of the second century, was rife with disaster, instability, and decline. Under the four Severans (193–235 C.E.), the empire moved toward military anarchy as pressure from the barbarians in the northern and eastern empire increased. Septimius

FIGURE 1.6. *The Roman Empire*

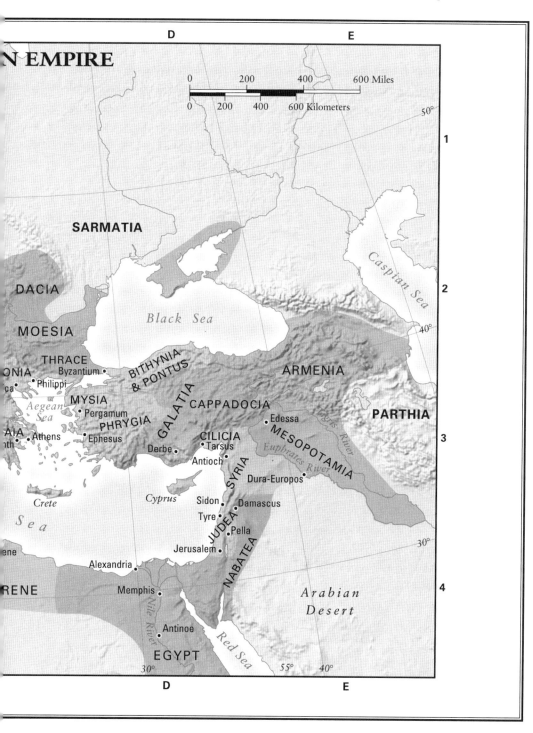

N EMPIRE

0 200 400 600 Miles
0 200 400 600 Kilometers

50°

SARMATIA

Caspian Sea

DACIA

Black Sea

MOESIA

THRACE

ONIA • Byzantium

ca • Philippi

MYSIA

Aegean Sea

BITHYNIA & PONTUS

ARMENIA

PARTHIA

• Pergamum

PHRYGIA

GALATIA

CAPPADOCIA

• Edessa

AIA • Athens

th

• Ephesus

CILICIA

MESOPOTAMIA

• Derbe

• Tarsus

Tigris River

• Antioch

SYRIA

Euphrates River

• Dura-Europos

Cyprus

Sidon •

• Damascus

Crete

Tyre •

JUDEA

• Pella

Sea

Jerusalem •

NABATEA

ene

• Alexandria

30°

RENE

Memphis •

Arabian Desert

Nile River

• Antinoe

Red Sea

EGYPT

30°

55° 40°

40°

30°

1

2

3

4

D

E

Severus's wife Julia Domna and her sister Julia Maesa came to Rome bringing their native Syrian culture and a religious syncretism that was perpetuated in their sons and grandsons, rulers of the Severan dynasty. Elagabalus, Julia Maesa's grandson, proved to be a voluptuary on the scale of Nero; as a hereditary priest of the sun god of Emesa, his devotion to that deity had a long-term effect on Roman religion. He introduced the worship of the sun god to Rome when he transferred the black conical stone, the god's sacred symbol, from Emesa to the *Elagaballium*, the huge temple he built to receive it on the Palatine Hill. This movement toward henotheism (the belief in a single god while acknowledging others) in the form of a sun god would be revived under Aurelian (270–275 C.E.) and then again by Constantine (306–337) who in some ways conflated the sun god with the God of the Christians. Severus Alexander, the cousin of the fanatical Elagabalus, returned the black stone of the sun god to Syria and promoted religious syncretism. According to his biography in the *Historia Augusta* (29.2), a collection of Latin imperial biographies that are widely considered dubious, Alexander Severus is even said to have counted Jesus among the gods in his palace shrine; and, according to Eusebius in his *Ecclesiastical History* (6.21.3) Alexander Severus' mother Julia Mamea sent an armed escort from Antioch to summon Origen, the great Alexandrian Christian theologian, to discuss Christian philosophy and doctrine with her.

From the time of Stephen, the Christian "proto-martyr" who was stoned to death in Jerusalem just after Jesus' death, there were isolated instances of the persecution of Christians who refused to worship the gods of the state or the divinity of the Roman emperor. Under Marcus Aurelius, Justin Martyr was beheaded in Rome in 165 C.E., and several Christians were martyred in Lyon in 177 C.E. In 202 C.E., during the reign of Septimius Severus, a group of Christians was sent into the arena against wild beasts for refusing to worship the state gods at the celebrations for Geta's birthday in North Africa. Among these martyrs was the young noble woman Perpetua, whose martyrdom is unusual in that it was told in her own voice. In her *passio*, "martyrdom," Perpetua insisted that she could not recant, that she could not renounce Christianity, despite the fact that her father was beaten before her eyes and her newborn baby was wrenched away from her so that she could be taken to prison and then die in the arena fighting against wild beasts.

In the fifty years following the Severans, the fabric of the empire frayed. Barbarian invasions, depopulation, civil wars, and natural disasters led the emperors to attempt to restore the traditional forms of worship in order to win the favor of the gods. The emperors variously termed themselves *reparatores*, "restorers," or *conservatores patriae*, "preservers of the fatherland." In this period, a certain fear took root, that Christians were too active in all levels of the imperial government and that the old religion was being abandoned in favor of Christianity, to the empire's detriment. Under the emperor Philip (244–249 C.E.), coins issued in celebration of Rome's millennium (247 C.E.) bore the inscription *Roma aeterna*, "eternal Rome." The political ideal of Rome's sacred mission and her *aeternitas*, "eternity," gained momentum, the more so as Philip was considered by some contemporaries to be a practicing Christian. In fact, it was very likely the fear that the steady crumbling of the empire was retribution for the impiety of the Christians that led to his murder. The new emperor Decius (249–251), a Pannonian officer and Roman traditionalist, was welcomed by the senate and dubbed a new Trajan. He was staunchly anti-Christian; he is even said to have claimed that he would rather meet a rival emperor in the field than a Christian bishop in Rome. For Decius, only the restoration of the state religious practices could preserve the empire. In the first general persecution of the Christians, he insisted that all citizens obtain a *libellus*, "certificate," as proof that they had poured a libation and sacrificed to the gods of the state and then tasted the sacrificial meat before a specially appointed commission. For Christians, this meant a denial of their faith. His conservative radicalism typified the new group of Illyrian soldiers that stood for traditional Roman values of which Diocletian and the tetrarchy were more severe examples.

Diocletian (284–305 C.E.), the son of slaves in the house of a senator, finally transformed the principate of Augustus into a theocracy (disguised as an absolute monarchy). Almost immediately upon taking office he proclaimed himself Augustus and associated himself with a subordinate co-ruler, and he reinstated the ancient Roman gods, most importantly *Iuppiter, conservator Augusti*, "Jupiter, the protector of Augustus." The co-rulers assumed the titles *Iovius* and *Herculius*,

where Diocletian was the supreme ruler (like Jupiter) and Maximian his Herculian co-ruler. Shortly thereafter, Maximian was promoted to co-Augustus and a Caesar or co-ruler appointed to each. This was the beginning of the tetrarchy (from the Greek *tetrarchia*, "rule of four"): the Augustus Diocletian and his Caesar Galerius ruled in the east; the Augustus Maximian and his Caesar Constantius Chlorus ruled in the west. These leaders were worshipped as though they were gods. They insisted upon a splendid court ceremonial and depicted themselves as personifications of the Roman virtues and of the Roman state. Their rare appearances featured the scepter and the orb and they wore purple robes embroidered with silk. An extravagant adoration gave rise to an aura of the divine supernatural that was reiterated in their building programs.

Highly successful in their various military campaigns, the tetrarchs reorganized the army and secured the empire's borders. From different and mobile locations around the empire, they regulated agriculture, industry, trade, and coinage. Moreover, this division of power was designed to ensure a peaceful succession.

Diocletian's first visit to Rome may have been on the occasion of his twenty-year anniversary, the *Vicennalia*, in late 303 C.E. He seems not to have been present even in 299 C.E. to dedicate his ample baths project, the largest bath complex ever built in Rome. In May of 305 C.E., he abdicated and forced his co-Augustus Maximian to do the same. The world at that moment could fairly be described as at peace, yet the tetrarchs had launched the longest and most virulent persecution ever undertaken against the church (303–313 C.E.). Why, after nineteen years of reforms and military victories and toleration for Christianity, Diocletian conceived of a superstitious fear that precipitated widespread persecution is unclear.

In February 303 C.E., by an edict of Diocletian, churches and scriptures were destroyed by fire; later that year, two more edicts were published requiring all ecclesiasts to make sacrifice to the gods. Only upon apostasizing could they be freed. In 304 C.E., a fourth edict required all Christians all over the empire to make sacrifices and pour libations to the gods. In a fifth and final edict in 308 C.E., all goods for sale in markets were polluted by sacrificial libations.

At Diocletian's abdication persecution in the west ended, partly because Constantius Chlorus had not implemented any but the first edict. In Rome, where Maximian's son Maxentius was quickly elected Augustus at his father's abdication, church property was restored immediately along with the freedom to worship the Christian God. Persecution continued in the east under Galerius until April of 311 C.E. When he knew he was dying, he freed confessors from prison and begged the Christians to pray to their God on his behalf. Maximinus Daia, however, the new Augustus in the east, continued the persecution even more horrifically. The church historian Eusebius (who cannot be considered unbiased) recorded seeing ninety-seven Christians, including children, en route to the mines, each missing the right eye and crippled in the left foot by hot irons, at Maximinus Daia's command.

Fourth Century: Constantine to Theodosius and the Primacy of the Church of Rome

Although the expectation was that Constantine, the son of Constantius, and Maxentius, the son of Maximian, would be appointed Caesars at the abdication of their fathers in 305 C.E., this did not happen. In the east, Galerius became the Augustus and appointed friends and relatives as his co-Augustus and their Caesars. This second tetrarchy fell into crisis at the death of Constantius in 306 C.E. His father's army immediately proclaimed Constantine the new Augustus and, shortly thereafter, Maxentius proclaimed himself *princeps*, "leader," in Rome. By 310 C.E., there were five different claims on the title of Augustus, and by October of 312 C.E., the two claimants in the west, Constantine and Maxentius, engaged in battle at the Milvian Bridge, just north of Rome. Here, just before the battle, Constantine is reported to have seen a vision in which he read the words *hoc signo vinces*, "by this sign you will conquer." He ordered his troops to mark their shields with the chi-rho symbol, the first two letters of the Greek χριστός ("Christ") superimposed upon one another. He was victorious in the battle and was quickly proclaimed Augustus by the senate. By imperial decree, the Christians were freed from persecution and from the enforced worship of the traditional religions of the empire.

In the scramble for power at the death of Constantius on July 25, 306 C.E., Maxentius, the son of the former Augustus Maximian, at first seemed to be the stronger contender. Over Constantine, the son of Constantius and Helen, who, according to Ambrose, was a tavern keeper, he could claim that he was the legitimate son of an emperor; and, too, he was married to the daughter of Galerius, Augustus in the east. Moreover, he had the support of Rome, still a glorious and formidable power (at least nominally) and fractious in response to the steady diminution of its political clout under the tetrarchs. Constantine's victory against Maxentius and the traditional *mos maiorum*, therefore, seemed all the more influenced by the divinity of his vision. His building program was designed to broadcast the fact that Christianity was now a favored religion but also to suppress the memory of Maxentius whose own extensive building program was dedicated to the history and civic values of the *mos maiorum*. The strong visualization of Christianity in sacred sites ultimately converted Rome into the Christian center of the church. Next to beautiful temples and statues commissioned by secular aristocrats were the Christian holy places, the basilicas commissioned by Constantine. In the catacombs, especially, pagan and Christian images are (sometimes jarringly) juxtaposed. Rome took on its unique pagan, imperial, and Christian character in precisely this period though Constantine founded and consecrated Constantinople, the modern Istanbul, as the new Christian capital in 330 C.E.

After Constantine, the only return to a pagan imperial government occurred during the reign of Julian (361–363 C.E.) who was Constantine's nephew. As a young boy, he had seen his own father and several male relatives murdered by his Christian relatives in dynastic rivalry. Though he was raised as a Christian he seems to have acquired an abiding love of Greek and Latin literature and philosophy. As a young man he apostasized from Christianity to worship a syncretistic religious philosophy. When he became emperor in 361 C.E., he immediately issued an Edict on Religious Toleration and ordered that pagan temples, altars, sacrifices, and priesthoods be reinstated. State support for Christianity was minimized although there was no overt persecution. His aim was to unite the empire under a shared high culture based upon the Greek ideal of education, called *paideia*. For Julian, the divine word of the gods, the way to true salvation, was revealed in the incomparable and quasi-divine literature of writers like Homer, Hesiod, and Demosthenes and in the culture such literature engendered. Christians, on the other hand, bereft of this literary culture, relied upon the strange (he called it "deranged") myth of Jesus Christ. Because they rejected Hellenism, Julian issued the Edict on Teaching in 362 C.E. that forbade Christian teachers to teach classical literature. In another anti-Christian directive later that same year, he ordered that the Jewish Temple in Jerusalem be rebuilt. Upon his death a year later, the Christian Jovian became emperor. That high-ranking polytheists in Julian's court (who could have) did not attempt to become emperor or to continue his reforms suggests that they did not fear the religious policies of a Christian emperor, and that Christians and non-Christians were not so clearly divided as our modern perspective suggests.

From Constantine to Theodosius the duality of pagan and Christian Rome persisted—in architecture, sculpting, painting, and literature. The east could boast shrines and sites with biblical and New Testament associations, but Rome had the bones of the martyrs Peter and Paul, the twin founders of the church. Yet this was not enough to make Rome the major see of the early church. In addition to the apostolic association Rome claimed through the martyrdoms of Peter and Paul, and in addition to Constantine's Christian building program, it was still necessary for Christians to appropriate a Christian antiquity. This they did in the Codex-Calendar of 354 C.E. and in the rise of the worship of saints, under Pope Damasus (366–384 C.E.).

The Codex-Calendar established a Christian identity for Rome that could be traced well into antiquity, parallel to its polytheistic heritage. By associating commemorations and feasts for the Christian martyrs with pagan religious festivals and celebrations, the Codex-Calendar melded pagan and Christian sacred time and authenticated a Christian history. In addition to the Codex-Calendar, Constantine's churches built around the periphery of the city formed a liturgical pattern of sacred commemorative spaces. The tombs of Peter and Paul secured the identity of *Roma Christiana*, that is, "Christian Rome," in the apostolic succession of churches. Pope Damasus effectively consecrated Rome as the center of pilgrim worship. Sainted bishops' and martyrs' tombs and their relics become popular pilgrimage sites, and under Damasus rites associated with relics, sacred Christian places, and Christian epigrams established Rome as a "new" Jerusalem.

Conclusion

Constantine adapted the vital tenet—*quid pro quo*—of polytheism to Christianity. He attempted to unify the empire in a single religious experience that had widespread appeal. The divinity, pleased by the broad worship, would (he anticipated) respond favorably. By establishing Christianity as a state religion and by inaugurating a vast and splendid Christian building program that invited all levels of society to convert, Constantine reestablished the old polytheistic pattern of common rituals and shared values. Among rival sects and heresies he promoted harmony, so that the state could receive the full benefit of the divinity's prescribed and united worship, just as had been insisted upon by so many previous emperors who persecuted the Christians for refusing to worship the state gods. Damasus oversaw the development of the cult of martyrs and saints whose relics and tombs formed a new Christian topography around which liturgies and pilgrimages developed. His interpretation, like that of Constantine, relied upon the same *quid pro quo* association with the gods that polytheistic Rome had demanded: pilgrims who performed the "sacrifices" properly, that is, who came to Rome to pray at the tombs of martyrs and saints, would be heard by God.

The literary debate over traditional polytheism and Christianity is played out in the texts of Symmachus and Ambrose who contend between themselves in a published correspondence about the removal of the altar of Victory from the Roman senate house. The identity of Rome was in the balance. Polytheism had the strength of antiquity, the traditional *mos maiorum*; Christianity had imperial support.

Through their combined efforts, Constantine, who institutionalized Christianity, Damasus, who organized Rome as a web of holy places, and the Christian emperors who passed legislation against pagan religious practices and gave legal sanction to Christianity created *Roma Christiana*, the new center of the Christian church, over and above Jerusalem and Constantinople.

STUDY QUESTIONS

1 What does the Latin phrase *quid pro quo* mean, and how does it apply to Roman cult practice?

2 Using the bibliographic resources provided at the end of this book, conduct further research into the differences and similarities—organization, relationships with native populations, treatment of the emperor, and so on—between the eastern and western imperial cults.

3 List the different sects of Jews that inhabited ancient Palestine and provide a brief description of each.

4 Is it appropriate to speak of early Christianity as a religion *adversus Judaeos* ("against the Jews")? At what point did early Christianity break away from Judaism, and on what points did the two faiths disagree?

5 Why did early Christians come into conflict with Roman authorities? What criminal charges were frequently raised against early Christians and why?

Chapter 2

JEWS AND CHRISTIANS:
The Dynasty of Herod the Great

The establishment of our religion at the very time when the Empire began so auspiciously was an unmixed blessing, and this is proved by this fact—from the reign of Augustus the Empire has suffered no damage; on the contrary everything has gone splendidly and gloriously, and every prayer has been answered.

—Eusebius, *Historia Ecclesiastica*, 4.26.5

Jesus was born during the reign of Augustus, the first Roman emperor (27 B.C.E.–14 C.E.), in the territory of Herod the Great, King of the Jews (40–4 B.C.E.). The reign of Augustus was a time of universal peace, or *pax Romana* and economic prosperity and so much new building that according to the Roman biographer Suetonius (c. 70–130 C.E.) the emperor used to boast that he had found Rome a city of brick and left it a city of marble. The verses of Isaiah 40–55 look forward to just such a universal peace and prosperity as they foresee the restoration of Israel during the long, peaceful rule of her anointed king, the Messiah. A descendant from the ancestral line of the biblical king David (c. 1050 B.C.E.), this Messiah would restore to the Jewish nation the glory of his reign and free the Jews from foreign dominance. The words of the ecclesiastical historian Eusebius (c. 260–339 C.E.) quoted above echo the Isaiah passages and see the *pax Romana* under Augustus as part of God's divine plan to unify and pacify the world for the birth of Jesus, who claimed to be the Messiah descended from the line of David.

Personalities in Christianity 2.1
EUSEBIUS OF CAESAREA

Bishop of Caesarea (c. 260–339 C.E.) who served as bishop from 313 C.E., the biblical scholar and commentator Eusebius has been called the "father of church history." His *Ecclesiastical History* is the most important history of the first centuries of the early church that we possess. It covers the period from the apostolic age down to his own time, which ended just after the final battle between Constantine and Licinius in 324 C.E., when Constantine became the monarch of the empire. The *Ecclesiastical History* is vitally important for its account of the history of the period; but it is also uniquely valuable in that it is filled with references to, and quotations from, many authors whose works are otherwise unknown. Versions survive in Greek, Latin, Syriac, and Armenian.

Eusebius's teacher and spiritual guide, Pamphilus, who was martyred in the persecution of Diocletian in 310 C.E., was the librarian (and a theologian in his own right) of Origen's academy in Caesarea, the Roman capital of Palestine. The great Christian theologian Origen had taught for almost twenty years in Caesarea at the academy he had established there, and at his death Pamphilus laboriously copied his texts and commentaries. Eusebius was proud of this "intellectual" lineage and even referred to himself as *Eusebius Pamphili*, which means "Pamphilus's Eusebius."

In the Arian controversy, Eusebius was equivocal: a strong promoter of Arius's teachings, he nonetheless signed the Nicene Creed, which upheld the orthodox view. It was at the Council of Nicea in 325 C.E. when Eusebius first met Constantine, who was impressed enough to invite him to deliver an address at his *Tricennalia*, the celebration of his first thirty years as emperor. This and the *Life of Constantine*, which Eusebius wrote after Constantine's death, are panegyrics, which are speeches filled with exaggerated praise. In them, Constantine is depicted as God's representative on earth, and his office is imbued with a religious sanctity. The *Ecclesiastical History* and the works on Constantine are only a sampling of Eusebius's voluminous works, which also include his important *Chronicle* of the world that compares the dates of the great ancient empires. This survives only in a Latin translation by Jerome. Among the apologetic works written to defend the church against its literary and political persecutors are the *Preparation for the Gospel* and the *Proof of the Gospel*, which argue that God had established the world and the empire. Among many other doctrinal, apologetic, and scholarly works, Eusebius wrote an eyewitness account of Diocletian's persecution as it was carried out in the area of Palestine, called the *Martyrs of Palestine*, and an interesting study of the topography of the Holy Land, called the *Onomasticon*.

But the local world into which Jesus was born was in reality a multicultural tinderbox ruled by the Herods—Herod the Great and his descendants, client kings under the Romans. While the Herods sought to unite Jew and gentile in a nation state with some independence from Rome, the Jews were divided among themselves over the increasing secularization of Judea and the increasing collaboration of their Jewish leaders with Rome. Internecine strife, continued warfare, and rivalries over succession were compounded by the general sense among the Jewish populace that their leaders were too secular, too Roman. Instead of unifying the Jews, the rule of the Herods only heightened the antagonism among the

Jews and between Jews and non-Jews, fanning the hope of a Messiah who would free the Jews from their rulers—both the Herods and Romans.

This chapter outlines the story of Jesus, a Jew born in Galilee who claimed that he was the long-awaited Messiah and who inspired the development of a Christian church that would quickly become distinct from its Jewish origins. As the gospel accounts of his life are considered against contemporary politics in the Roman territory of Judea, four historically important intersections between early Christians and the Herods emerge: the birth of Jesus under Herod the Great; the death of John the Baptist at the order of Herod Antipas

TABLE 2.1

Rulers of Judea

Hasmoneans
Judas Maccabeus 166–161 B.C.E.
Jonathan 161–142
Simon 142–135
John Hyrcanus (I) 135–104
Aristobulus I 104–103
Alexander Janneus 103–76
Salome Alexandra 76–67
Hyrcanus II 67, 63–40
Aristobulus II (king) 67–63
Antigonus (king) 40–37

Herods
Herod the Great 37–4
 Judea, Samaria, Galilee, Perea, Batanea, Trachonitis
Archelaus (son by Malthace)

Judea 4 B.C.E.–6 C.E.
Antipas (son by Malthace)
 Galilee and Perea 4 B.C.E.–39 C.E.
Philip (son by Malthace)
 Iturea and Trachonitis 4 B.C.–34 C.E.

Agrippa I (grandson of Herod)
 territory of Philip from 37
 Judea 41–44

Herod of Chalcis (brother and son-in-law of Agrippa I)
 Chalcis 41–48

Agrippa II (son of Agrippa I)
 Chalcis 48–53
 Batanea, Trachonitis, Gaulanitis from 53
 parts of Galilee and of Perea from 61–93

(4 B.C.E.–39 C.E.); the persecution of the early Christians in Jerusalem under Herod Agrippa I (41–44 C.E.); and the meeting in Caesarea of Agrippa II (27/8–c. 100 C.E.) and Paul, the "apostle to the gentiles," just before he began his missionary journey to Rome. Despite the capable sovereignty of each successive Herod, the antagonism between the Jews and the Romans and between the Jews and the emerging "Christian" Jewish sects intensified, until, in the end, the Jewish kings could not prevent the complete dissolution of Jewish-Roman relations, or forestall the spread and growth of the new Christian church.

These priest-kings had united a powerful group of "traditionalists" who were opposed to some forms of Hellenization. It would be an oversimplification, however, to view the "traditionalists" as a homogeneous group since there was a wide range of levels of cooperation—from complete Hellenization to complete resistance—that characterized them. In fact, it was the Hasmoneans' ability to mediate between a political and social Hellenization and a native religious traditionalism that won them a following.

The Hasmonean line of high priests and ethnarchs established their rule in Judea and

Rise of Herod the Great

Jewish-Greco-Roman Conflict

In their long history, the Jews were alternately ruled by the Assyrian, Babylonian, Persian, Greek, Seleucid, Ptolemaic, and Roman empires; they were internally diverse, often fractious, and some were imperturbably defiant. Beginning in 40 B.C.E., Roman rulers appointed Herod the Great, and after him his son Antipas, then Herod's grandson Agrippa I, and then his son Agrippa II as client kings in Palestine. These titular Jewish rulers were forced to straddle the multicultural demands of wide territories plagued by centuries-old conflicts between the Jewish people and their rulers regarding accommodation, collaboration, and resistance. In the second century B.C.E., these conflicts had reached a climax that resulted in the establishment of an earlier dynasty of Jewish rulers—the Hasmoneans.

FIGURE 2.1. *Coin of Herod the Great. This bronze coin with a tripod and Greek inscription dates from the period of Herod the Great, King of Judea (37–44 B.C.E.).*

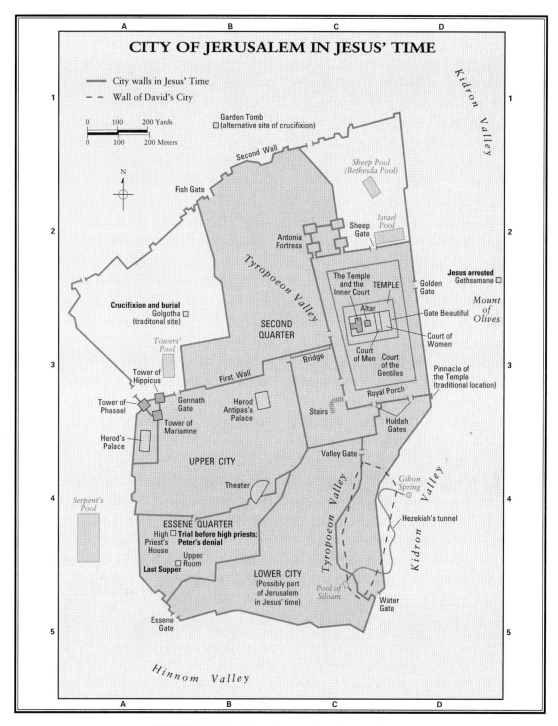

FIGURE 2.2. *City of Jerusalem in Jesus' time*

the larger area of Palestine after the revolutionary Judas Maccabeus, which means "the Hammer," led a revolt in 166 B.C.E. against the Seleucid ruler Antiochus IV Epiphanes (175–164 B.C.E.). Antiochus had attempted to forcibly Hellenize the Jewish state. He banned Temple rites, circumcision, the sanctity of the Sabbath, and the possession of the Torah and Jewish scriptures; everything that identified the religious, ethnic, or political separation of the Jews was restricted. The biblical account of the Maccabean revolt states that in some places mothers were thrown from the city wall with their circumcised babies tied around their necks. To the Jews, Antiochus's final abomination was during the rededication of the Temple in Jerusalem to Zeus Olympios, the Syrian god Ba'al Shamim: at the ceremony, he sacrificed swine on the altar and spattered blood and grease on the walls. After three years of guerilla warfare, Judas Maccabee forced Antiochus IV Epiphanes to restore to the Jews their right to worship in the Temple in Jerusalem (now rededicated to the God of Israel) and to enforce their food laws as previously. Just before his death in 161 B.C.E., Judas also secured an *amicitia*, "treaty of alliance," with Rome, and this alliance was renewed by his successors.

Judas Maccabee's brothers and their sons continued to rule Judea until 63 B.C.E. The high point of Maccabean power was under John Hyrcanus (135–104 B.C.E.), who established a Jewish state loyal to the Temple in Jerusalem and annexed wide territories, including Samaria and Galilee to the north and, to the south, Idumea, the territory of Herod.

Semitic descendants of the biblical Edomites, the Idumeans were hereditary enemies of the Jews. In 109 B.C.E., when their territory was annexed, they were forced against their will to convert to Judaism and to accept circumcision; however, they soon zealously embraced their new faith and considered themselves Jews. When the Romans placed the Idumean Herod on the throne of Judea in 40 B.C.E., it was this conversion that allowed him to justify his role as the religious and civil head of state. Yet, his Judaism was always a matter of controversy among the Jews of more ancient Jewish ancestry. Herod was Idumean by ethnicity and a Jew because of the conquest of Idumea by Hyrcanus; culturally, however, he was a Hellenist.

The Roman Conquest of Jerusalem

The internal wars for succession between the Hasmonean grandsons of John Hyrcanus— Aristobulus II and Hyrcanus II—first made Judea susceptible to intervention by the Roman triumvir Gnaeus Pompeius Magnus, Pompey the Great (106–48 B.C.E.). Pompey was in the east on other business. Pirates had taken control of the Mediterranean Sea and the economic impact on Rome's Mediterranean trade resulted in government intervention.

In 67 B.C.E., the *Lex Gabinia* granted Pompey a three-year *imperium*, "authority of the government," over the entire Mediterranean to eradicate the pirates. He accomplished this in three months rather than in the anticipated three years. While he was in the east, he made Syria a Roman province under the control of a Roman legate. This imperialistic decision,

FROM AN ANCIENT TEXT ❖ 2.1

Plutarch and the Pirate Menace

In this excerpt, Plutarch (46-122 C.E.), the well-known Greek biographer, recounts the story of the Cilician pirates who captured Julius Caesar while he was en route to Rhodes to study oratory (75 B.C.E.). It is an apt illustration of the pirates' ubiquity and the statesman's audacity.

To begin with, then, when the pirates demanded twenty talents for his ransom, he laughed at them for not knowing who their captive was, and of his own accord agreed to give them fifty. In the next place, after he had sent various followers to various cities to procure the money and was left with one friend and two attendants among Cilicians, most murderous of men, he held them in such disdain that whenever he lay down to sleep he would send and order them to stop talking.

For thirty-eight days, as if the men were not his watchers, but his royal bodyguard, he shared in their sports and exercises with great unconcern. He also wrote poems and sundry speeches, which he read aloud to them, and those who did not admire these he would call to their faces illiterate barbarians, and often laughingly threatened to hang them all. The pirates were delighted at this, and attributed his boldness of speech to a certain simplicity or boyish mirth.

But after his ransom had come from Miletus and he had paid it and was set free, he immediately manned vessels and put to sea from the harbor of Miletus against the robbers. He found them, too, still lying at anchor off the island, and got most of them into his power. Their money he made his booty, but the men themselves he lodged in the prison at Pergamum, and then went in person to Junius, the governor of Asia, on the ground that it belonged to him, as praetor of the province, to punish the captives. But since the praetor cast longing eyes on their money, which was no small sum, and kept saying that he would consider the case of the captives at his leisure, Caesar left him to his own devices, went to Pergamum, took the robbers out of prison, and crucified them all, just as he had often warned them on the island that he would do, when they thought he was joking.

Source: Plutarch, *Julius Caesar* 2 in *Plutarch*, tr. Bernadotte Perrin, Loeb Classical Library, 11 vols. (Cambridge, Mass.: Harvard University Press, 1949), vol. 7, *Parallel Lives*, pp. 445–447.

ostensibly to protect Syria from being taken over again by pirates and warring rival kings, effectively laid the groundwork for the great Roman expansion called the *pax Romana*, which Augustus would establish over the eastern empire. Although not directly annexed, Judea was also subject to the legates of Syria. When Pompey arrived in Syria in 63 B.C.E., delegations from both Aristobulus II and Hyrcanus II arrived from Judea laden with gifts and bribes in order to gain his support. This meeting in Damascus between Pompey and the rivaling Hasmonean brothers inaugurated almost two centuries of Judeo-Romano relations that saw the status of Judea change: an independent nation under the Hasmonean priest-kings, Judea became a client kingdom of Rome under the Herods, and, finally, a subject kingdom under direct Roman rule.

At the meeting in Damascus, Pompey recognized Hyrcanus II as high priest and ethnarch, but he left civil authority in the hands of the legate of Syria. In belligerent indignation Aristobulus II returned to Judea to prepare for war. Almost immediately, Pompey followed him and marched on Jerusalem in 63 B.C.E. According to Josephus, within three months of arriving there Pompey had captured and desecrated part of the Temple and killed some 12,000 Jews. The true extent of Rome's control was revealed when Aristobulus II and his sons were forced to march in humiliation in Pompey's triumph in Rome while several Greek cities that had been conquered and annexed by the Maccabee kings were reestablished independent of Judea. In a further decentralization of Maccabean power, Hyrcanus II was permitted to retain only the office of high priest but was relieved of the title of king.

Antipater and Herod: Allies of Rome

Antipater, the chameleonic governor of Idumea, and his son Herod were able to mitigate the impact upon Judea of the tumultuous years of late Republican Rome. They had the uncanny ability to ally themselves with each new leader who emerged from the crumbling Roman Republic, changing loyalties as often as Rome changed governments. Their careers spanned those of the commanders who engineered the birth of the Roman Empire—Julius Caesar, Cassius and Brutus (Caesar's assassins), Mark Antony and Octavian (Caesar's avengers), Cleopatra, and, finally, Octavian, who emerged as the sole ruler and the first Roman emperor.

After the conquest of Jerusalem in 63 B.C.E., Antipater understood quickly that Judea's statehood would not be restored and that only cooperation with Pompey, its new Roman ruler, would ensure his personal financial security and power. Nonetheless, when Pompey was defeated and assassinated by Julius Caesar in 48 B.C.E., Antipater readily changed allegiances and promoted Caesar's interests. Caesar and Antipater together reconfirmed Hyrcanus II as high priest and ethnarch, and together they restored Judea to the status of a client kingdom rather than a Roman province. For his part in these affairs, Josephus tells us that Antipater received the privileges of Roman citizenship with exemption from taxes as well as other honors and marks of friendship. Hyrcanus II held titular power as high priest and king. Antipater, however, seems to have held the real power—financial, popular, and military—and was emboldened to appoint his son Herod as governor of Galilee.

Herod shared his father's genius for chameleonic politics. Twice he overcame the stigma of a previous alliance with their enemies to

FIGURE 2.3. *Model of Herod's Temple. On display at the Holy Land Hotel in Jerusalem, this model represents the Temple of Jerusalem before its destruction in 70 C.E.*

win the confidence of new rulers. In the first instance, he allied himself with Julius Caesar's assassins, Brutus and Cassius, who promised to establish him as king of the Jews after their war with Mark Antony and Octavian. But in 42 B.C.E. that outcome was reversed: Mark Antony and Octavian defeated Caesar's assassins at the Battle of Philippi. Despite the fact that he had cooperated with his enemies, Mark Antony appointed Herod King of the Jews, the chief administrator of the whole of Judea. The Roman Senate acted quickly to confirm Herod's appointment with the expectation that he would reclaim Palestine from the Parthians, who had invaded Syria, Phoenicia,

and Palestine in 40 B.C.E. But Herod was King of the Jews only in Rome. After seven short days of festivities, including a banquet given by his former enemy Mark Antony, Herod returned to Judea where it took him three years to subdue the anti-Roman factions.

In the second instance, Herod was again allied with defeated Roman generals and was forced to win the confidence of his victorious former enemy. When the combined forces of Mark Antony and Cleopatra challenged Octavian at the Battle of Actium in 31 B.C.E., Herod was working for Mark Antony on a campaign against his belligerent neighbors to the east, the Nabateans. Despite this alliance

Personalities in Christianity 2.2
HEROD THE GREAT

Herod's father Antipater was governor of Idumea during the Roman civil wars. When the territory of Judea and the larger area of Palestine (including Idumea) came under Roman rule, Antipater associated himself with the Roman rulers that arrived there in 63 B.C.E., and he appointed his sons, Herod (73–4 B.C.E.) and Phasel, as rulers in adjacent areas. Herod was governor of Galilee in 47 B.C.E. and by 40 B.C.E., after managing to support the victorious Roman general in each of a series of rivalries, he was confirmed as King of the Jews by the Roman senate. However, it took him three years to quell the disturbances in Judea and actually claim his throne.

In the spring of 37 B.C.E., just before he captured Jerusalem, Herod arrogantly left the battle to visit Samaria and marry the Hasmonean Mariamme, who was the granddaughter of Hyrcanus II (ruled 79–40 B.C.E.) and Aristobulus II (ruled 66–63 B.C.E.), brothers and rival Hasmonean princes who had alternately ruled Judea as priest kings. By this marriage, Herod sought to join his Idumean line with the royal line of Hasmonean priest kings; but he also hoped to ingratiate himself with the Jews who still felt that, as an Idumean, Herod was not a *real* Jew, but only a recent convert to Judaism. (Idumea had been conquered and its inhabitants forced to convert under John Hyrcanus I [135–104 B.C.E.] and so were regarded as outsiders.)

Herod was ruthless but effective. During his long and relatively peaceful reign in Judea, he sponsored a building program that echoed the lavish and magnificent building program of Augustus. In addition to the harbor of Caesarea Maritima, an architectural wonder, and in addition to the famed Temple in Jerusalem, Herod undertook vast building projects all over his territories, including theatres, amphitheatres, and fortresses. In his personal life he was plagued by disputes among his ten wives and their children, especially the potential successors among his sons. In 29 B.C.E., he executed Mariamme and then in 7 B.C.E., their two sons. He ordered his eldest son, from a different marriage, to be killed just days before he himself died. At his death, his kingdom was divided among three other sons, Herod Antipas, Archelaus, and Philip. Archelaus ruled Judea, Idumea, and Samaria; Antipas ruled Galilee and Perea; and Philip ruled the territories north and east.

It was (probably) during the reign of Herod that Jesus was born in Bethlehem, an event that heightened the tensions surrounding Herod's dynastic disputes. According to the account in Matt 2:1-12, when he learned from traveling magi that a new king of the Jews had been born in Bethlehem, he ordered that all male children under the age of two be slaughtered to prevent this new *king* from challenging his dynastic plans.

with Mark Antony, Herod won the support of the victorious Octavian. Just after the Battle of Actium, on the island of Rhodes in 30 B.C.E., Herod put aside his royal diadem as an act of submission and asked Octavian not to consider the fact that he had been loyal to Mark Antony, but rather how loyal he had been; and he promised to be just as loyal to Octavian. Octavian acted quickly to reaffirm Herod's title as King of the Jews and soon thereafter vastly expanded his territory.

From 20–14 B.C.E., Herod's kingdom echoed the peace and flourishing prosperity of the renowned *pax Romana* under Augustus that Eusebius later claimed was achieved by God's divine plan to prepare the world to receive Jesus as Christ the Messiah. This golden period in Herod's long reign was marked by lavish entertainments, luxurious building projects, and the construction of vast and splendid cities: Greco-Roman theatres, amphitheatres, fortresses, palaces, colonnades, and temples decorated his territories. His own palace was filled with sculptures and embellished with silver, gold, and other precious materials; a new city, Caesarea, took twelve years to build and was an architectural marvel. The Temple in Jerusalem, however, was the most magnificent of all his building projects. Herod began the project in 20 B.C.E., and it was not completed until 64 C.E., just a few years before the Romans destroyed it. Its massive size and unspeakable riches are proverbial, and the fact that portions of it still remain standing despite the Romans' best effort to raze it illustrates the drama of its scale.

FROM AN ANCIENT TEXT ❖ 2.2

Herod Assumes the Role of King of Judea

Finally, in 37 B.C.E., after a two-month siege during which Herod's troops slaughtered great numbers of Jews, Jerusalem fell and Antigonus surrendered to the Romans who sent him to Antony to be killed. In the melee, Herod could barely control his Roman allies who rushed to plunder the city, as this account from Josephus documents.

And now all parts were full of those that were slain by the rage of the Romans at the long duration of the siege, and by the zeal of Jews that were on Herod's side, who were not willing to leave one of their adversaries alive; so they were murdered continually in the narrow streets and in the houses and as they were flying to the temple for shelter, and there was no pity taken of either infants or the aged, nor did they spare even the women. Although the king sent about and besought them to spare the people, yet none restrained their hand from slaughter, but as if they were a company of madmen, they fell upon persons of all ages, without distinction.

Source: Josephus, *Jewish Antiquities* 14.479-80 in *The Works of Josephus*, tr. William Whiston (Peabody, Mass.: Hendrickson, 1987), p. 396.

FROM AN ANCIENT TEXT ❖ 2.3

Universal Peace in the Reign of Augustus

We possess two contemporary accounts of this universal peace, one from Augustus himself and one from his court poet, Publius Virgilius Maro (Virgil).

Augustus

The peace of Augustus is commemorated in his Res gestae divi Augusti *(34), a personal account of his political accomplishments in which we learn that in 27 B.C.E. his universal peace and personal influence resulted in his receiving the title of "Augustus," a word associated with divinity.*

In my sixth and seventh consulates (28–27 B.C.E.), after putting out the civil war, having obtained all things by universal consent, I handed over the state from my power to the dominion of the senate and Roman people. And for this merit of mine, by a senate decree, I was called Augustus and the doors of my temple were publicly clothed with laurel and a civic crown was fixed over my door and a gold shield placed in the Julian senate-house, and the inscription of that shield testified to the virtue, mercy, justice, and piety, for which the senate and Roman people gave it to me. After that time, I exceeded all in influence, but I had no greater power than the others who were colleagues with me in each magistracy.

Source: P. A. Brunt and J. M. Moore, *Res Gestae Divi Augusti. The Achievements of the Divine Augustus* (Oxford: Oxford University Press, 1983), pp. 35–37.

Virgil

In a similar description from Virgil, Aeneid *6.791–797, we read that the constitutional agreement reached in 27 B.C.E. between Augustus and the Senate inaugurated a new Golden Age.*

This is the man whom you so often have heard to be promised to you, Augustus Caesar, son of a god. He will again establish a Golden Age in the fields once ruled by Saturn, and he will spread his empire beyond the Garamants and Indians, to a land beyond the stars and the paths of the year and sun.

Source: Robert Fitzgerald, *The Aeneid* (New York: Random House, 1983), pp. 187–188.

On the one hand, Herod's reign was characterized by the grand entertainments, reduced taxes, general peace, and brilliant cultural achievements of a ruler who enjoyed Augustus's imperial favor; on the other hand, however, his reign was characterized by a personal life rent by intrigue, murder, and anguish. Beginning in 29 B.C.E., when he had his wife Mariamme murdered on a trumped-up charge of disloyalty, until his death, just about the time of Jesus' birth, Herod's reign steadily devolved into despotism.

In the years just before his death, Herod's sons from his multiple wives—Antipater, Alexander, Aristobulus, Archelaus, Antipas, and Philip—were embroiled in succession rivalries. Antipater, Herod's son by his first wife, sought to undermine his half-brothers Alexander and Aristobulus, Herod's sons by the Hasmonean Mariamme, his second wife. Their intrigues reached such an intolerable level that Herod had Mariamme's sons killed in 7 B.C.E., and, soon thereafter, Antipater was charged with conspiring to kill his father. In 4 B.C.E., in the final days of his life, Herod had Antipater killed, too. His will named his three other sons—the brothers Archelaus and Antipas, and their half-brother, Philip—as his successors.

Although Augustus allowed Herod's three sons to divide his kingdom at his death in 4 B.C.E., he deposed the eldest, Archelaus, in 6 C.E., and sent him to exile in Vienne. At his brother's deposition, Antipas received the dynastic title Herod; he ruled over a predominantly Jewish Aramaic-speaking population in Galilee and Perea, the areas north and east of Judea, until 39 C.E. It was in his territory that Jesus had been born while his father still ruled; it was under his rule that Jesus was baptized by John the Baptist; and it was in his territory that Jesus preached and taught that a new God, a loving Father, was accessible by prayer to a new community of the faithful. Jesus' teaching was unique and Jesus was called the prophet promised by all the prophets, come to lift the Jews from the oppression of Rome and the defilement of Hellenization.

Life of Jesus

Birth of Jesus

The principal sources for Jesus' life are the four canonical gospels (c. 90 C.E.) by the evangelists Matthew, Mark, Luke, and John. Several non-canonical Christian texts called *apocrypha* or *pseudepigrapha* also depict stories of Jesus' life, but these are not included in the New Testament. Written in Greek, although Jesus himself spoke Aramaic, the gospels of Matthew, Mark, and Luke are called the *synoptic* gospels because they all correspond closely and share a common perspective. The gospel of John is more philosophical and was written a bit later, perhaps 90–100 C.E.

In the gospel accounts (notably Luke), the story of Jesus begins with the story of his conception. When she was a young girl, his mother Mary was engaged to a carpenter, Joseph. During this time the angel Gabriel appeared to Mary, who was a virgin, and told her that she was carrying a child, a boy to be named Jesus who was the Messiah. Mary told her cousin Elizabeth, the mother of John the Baptist, of the angel's visit, and the angel also appeared to Joseph in a dream to tell him that Mary had conceived a child through the Holy Spirit. Mary and Joseph then married. Toward the end of Mary's pregnancy, although they lived in Nazareth, Mary and Joseph were required to travel to Bethlehem to be counted as part of the census organized by the Romans to assess taxes in the province. Because Bethlehem was crowded with travelers coming there for the census, Mary and Joseph could not find a room at any inn. Mary was in labor and instead of turning them away completely, one innkeeper allowed them to sleep in the stables. There, in the last years of Herod's despotic reign, Jesus was born.

Herod and the "Slaughter of the Innocents"

Of the four gospel accounts only Matthew writes of the magi, eastern astrologers who had interpreted the appearance of a new star to mean that a ruler was to be born among the Jews. According to Matthew's account (2:1-12), when the magi (commonly called the Three Wise Men) arrived in Jerusalem and asked King Herod where the new king of the Jews would be born, he convened his scribes and chief priests to consult with them on the matter. They advised him of the prophecy that a ruler would come from Bethlehem to shepherd the people of Israel, and so it was to Bethlehem that Herod directed the magi. He then asked the magi to return to Jerusalem after paying homage to the new king, to tell him exactly where he could find the child and pay homage himself. In reality, according to the gospel account, Herod intended to learn

Personalities in Christianity 2.3
HEROD ANTIPAS

Antipas (20 B.C.E.–c. 39 C.E.) was the youngest son of Herod by his wife Malthace. Upon his father's death in 4 B.C.E., Antipas became tetrarch of Galilee and Perea. He was a competent ruler who continued his father's building projects in the former capital city Sepphoris and built the new capital city Tiberias, named in honor of Emperor Tiberius. Thereafter, this new city, which included a stadium and a palace on the model of a Greek city, was the capital of Galilee.

Antipas was married to the daughter of Aretas IV, the Nabetean king. When he divorced her to marry his own niece Herodias, who was also his half-brother's wife, a series of civil wars erupted between Aretas and Antipas. Moreover, the marriage offended the Jews because it violated Mosaic Law and so was vociferously condemned by John the Baptist (Matt 14:4; Mark 6:18). Herodias and her daughter Salome are said to have requested the beheading of John the Baptist from Antipas, but by some accounts (Matt 14:9; Mark 6:26) he was distressed that exactly where the child was so that he could have him killed.

The magi did not return to Herod because they had been in a dream warned of his malevolence. Their inquiry, however, had unnerved him; he was deeply mired in rivalries, murders, and intrigues concerning his succession. Despite the failure of the magi to give him any news, rumors abounded about the birth of the Messiah, and King Herod became desperate in his search for the baby. Upon hearing news that the Messiah had been born in Bethlehem, King Herod dispatched his troops there with orders to kill every male child they found under the age of two years. This event, called the Slaughter of the Innocents, is known only from the account in Matthew 2:16 which speaks more to its qualities as an interpretive rather than historical narrative. Some scholars accept that the story sets up an obvious literary parallel with the account in Exodus (1:22) of the murder of the Israelite children and that it is intended to associate Jesus with Moses and Herod with Pharaoh. Others consider the story a fictional elaboration upon Herod's murder of his own sons, or a representative expression of the more general distraction and paranoia that punctuated his reign.

Jesus was not killed in the slaughter ordered by Herod because an angel again had visited Joseph, this time to urge him to flee to Egypt where he and his family lived safely until Herod's death. When he learned of Herod's death, Joseph eventually resettled his family in Nazareth in the area of Galilee, north of Judea. Jesus' youth in Galilee must have put him in touch with the revolutionary tradition for which it is famous: Judas the Galilean had led revolts against Herod and also against the

he had agreed to grant their request and even feared that Jesus was a resurrected John (Matt 14:2). Antipas ruled for the entirety of Jesus' ministry, his trial, and his death.

According to the account in Luke 23:6-12, Antipas was in Jerusalem for the feast of the Passover when Jesus was condemned by the Sanhedrin and by Pontius Pilate for, respectively, blasphemy and subversion. Before he passed final judgment, Pilate sent Jesus to Antipas, perhaps thinking that because Jesus was from Galilee and Antipas was tetrarch of Galilee it fell more properly to Antipas to pass judgment. Antipas, however, refused to make any legal decision about Jesus; after allowing his soldiers to dress him as a king in mockery, he sent him back to Pilate. This exchange seems to have resulted in a new cordiality between Pilate and Antipas, who previously had complained directly to the emperor about Pilate's insensitivity to Jewish religious principles.

Several times during his reign, Antipas unsuccessfully petitioned Roman emperors for greater territory. Finally, in 39 C.E., after one such petition for more territory and authority, Caligula exiled him to Gaul (modern France) and transferred his territories to his nephew Agrippa I, Herodias's brother and the grandson of Herod through his father Aristobulus.

FIGURE 2.4. *The Adoration of the Magi. Painted by Antonio Vivarini (c. 1418–1476), this is a particularly lush treatment of the story of the Three Wise Men (or magi) from the east who followed a star that they believed heralded the birth of a new king of the Jews. When they passed through the territory of Herod the Great, he directed them to Bethlehem and, according to Matt 2:1-17, he then prepared to slaughter all children under the age of two, to ensure that his own sons would inherit his title.*

Romans; he claimed that the Jews owed allegiance only to God and that they should not be forced to pay taxes to the Romans.

For the first thirty years of his life Jesus lived quietly in Nazareth with one exception. When he was about twelve, Mary discovered that Jesus was missing from the group of travelers who had returned to Nazareth from Jerusalem after celebrating the Feast of Passover (Luke 2:41-49). She searched for him for three days before she found him in the Temple in Jerusalem, astounding the priests and rabbis

there with his knowledge. When she chided him for causing her and Joseph such anxiety, Jesus cryptically remarked, "Why were you looking for me? Did you not know that I must be in my Father's house?"

Baptism of Jesus

According to the gospel accounts, Jesus was about thirty years old when his cousin John baptized him (c. 26 C.E.). This event marked the beginning of his ministry—his preaching and teaching in Galilee and Judea. The fact that his baptism is recorded in all four of the gospels (Matt 3:13-17; Mark 1:9-11; Luke 3:21-22; John 1:29-34) marks it as a significant turning point in the story of his life. According to each account, Jesus arrived to the Jordan River in Bethany from Nazareth to submit to the purification of his cousin John's baptism. John was an ascetic prophet and preacher who lived in the wilderness. Perhaps a member of a monastic community, he wore clothing made of camel's hair, ate locusts and honey, and demanded repentance and baptism for anyone who wished to prepare for the coming of the kingdom of God. He denied that he was the Messiah and he promised that someone was yet to come who would baptize with the Holy Spirit and fire and whose sandals he was not fit even to carry (Matt 3:11; Mark 1:7-8; Luke 3:16; John 2:26-27). In the synoptic gospels (Matt 3:17; Mark 1:11; Luke 3:22), when Jesus entered the Jordan River to be baptized by John, the heavens opened and the dove of the Holy Spirit appeared; as he emerged from the water, a voice was heard proclaiming, "This is my beloved son in whom I am well pleased."

The Death of John the Baptist

In two gospel accounts (Matt 14:3-12 and Mark 6:17-26), Herod Antipas ordered the beheading of John the Baptist not long after he had baptized Jesus. According to these

FIGURE 2.5. *The Slaughter of the Innocents. This fresco of Domenico Ghirlandaio (1449–1494) is located in the Tornabuoni Chapel in the Basilica of Santa Maria Novella in Florence.*

accounts, in 27 B.C.E., Antipas visited his half-brother Herod Boethus while en route to Rome. Boethus was married to his own niece Herodias, a granddaughter of Herod the Great and the Hasmonean Mariamme. During this visit, Antipas and Herodias seem to have agreed that when he returned from Rome she would divorce Boethus to marry him. When Antipas' wife, the daughter of the neighboring Nabatean king, Aretas IV (9 B.C.E.–40 C.E.), heard of this plan, she escaped to her father's kingdom to report the insult. King Aretas was enraged, but even the threat of war was not enough to make Antipas reconcile with his wife and appease his father-in-law. Instead, as they had planned, Antipas married his half-brother Boethus' wife Herodias. Salome, the daughter of Boethus and Herodias, joined her mother when she moved to the territory of her new husband.

Herod Antipas's marriage to his half-brother's wife contravened Jewish law, which states that no man may marry the wife of his brother. This is an act of incest according to Lev 18:16 and 20:21. John the Baptist, who was then preaching in Perea, condemned the marriage. Antipas feared that John's influence over the people could lead to political unrest, even his own deposition, and so he had him arrested and sent to the fortress on the east end of the Dead Sea, at Macherus. John seems to have been in prison there on the evening when Antipas together with his many guests celebrated his birthday at an infamous banquet.

As part of the banquet entertainment, Salome performed a dance for Antipas and his guests. Antipas was said to have been enchanted by her performance, so enchanted that he promised to grant her any request that she made. She briefly consulted with her mother who, perhaps because she was still harboring resentment against him for his condemnation of her marriage to Antipas (Mark 6:19), prompted her to ask for the head of John the Baptist on a platter.

Josephus's account of the death of John the Baptist is less dramatic than the accounts in the gospels and highlights Herod's fear that John would incite a rebellion. He makes no mention of the role of Herodias and Salome. Instead, he concentrates upon the divine wrath visited upon Herod Antipas for what he considers an unjust murder, that of John the Baptist. In 36 C.E., what began as a series of border disputes between Aretas IV and Antipas resulted in a full-blown war between the two nations. Antipas's army was soundly defeated. Josephus suggests that Antipas's defeat by Aretas IV was God's retribution for the tetrarch's rejection of his wife (the king's daughter), his illicit marriage to his brother's wife Herodias, and his capricious murder of John, whom Josephus calls a good man who preached virtue, righteousness, and piety.

Ministry of Jesus

Among Jesus' public acts during his ministry, one of the best known is called the Miracle at the Wedding at Cana (John 2:1-12), when Jesus changed water into the finest of wines. In this account, Jesus and his mother Mary attended a wedding at Cana, in Galilee. During the feast Mary told Jesus that the hosts had run out of

FROM AN ANCIENT TEXT ❖ 2.4

Two Gospel Accounts of the Death of John the Baptist

There are two gospel accounts of the dance of Salome and her request to have the head of John the Baptist on a platter. They differ in that the account in Mark is more detailed, but the important fact that Herod was distressed when he heard that the price of Salome's dance would be the death of John is central to both. Although in Matthew's account (14:3-12), Herod regrets that he had to abide by his promise to Salome and order John's death, he also feared John's power as a prophet and wanted to kill him.

Matthew 14:3-12

Now Herod had arrested John, bound him, and put him in prison on account of Herodias, the wife of his brother Philip, for John had said to him "It is not lawful for you to have her." Although he wanted to kill him, he feared the people, for they regarded him as a prophet. But at a birthday celebration for Herod, the daughter of Herodias performed a dance before the guests and delighted Herod so much that he swore to give her whatever she might ask for. Prompted by her mother, she said, "Give me here on a platter the head of John the Baptist." The king was distressed, but because of his oaths and the guests who were present, he ordered that it be given, and he had John beheaded in prison. His head was brought in on a platter and given to the girl, who took it to her mother. His disciples came and took away the corpse and buried him; and they went and told Jesus.

Mark's account (6:17-28) is almost identical to that of Matthew except that here Herod does not fear John and is deeply distressed that he must order his death.

Mark 6:17-28

Herod was the one who had John the Baptist arrested and bound in prison on account of Herodias, the wife of his brother Philip, whom he had married. John had said to Herod, "It is not lawful for you to have your brother's wife." Herodias harbored a grudge against him and wanted to kill him but was unable to do so. . . . She had an opportunity one day when Herod, on his birthday, gave a banquet for his courtiers, his military officers, and the leading men of Galilee. The daughter of Herodias came in and performed a dance that delighted Herod and his guests. The king said to the girl, "Ask of me whatever you wish and I will grant it to you." . . . She went out and said to her mother, "What shall I ask for?" She replied, "The head of John the Baptist." The girl hurried back to the king's presence and made her request, "I want you to give me at once on a platter the head of John the Baptist." The king was deeply distressed, but because of his oaths and the guests he did not wish to break his word to her. So he promptly dispatched an executioner with orders to bring back his head. He went off and beheaded him in prison. He brought in the head on a platter and gave it to the girl. The girl in turn gave it to her mother.

wine. At first, Jesus told his mother that it was not yet time for him to reveal his glory, but then he ordered the servers to fill six water jars to the brim and to draw some out for the head-waiter to taste. The servers had filled the jars so they knew it was water, but the headwaiter did not; when he tasted it, he marveled at the fact that such a fine wine was to be served so late in the celebration. After that event, Jesus began to preach all through the area of Galilee that all should repent and prepare for the kingdom of heaven—the end of time, which was soon to appear on earth. Jesus traveled around teaching, preaching, and performing miracles, including healing the sick, curing lepers, making blind men see, deaf men hear, and lame men walk, and bringing back to life a dead man named Lazarus. He embraced lepers and welcomed sinners, urging all to believe in God and to be redeemed. His fame traveled as far as Syria and crowds gathered wherever he went.

Among Jesus' followers were twelve disciples ("students") or apostles ("those sent out"), men later regarded as forming the foundation of his new church. Following John the

---

FROM AN ANCIENT TEXT ❖ 2.5

Josephus's Account of the Death of John the Baptist

Josephus's account of the death of John the Baptist attributes John's imprisonment and murder to Antipas's fear that he will incite the people to rebellion.

Now, some of the Jews thought that the destruction of Herod's army came from God, and that very justly, as a punishment of what he did against John, who was called the Baptist: for Herod slew him, who was a good man, and commanded the Jews to exercise virtue, both as to righteousness towards one another, and piety towards God, and so to come to baptism; for the washing would be acceptable to him, if they made use of it, not for the remission of some sins, but for the purification of the body; supposing still that the soul was thoroughly purified beforehand by righteousness. Now, when others came in crowds about him, for they were greatly moved by hearing his words, Herod, who feared lest the great influence John had over the people might put it into his power and inclination to raise a rebellion (for they seemed ready to do anything he should advise), thought it best, by putting him to death, to prevent any mischief he might cause, and not bring himself into difficulties, by sparing a man who might make him repent of it when it should be too late. Accordingly he was sent a prisoner, out of Herod's suspicious temper, to Macherus, the castle I before mentioned, and was there put to death. Now the Jews had an opinion that the destruction of this army was sent as a punishment upon Herod, and a mark of God's displeasure against him.

Source: Josephus, *Jewish Antiquities* 18.5 in *The Works of Josephus*, tr. William Whiston (Peabody, Mass.: Hendrickson, 1987), p. 484.

Personalities in Christianity 2.4
JOSEPHUS

The primary sources for Jewish history from 400 B.C.E. to approximately 100 C.E. are the books of the historian Flavius Josephus (38–c. 100 C.E.), a Jew who wrote in Greek and lived in Rome under the protection of the Flavian court. His sources include the Bible, a rich collection of Hellenistic texts, and his own experience; his corpus represents the continuity of Jewish history from creation to the revolt against the Romans in 66 C.E. Additionally, it is the source of Jewish theological doctrine and moral and social conduct, and a reflection of Jewish historical consciousness.

Born in Jerusalem in 37 or 38 C.E., Joseph ben Mattathias, called Josephus, was a member of one of the most important families of the priesthood. At twenty-six, in the year 63 C.E., Josephus led a deputation to Rome on behalf of imprisoned Jewish priests who had been sent to Rome by the governor Felix to be tried before Nero. He secured their release through Poppea, the wife of Nero. Upon returning to Jerusalem, he entered into the First Jewish Revolt by commanding a garrison in Galilee. During his short time there he seems to have been in conflict with other Jewish leaders because he did not want to oppose Rome. He was captured but later defected to the Romans and earned the patronage of Vespasian when he predicted that he would become emperor. Josephus accompanied Titus on the final siege of Jerusalem in 70 C.E. as an official historian and there he attempted to persuade the rebel Jews to surrender. After the fall of Jerusalem, Josephus returned to Rome with Titus where he was rewarded with citizenship and adopted by the Flavians. Thus, he was not an impartial historian: he was made a Roman citizen, received a lifetime pension, and enjoyed the imperial friendship and favor of the Flavians, even taking their family name as his own.

Both a Jewish historian and a Roman apologist, Josephus wrote on the premise that no one could challenge Rome. Four of his works are extant. The *Jewish War* (*Bellum Iudaicum*) in seven books must have been composed in the 70s since Titus authorized its publication in 79–81 C.E. The general themes of the book reiterate his basic tenet, that Rome was invincible and that only a small volatile group of Jews was responsible for inciting the revolt. The book begins with the reign of Antiochus IV and the Maccabean revolt and ends with the capture of Masada in 73 or 74 C.E.

His *Jewish Antiquities* (*Antiquitates Iudaicae*) was completed in 94 C.E. This work was an apology for the Jews, an attempt to present Judaism to the Greeks and Romans in a positive light by emphasizing its antiquity and by illustrating points of contact with Greco-Roman thought. Using the Septuagint rather than the original Hebrew scriptures, books 1–10 retell the history of the Jews according to the Old Testament. The *Life* (*Vita*) was published in 95 C.E. as an appendix

to the *Antiquities*. A defense of his actions, especially in Galilee during the First Jewish Revolt (66–67 C.E.), this can be usefully compared to the same account in Book 2 of the *Jewish War* for an appreciation of how Josephus' motives affected his historical accounts.

Josephus' final work is *Against Apion* (*Contra Apionem*), an Alexandrian Greek who appeared with the delegation to Claudius in 41 C.E. to accuse the Jewish community in that city of misconduct. One of the earliest examples of Judeo-Christian apologetic literature, Josephus' response to Apion provides details of specific contemporary anti-Semitic attitudes.

Baptist, they believed him to be the Messiah, the one about whom Moses and the prophets had written. The first to become disciples were the fishermen Simon and his brother Andrew. As they were casting their nets into the Sea of Galilee, Jesus called them to follow him and become "fishers of men." Included among the Twelve were (Matt 10:1-4): the "fishers of men" Andrew and his brother Simon, whom

Jesus renamed Peter; James, son of Zebedee, and his brother John; Philip, Bartholomew, Thomas, Matthew, the tax collector; James, son of Alphaeus; Thaddeus; Simon the Cananean; and Judas Iscariot, who later would betray Jesus to the Romans. Before commissioning them to go out and preach the coming of the kingdom, Jesus gave the disciples the authority to cure diseases, raise the dead, cleanse lepers, and dispel demons. In giving them this injunction, he predicted that they would suffer persecution; he told them that he knew sending them out to preach what he was teaching was like sending sheep into the midst of wolves (Matt 10:16).

Jesus' teaching often took the form of parables—short narratives with morals attached—such as the parable of the prodigal son who returned to his father's home after spending his patrimony (Luke 15:11-32). His arrival was celebrated with a great feast while his brother, who had worked loyally for the entire time his brother was gone, had never enjoyed that extravagant a display of affection from his father. The moral of this parable is that when someone returns from a life of dissipation to one of honest living it should be celebrated and that honest living is in itself a reward. His parables often confused even his

FIGURE 2.6. *Jesus the Good Shepherd. The image of Jesus as the Good Shepherd adopts the classical* Κριοφόρος *(the "ram-bearer"), a figure that commemorates an ancient religious sacrifice. Jesus calls himself the Good Shepherd (John 10:1-21). This fourth-century drawing is in the Museo Epigrafico, Rome.*

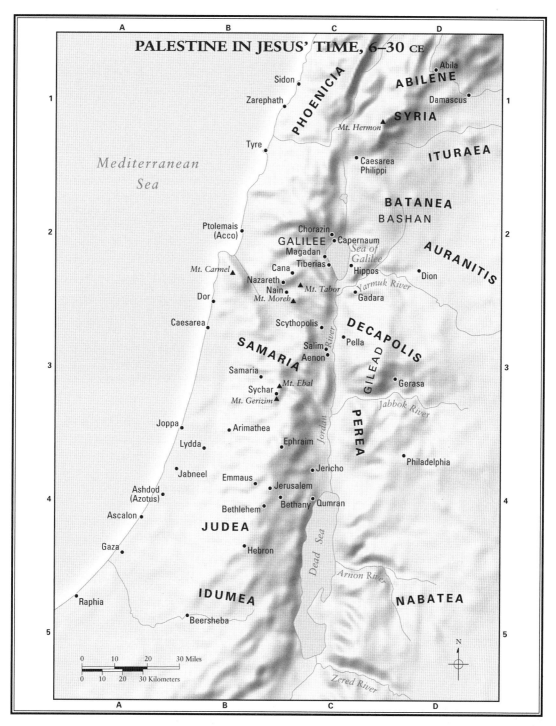

FIGURE 2.7. *Palestine in Jesus' Time, 6–30 C.E.*

FIGURE 2.8. *Funerary stele of Licinia Amias. One of the most ancient Christian inscriptions, the fish (from the Greek, ΙΧΘΥΣ or ΙΧΘΥC) became a well-known Christian symbol and acrostic in Augustine's* City of God *(18:23). The initials spell the Greek words for "Jesus Christ Son of God Savior."*

disciples who would listen to Jesus deliver one and then later ask him to explain its application (Matt 13:36).

Jesus performed miracles for large crowds and also while alone with his disciples. All four gospels include the story of the Multiplication of the Loaves or the Feeding of the Five Thousand (Matt 14:13-21; Mark 6:34-44; Luke 9:10-17; John 6:1-13): Jesus attracted so many followers that once when he was in a small boat in shallow water, thousands of people had gathered on the deserted shore nearby to hear him speak. When it grew late and there was no village nearby where they could buy food, Jesus asked his disciples to bring him all the available food. He blessed the five meager loaves of bread and two fish and turned them into enough food to feed the multitudes, and enough to fill twelve baskets with leftovers. Shortly after this miracle, Jesus performed another miracle that only his disciples saw—he walked on water (Mark 6:45-48; John 6:16-19). After the crowds of his followers had eaten, Jesus withdrew to a nearby mountain and sent his disciples ahead by boat across the sea to Capernaum. A few miles out in the open sea the disciples could no longer row against the wind and churning waves. Suddenly, out of the storm, they saw Jesus walking on the water approaching the boat. In Matthew's version of the miracle (14:22-25), Peter then climbed out of the boat and began to walk toward Jesus, but he began to sink and Jesus rebuked him for his lack of faith. When Jesus got into the boat the stormy waters calmed, but the combination of the two miracles had frightened and astounded even his disciples.

Death of Jesus

When Jesus was in his thirties he went with his disciples to Jerusalem to celebrate Passover. As Jesus came to Jerusalem for the Passover festival, the fears of the Jewish leaders—priests, scribes, and elders—were realized. Palms were strewn on the road as he entered in triumph accompanied by shouts of joy and acclamation (Mark 11:9-10): "Hosanna! Blessed is he who comes in the name of the Lord. Blessed is the kingdom of our father David that is coming! Hosanna in the highest!" Once in the city, he denounced the chief priests and scribes who were looking for a way to stop his rising popularity. Not only did they fear the social unrest and the possibility of an insurgency as a result of this religious fervor, but they also feared the reprisal of Rome. In John 11:48, the convened priests worry that if they do nothing about the crowds following Jesus, the fanaticism will escalate to such a point that the Romans will come and take away both their land and their nation. Caiaphas, the high priest, argued that Jesus had to die for the good of Israel, to save the nation of Jews from the wrath of Rome. While the Jewish leaders were considering how to control his restive crowd of zealots, Jesus dramatically chased the moneychangers out of the Temple. This was an open challenge to the priests who called him before them and asked by what authority he did these things. Hostility escalated and the authority of the Jewish leaders was pit against the messianic expectations popularized by the new teaching of Jesus.

The night before he died, Jesus celebrated the Passover supper with his disciples. After the supper, Jesus went with some of his disciples to the Garden of Gethsemane. There he prayed that either he might not have to suffer the death that seemed inevitable or that he would find the strength to acquiesce to God's will. Led by Judas Iscariot, Roman soldiers found Jesus in the Garden of Gethsemane and brought him before the high priest Caiaphas, who asked him whether he was the Messiah. When Jesus answered that he was the Son of Man, the assembled council was outraged at the blasphemy and he was taken immediately before the Roman governor Pontius Pilate. Before Pilate, he was accused of preaching that he was the Son of God and King of the Jews. According to the account in Matt 27:1-26, Pilate attempted to persuade the priests and other accusers that he had not done anything to merit punishment, but the crowd only became more agitated.

Herod Antipas was also in Jerusalem for the Feast of the Passover during the trial. Since he was the ruler of Galilee, Pilate thought it prudent to defer to him on the matter of the Galilean Jesus. He sent him as a prisoner to Antipas so that he could pass judgment on the charges. In Luke 23:6-11, we read that Antipas was eager to meet Jesus because he wanted to see him perform one of the miracles he had heard so much about; but when Jesus refused to perform, Antipas was content to mock him by dressing him in royal clothing before sending him back to Pilate. Finally, Pilate dramatically washed his hands of the affair and offered the customary Passover liberation of a criminal of their choice. The crowd chose the notorious criminal Barabbas and called for Jesus to be crucified.

Under Roman rule, divinity was an honor accorded only to the Roman emperor and there could be no king but Caesar. Therefore, Jesus' claim that he was the Messiah, the Son of God and King of the Jews (Luke 22:66—23:5) was considered an act of treason against the Roman state. Pilate, as the Roman ruler of Judea, had no choice but to order Jesus to be killed for claiming to be divine. He was crucified under a wooden sign that read King of the Jews in Hebrew, Latin, and Greek (John 19:20). (The first letter of each of those words in Latin [*Iesus Nazarenus Rex Iudeorum*, "Jesus the Nazarene King of the Jews"] is the source of the well-known *INRI* Christian symbol.)

FROM AN ANCIENT TEXT ❖ 2.6

Josephus's Account of the Trial and Death of Jesus

Jesus' trial and death are passed over in silence among the writers of the first century C.E. and receive little more than a note in passing in the works of Josephus. This single brief reference to a defining event in the early Christian movement in Jerusalem reminds us that from the prospective of the Jews and the Romans, Christianity was only one of many small religious groups with a messianic vision in the tense multiethnic areas around Jerusalem in the first century C.E. Nonetheless, though hardly more than a footnote, within three years of his death the incipient church of Jesus had spread well beyond the borders of Jerusalem.

Now there was at this time Jesus, a wise man, if it is lawful to call him a man, for he was a doer of wonderful works—a teacher of such men as receive the truth with pleasure. He drew over to him both many of the Jews, and many of the gentiles. He was the Christ; and when Pilate, at the suggestion of the principal men amongst us, had condemned him to the cross, those that loved him at the first did not forsake him for he appeared to them alive again on the third day, as the divine prophets had foretold these and ten thousand other wonderful things concerning him; and the tribe of Christians so named from him are not extinct at this day.

Source: Josephus, *Jewish Antiquities* 18.3.63–4 in *The Works of Josephus*, tr. William Whiston (Peabody, Mass.: Hendrickson, 1987), p. 480.

Separation of Judaism and Christianity

Agrippa I and the Persecution of the Jews in Alexandria

In 38 C.E., Caligula crowned his childhood friend Agrippa I, the brother of Herodias and grandson of Herod the Great, King of the Jews. When he set out from Rome for Palestine to assume the throne, Agrippa stopped in Alexandria. His presence there seems to have provoked severe riots between the Jews and the Greeks and Egyptians. In collusion with their Roman governor A. Avillius Flaccus, the Alexandrians insulted Agrippa by staging a mock homage to his kingship. Agrippa had processed through the city surrounded by bodyguards in bright gleaming armor and the Alexandrians derided the pompous arrival by crowning their own "king of the Jews" and parading him through the streets. Flaccus permitted further outrages against the Jews: emperor images were installed in the synagogues; Jews were stripped of their rights as citizens; and a general persecution was approved. Because they refused to worship the emperor, Jews were dragged into the theater and flogged or forced to eat pork. Agrippa left Alexandria hurriedly but not before sending a letter to Caligula in which he reported the abuses of Flaccus. This, Agrippa's first act as King of the Jews, resulted in Flaccus's arrest and banishment.

Agrippa I and the Gilded Statue of Caligula

When Agrippa arrived in Palestine, his sister Herodias was envious of his title. This new King of the Jews had been obliged a few years before to ask for help from her husband Herod Antipas, who had been serving as tetrarch since his father's death in 4 B.C.E. Hoping that Caligula would recognize her husband as king, Herodias urged Antipas to go to Rome and petition a royal title for himself. Instead of rewarding him with a title, however, Caligula deposed Antipas, banished him to Lugdunum in Gaul and, in 39 C.E., added his tetrarchy to Agrippa's already substantial territory. Later that year, when Agrippa was in Rome, a situation similar to the one he had experienced the year before in Alexandria came to a head in Palestine.

In Jamnia, near Jerusalem, Jews destroyed an altar that a group of non-Jews had erected so that they could perform rites associated with emperor worship. In retaliation, Caligula ordered that a large gilded statue of himself be set up in the Temple in Jerusalem, a defilement that recalls the abominations of Antiochus IV Epiphanes. Anticipating a response like that of the Maccabeans to Antiochus, Caligula took the precaution of ordering Publius Petronius, the governor of Syria, to be ready with troops if any Jews resisted. The Jews heard about the emperor's plan to install his effigy in the Temple and went *en masse* to Petronius to beg him not to allow Caligula's effigy in the Temple. In addition, they threatened not to till the land, which would have severely crippled the economy and prevented payment of the tribute money due to Rome. Agrippa knew nothing of the events in Palestine, since he was traveling to Rome to meet Caligula who was returning from a campaign in Germany.

Consequently, when he met the emperor, he was shocked and bewildered to find the emperor enraged about a fractious situation in Jerusalem. Upon learning the cause, he dissuaded the emperor from going through with his planned profanation of the Temple. But it was only Caligula's death in January 41 C.E. that forestalled the outbreak of more hostilities in Jerusalem, where he had ordered altars to be erected in several localities so that he could be worshipped.

Agrippa was still in Rome at Claudius's accession (41 C.E.). In the hope that King Agrippa would be able to pacify tensions in Palestine, Claudius added to his territories so that he now ruled the same kingdom that his grandfather Herod the Great had ruled. Agrippa returned to Jerusalem in May of 41 C.E. and revived some of the former glory of the Jewish state by adding a third north wall to enclose a large residential area outside of the original walls. Josephus (*Jewish Antiquities* 19.331) tells us that he observed the Mosaic Law in Jerusalem and defended it abroad by demonstrating every act of piety, and that he performed the appointed sacrifice for each day in the calendar. For the duration of his brief reign (41–44 C.E.), he seems never to have left Judea again but to have been a beneficent and obliging ruler and an advocate for the Jews.

Agrippa I and the Persecution of the Christians in Jerusalem

Agrippa had become so devoted to Judaism, in fact, that he allowed an attack against the Christian church in Jerusalem, now headed by the apostle James, the brother of John

and son of Zebedee. In these early days of the church in Jerusalem there was a growing antagonism between the Christian Hellenists and the Christian Hebrews. We read in Acts 10 that Peter baptized the first gentile and that Hellenized Jewish Christians were proselytizing and preaching in synagogues both within and outside of Jerusalem. The mission to the gentiles was aggressive and characterized by a new leniency: whereas in the past Jewish converts were forced to take on all aspects of Jewish law, now uncircumcised gentiles were welcomed into the church. This, along with the failure of the new converts to observe the food laws or the Sabbath and the fact that they preferred the Greek Septuagint to the Hebrew or Aramaic Bible, forced a breach to develop in the incipient Jewish-Christian community between conservative Jewish-Christians and those, like Peter and Paul, who baptized and preached to the gentiles as well as to the circumcised Jews. To summarize the distinction: the Aramaic-speaking Jewish Christians still regarded the Torah and Temple worship in Jerusalem as the central features of their worship; the Hellenized Jewish Christians considered Jesus the Messiah and thought that his authority had eclipsed that of Moses. These two groups were further divided on the question of whether all converts to Christianity were to be circumcised as well as baptized.

According to Acts 12:1-3, Agrippa had authorized an attack against the Jewish believers in Jesus in Jerusalem. Agrippa further ordered the apostle James, brother of John, to be killed, and then "after he saw that this pleased the Jews," he had the apostle Peter

Personalities in Christianity 2.5
PETER

Peter (died c. 65 C.E.) is included among the twelve apostles every time they are mentioned in the gospels, where he is variously called a "fisherman" or a "fisher" of men. In John 1:35, Peter is called Cephas, an Aramaic word that in Greek means "rock," and in Matt 16:13-20, when he declared that Jesus was the Christ, the Son of the living God, Jesus played upon his name [Rock] by answering, "You are Peter (Rock) and on this 'rock' I will build my church." In the same passage, Jesus gives Peter the keys of heaven and adds, "Whatever you bind on earth shall be bound in heaven and whatever you loose on earth shall be loosed in heaven." This apostolic succession became the bedrock of Rome's claim to primacy and papal infallibility.

At the Last Supper, just after Peter had assured Jesus that he would not only go to prison with him but would die with him, Jesus predicted that Peter would deny him three times before the cock crowed (Luke 22:34). In fact, after Jesus was arrested on the Mount of Olives (Luke 22:47-53) Peter did deny on three separate occasions that he was one of his followers (Luke 22:54-61). Peter was one of the first apostles to arrive at Jesus' tomb after it had been reported empty, and later that same day he met Jesus while walking to a nearby village. Jesus walked to the village with him but did not reveal himself until that evening when he appeared to the apostles as they prayed (Luke 24:13-32).

In Acts 1, Peter assumed leadership of the church after Jesus' death. Several miracles were attributed to him (Acts 5:15), and at the Council of Jerusalem (51 C.E.) he was the acknowledged leader of the mission to the Jews, in contradistinction to Paul's mission to the gentiles (Acts 15:7-11).

The tradition connecting Peter with Rome cannot be substantiated by canonical texts. The two epistles of Peter suggest, in fact, that Peter was last seen in Asia Minor where he was concerned with refuting certain false doctrines. The apocryphal *Acts of Peter* (written c. 150–225 C.E.), however, provide the basis for several legends concerning Peter's preaching in Rome, his meeting with Paul, and his martyrdom under Nero. Among the earliest of the apocryphal acts, the text is a compilation of several traditions. There is a short episode in Coptic, a Latin portion called the *Vercelli Acts* (named for the single manuscript containing the text, which was found in Vercelli, in northern Italy), and there are also several separate accounts of the martyrdom, in Greek, Latin, Arabic, Ethiopic, Coptic, Syriac, and Armenian.

According to this compilation, Peter sailed from Jerusalem to Puteoli and from there traveled to Rome. Upon his arrival in Rome, Peter immediately confronted the Gnostic teacher Simon Magus, someone pretending to preach in Jesus' name and pretending to perform miracles. In a short time, Peter gained Simon's followers, including Simon's wealthy patron Marcellus.

Peter revealed Simon to be an imposter and performed miracle after miracle winning many new converts to the church. The *Acts of Peter* concludes with the account of Peter's martyrdom after meeting Jesus outside of Rome.

In this account, Peter had been warned by several of his followers to leave the city for his own safety. At first he refused, arguing that he did not want to run away from persecution. But he was convinced by their arguments that he might do more good for the church by remaining alive than by dying at the hands of his persecutors. As he left the city, he met Jesus, who was walking the opposite way, toward the city, and was convinced by him to return and be martyred. According to Eusebius (*Ecclesiastical History* 3.1.2) Peter was crucified upside down at his own request during the reign of Nero, at the same time as Paul (2.25.5–8). A Constantinian basilica, today the Basilica of San Pietro, was built on the supposed site of his martyrdom.

imprisoned. The well-known story of Peter's escape, drawn from Acts 12:3, relates that even though Peter was under constant surveillance, his cell was illuminated by an angel who loosened his chains and opened the prison as the guards slept. Fleeing to a gathering of fellow Christians, he reported the miracle and then withdrew to "another place." According to tradition, it was just after his escape from prison, in the reign of Claudius, that Peter went to Antioch and, later, to Rome.

Agrippa died suddenly at Caesarea in 44 C.E., after only three years as king of the broad territories governed by his grandfather Herod the Great. His children—Berenice, Mariamme, Drusilla, and Agrippa II—were too young to assume his throne and so Palestine was taken over as a Roman territory under a procurator who answered to the governor of Syria. By most accounts his short reign was marked by his advocacy of Judaism and the revitalization of Jewish Temple worship. Yet, the accounts of his "persecution" of the Hellenized Jewish-Christian church in Jerusalem contradict that

picture. In this view, Agrippa's persecution of the early church must be considered the catalyst in its final separation from Judaism.

The Missionary Church

Agrippa II and the Romans

Marcus Julius Agrippa II (50–100 C.E.) was in Rome in 44 C.E. when his father died. Sometime after 52 C.E. he assumed the government of a small kingdom that Claudius granted him as recompense for the loss of his father's vast kingdom. By 53 C.E., however, he had received wider territories in Palestine that were increased again in 54 C.E. at the accession of Nero. His reign may be defined as unconditionally Roman. When called upon, he provided troops for all Roman ventures in the area, and he named (and renamed) his cities in honor of the Roman emperors, who also appeared on the coins minted during his reign. His sister Drusilla was married to Antonius Felix, governor of Judea from c.

52–60 C.E., a marriage to which the Jews were intensely opposed and resentful: shortly after he arrived to assume his duties as procurator, Felix had lured the sixteen-year-old from her then new husband Azizus, the king of Emesa, whom Agrippa had required to convert before he would agree to the marriage.

Under Porcius Festus (60–62 C.E.), the next procurator, the seething hatred of Rome coalesced into near anarchy. Two events stand out in the reign of Agrippa II that illustrate the mounting tensions between the Romans and the Jews and their respective attitudes to the growing Christian movement: the trial of

Personalities in Christianity 2.6
HEROD AGRIPPA I

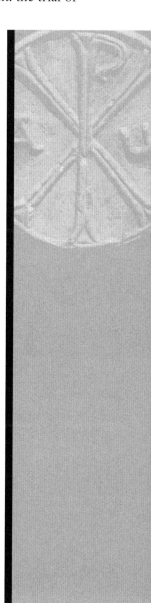

Agrippa (10 B.C.E.–44 C.E.) was the son of Herod's second son Aristobulus (the son whom Herod murdered in 7 B.C.E.) and Berenice, a daughter of Herod's sister Salome. Like his father and his father's brothers, Agrippa was educated in Rome together with the future emperor Claudius and Drusus, the son of Tiberius. When Drusus died in 23 C.E., Tiberius refused to see his son's friends any longer. Without his influential patron, Agrippa was forced to leave Rome and return to Judea. By this time, his sister Herodias was already married to Herod Antipas, who, at his wife's request, gave his brother-in-law an appointment as overseer of the markets in his capital Tiberias. Agrippa was not successful in the appointment and quarreled with Antipas before moving on to the court of an old friend from Rome, L. Pomponius Flaccus, the legate of Syria. There, too, he soon disappointed his patron and was forced to borrow heavily to return to Rome in 36 C.E. where he appealed to Tiberius for help. Tiberius was accommodating until he learned that Agrippa had offhandedly commented that he wished the old emperor dead so that his friend Caligula could succeed to the throne and relieve his debts. Tiberius had him imprisoned for his indiscreet remarks and he remained there until March of 37 C.E. when Tiberus died.

Appointed by Caligula as King of the Jews in 41 C.E., Agrippa traveled from Rome to Jerusalem via Alexandria where his visit sparked a series of riots by the Greeks and Egyptians against the Jews. His territories were considerably expanded in 39 C.E. when he received Galilee and Perea at the deposition of Antipas. In the end, he governed as large an expanse as had his grandfather Herod.

In Jerusalem, Agrippa opposed Caligula's plan to place a gilded effigy of himself in the Temple and further supported conservative, i.e., non-Christian, Jews by persecuting the Christian Jews (Acts 12:1-3). In 44 C.E., he had the apostle James, son of Zebedee, killed and Peter imprisoned. Agrippa died suddenly while sitting on a throne during public games in Caesarea leaving his young son as his legitimate successor.

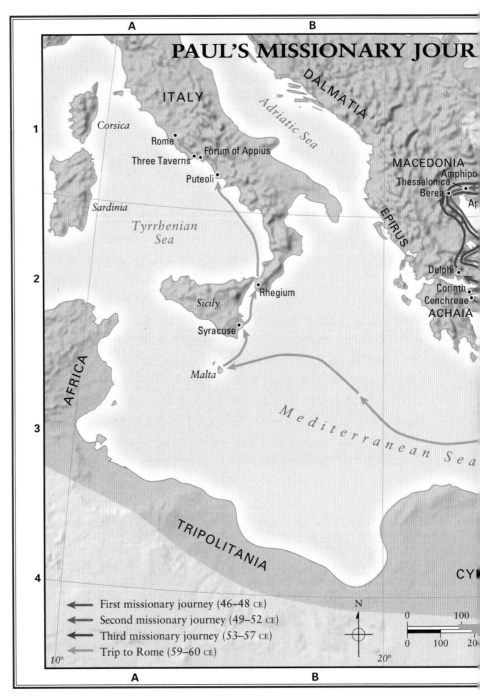

FIGURE 2.9. *Paul's Missionary Journeys according to Acts*

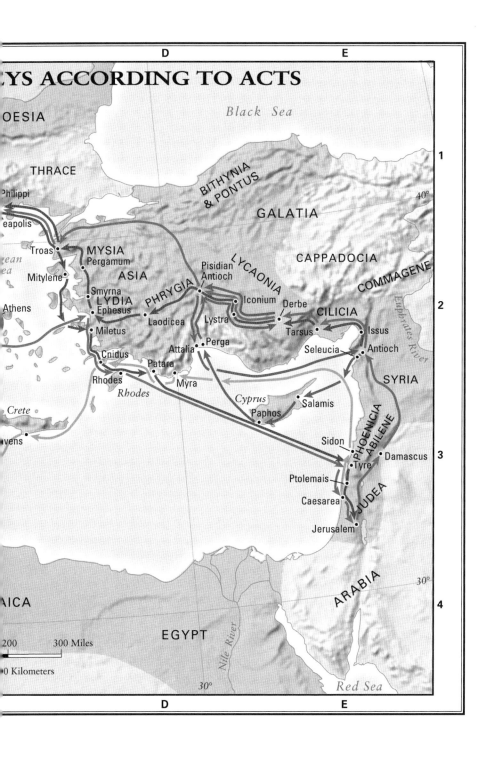

...EYS ACCORDING TO ACTS

Paul before Festus, Agrippa, and Berenice; and the martyrdom of James, the brother of Jesus.

Agrippa II and the Meeting with Paul

We read in Acts 9:3-8 that in about 35 C.E. when he was on the road to Damascus where he intended to persecute Christians, Paul encountered a vision of the resurrected Jesus and was converted. He began to preach a Jesus-centered eschatology to Jew and gentile alike. His first mission was in Antioch, Syria, where the followers of Jesus were called *Christianoi* for the first time. There, Paul taught that non-Jews were not compelled to keep the law of Moses, that is, they did not have to follow the food laws, the laws of purification, and, most importantly, they did not have to undergo the rite of circumcision. His interpretation opened Christianity to everyone who had faith in Jesus as the savior. These new beliefs held that after Jesus' sacrifice for mankind there was no need for blood sacrifices; his death was considered a victory over death and it was recalled each time Christians met for commensality. Transcending powerful traditional categories, Jews and gentiles, slaves and free men and women, educated or not, were all bound together in this new faith.

When Paul returned to Jerusalem in 58 C.E., he had been engaged in missionary activities among the gentiles for over a decade. The church leaders there insisted that Paul conform to their own brand of Christianity. He was forced to perform a ritual test in the Temple to prove his orthodoxy. When he invited gentile converts to accompany him, he was charged with the capital crime of defiling the Temple since no gentile could enter the Temple. Roman soldiers rescued him from an angry mob and brought him before the Sanhedrin for a hearing, which was inconclusive. For his own safety, the Romans decided to transport him to Felix, the procurator in Caesarea Maritima, to get him out of Jerusalem. There he preached to Felix and Drusilla about the coming judgment, an apocalyptic vision that frightened Felix, who sent him back to prison. To many historians, the fact that Paul stayed in prison for two years in Caesarea is indicative of the fact that Felix could not maintain order among the religious and political polarities terrorizing Palestine. Though typical legal proceedings under the procurators suggest that Felix was waiting for Paul to offer him a bribe for his release, the situation in Palestine was quickly devolving into a full-scale revolt against the Romans. Paul was considered another pseudo-messiah portending the end of Roman rule, and he had as large a crowd of enemies as followers. In 60 C.E., Nero recalled Felix, realizing that the situation was beyond his control.

Porcius Festus (c. 60–62 C.E.) was the new governor, appointed by Nero in the hope that he would quell this near-anarchy. Paul was charged with taking gentiles into the Temple and with undermining the authority of the emperor in his preaching. When he had heard the charges, Festus asked Paul if he would be willing to go to Jerusalem for a trial. Rather than return to Jerusalem to stand trial, however, Paul invoked his right as a Roman citizen to appeal his case to the emperor (Acts 25:12). "You have appealed to Caesar," Festus responded. "To Caesar you shall go."

According to Acts 25:13-27, Agrippa II and his sister Berenice were attending the festivities associated with Festus' accession when they heard about Paul and his dissension with the Jews in Jerusalem over a certain Jesus who had died, but who, Paul contended, was still alive. Agrippa and Berenice were both intrigued and wished to meet Paul. The next day Agrippa and Berenice entered the court in great pomp and heard Paul present his defense. Agrippa's response, as reported in Acts 26:28, was curious and may refer to the popular charge that he was more Roman than Jew: "Paul, you will soon persuade me to play the Christian." Festus and Agrippa agreed, in opposition to the Jewish priests, that Paul had done nothing to deserve prison or death. Though he might have been set free if he had not requested a hearing from the emperor, in the event, he was sent to Rome, to the emperor.

Death of James, the Brother of Jesus

At the death of the Roman governor Festus, Lucceius Albinus (62–64 C.E.) succeeded as governor of Judea. By this time, the two factions of Jewish Christians in Jerusalem (both the Greek-speaking Hellenized Christian Jews and the conservative Hebrew Christian Jews) together with the chief priests and Jewish leaders, King Agrippa II and his sister/queen Berenice, and the Roman governors were all embrangled in a multifarious social web of competing political and religious interests. In the interregnum between the death of Festus and the arrival of Albinus, events came to a head: James, the brother of Jesus, was stoned to death by the Jewish leaders who feared the unrest in Jerusalem caused by the agitated expectation of the imminent kingdom of God on earth.

This James had led the Hebrew-Christian community in Jerusalem from 42–62 C.E. and was among those who had tried to tone down Paul's new universalism. His own Hebrew-Christian church, which included the conservative followers and apostles of Jesus, resented Paul's mission to the gentiles. As a result, James could no longer mediate among his own conservative Hebrew Christians, the Hellenized Christians led by Peter and Paul, and the Sanhedrin Jewish priests and leaders. Paul had been removed from Jerusalem by the Romans and remained under house arrest in Caesarea, but the Sanhedrin priests did not forget that they had been foiled in their attempt to have him executed.

As they watched the Christian movement spread beyond the borders of Palestine and as they observed the uproar in the city as Jesus worshippers gathered for the Passover celebration, the Jewish priests and leaders must have felt their power waning. In desperation, they asked James to intervene and address the crowd from the Temple parapet, to explain that Jesus was not the Son of God. Instead, James delivered an uncompromising eulogy on the Son of Man, which incited rather than calmed the crowd. The Jewish leaders were outraged. They reacted with violence. Although they did not have the right to inflict capital punishment, which was the exclusive prerogative of the Roman governor, they called James to account for his sermon. Then, according to both Hegesippus (as he was quoted in

Personalities in Christianity 2.7
PAUL

Paul (died c. 65 C.E.) was a Pharisee (Acts 22:3; 26:5) originally named Saul, and a Roman citizen. A native of Tarsus, he lived in Jerusalem in the early years of the Christian-Jewish church. He was well educated in Mosaic Law and Hebrew scriptures and he knew Greek. In 35 C.E., Saul was involved (Acts 7.58) in the stoning of Stephen, a Christian-Jew who argued that Jesus had replaced Moses. He was en route to Damascus pursuing other Christian-Jews who he believed had contravened the law when he saw (according to Acts 9:1-19; 22:5-16; 26:12-18) a great light and heard the words: "Saul, Saul, why do you persecute me?" Paul believed that Jesus had appeared to him and had "consecrated" him as one of his apostles. He considered it his unique mission to spread Jesus' teaching to the gentiles. Upon arriving in Damascus, he was baptized by the priest Ananias (Acts 9:17) and went into the desert to pray in solitude (Gal 1:17). He returned to Damascus and had to escape by shimmying down the side of the city wall in a basket (Acts 9:23-25; 2 Cor 11:32). From Damascus he returned to Jerusalem where he presented himself to a Jewish-Christian community that was skeptical of his missionary work.

It was three years before his fellow missionary, the wealthy Cypriot convert Barnabas, set out with him to preach in Antioch (Acts 11:25). His first missionary journey began almost ten years after the stoning of Stephen, when he set out with Barnabas (Acts 12:25) to Cyprus. Two other apostles joined them—John and Mark—but Mark left after they had gone on to Asia Minor (probably because he quarreled with Paul). The missionaries preached first in synagogues, where they attempted to convert Jews to a Christian-Jewish belief. Gradually, Paul and Barnabas preached also to non-Jews (Acts 13:48). Jews openly (and violently) opposed them, even turning them over to local authorities. By 49 C.E., Paul and the missionaries had completed their first missionary journey. They had traveled to Antioch, Cyprus, Perga, Iconium, Lystra, Derbe, and back to Antioch preaching alike to Jews and gentiles (Acts 14:27). Theirs was a radical Christian-Judaism that proclaimed "new" things (2 Cor 5:17). Jesus, the Messiah, had been resurrected and promised a means to salvation that the law of Moses did not promise. In Athens, when Paul preached of the resurrection of Jesus at the Areopagus, the Greek council laughed him out of its meeting. In other places, his message was so misinterpreted that he and Barnabas were themselves proclaimed as gods (Zeus and Hermes).

In 51 C.E., Paul was at the Council of Jerusalem (Gal 2:7-9) where he argued that gentile converts to the Christian-Jewish church should not feel compelled to be circumcised

(Acts 15:11). Converts were enjoined, however, to follow Jewish teaching, that is, to abstain from meat sacrificed to idols and from illicit sexual union, and to abstain from the meat of strangled animals and from blood. From Jerusalem, he set out on his second missionary journey, which included Phoenicia, Samaria, Antioch, Phrygia, Galatia, Mysia, Troy, Philippi, Thessalonica, Athens, Corinth, and Ephesus. By 59 or 60 C.E., he was back again in Jerusalem. By this time, the Christian-Jewish church of Jesus had split into two sects: a more Hellenistic Greek-speaking, Jewish-Christian community, which participated in the larger intellectual and cultural environment of the Greco-Roman world, and the Hebrew or Aramaic-speaking Jews, who tended to maintain Jewish nationalistic ideals and on the whole were more conservative, legalistic, and exclusive in practicing Jewish rituals associated with the Temple. The first group has been identified by some scholars as Pauline Christians, and the second, as Petrine Christians. Jesus' brother James emerged as the leader of the Jewish-Christian community in Jerusalem, and Peter and Paul were the chief missioners (Gal 2:7-8), the one to Jews and the other to gentiles.

In 59 C.E., when Paul returned to Jerusalem there was friction between the two sects and he was charged with contravening Jewish law. The charges against him were that he had allowed gentiles to abandon Moses, abstain from circumcision, and renounce the Jewish law. He was brought before the Sanhedrin and chief priests and he claimed in that trial that he was being attacked for preaching the resurrection, a doctrine about which the Sadducees and Pharisees disagreed. Paul was released, but when a plot to kill him was discovered, he was sent to Felix, the Roman governor in Caesarea, for his own protection. Felix found the charges against Paul to be without merit but held him under house arrest for two years. During that time a new procurator, Festus, replaced Felix. At the ceremony of his accession, the King of the Jews, Agrippa II, and his sister, queen Berenice, were invited to hear Paul defend himself against the charges of the Jewish-Christians and the Sanhedrin. When they agreed that the charges were unfounded and advised him to return to Jerusalem to stand trial (and presumably clear himself there), Paul invoked his right to appeal his case as a Roman citizen, which meant that he would take his case to the emperor in Rome.

En route to Rome, Paul was shipwrecked on the island of Malta before arriving to Syracuse (Sicily), then to Puteoli (southern Italy), and then, via the Appian Way, to Rome. There, he ministered to the Christian and Jewish communities teaching that the judgment was at hand and that the new law of Christ the Messiah had superseded Jewish law. According to tradition, Nero had Paul beheaded in a widespread persecution of the Christians, on the same day and at the same time as Peter, the only other apostle believed to have traveled to Rome.

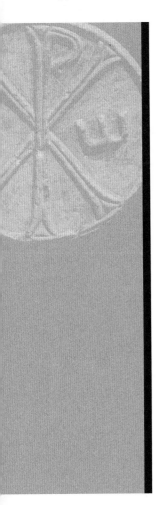

Personalities in Christianity 2.8
HEROD AGRIPPA II

King of the Jews from 50 C.E., Agrippa II (27–100 C.E.) had been educated in Rome just as his father and so many uncles. At his father's death, he was considered too young to rule, and Judea reverted to the status of a Roman province under the rule of a procurator. By 53 C.E., however, Claudius had restored many of the territories of his father and of the tetrarch Philip, and Agrippa ruled together with the Roman procurators. It was the first procurator, Marcus Antonius Felix (52–58 C.E.), who held Paul under house arrest for two years (56–58 C.E.) while, reputedly, waiting for bribes. Felix was recalled in 58 C.E. and it was at the accession ceremony of the new procurator, Porcius Festus (58–62 C.E.) that Agrippa and his sister Berenice heard Paul preach his Christian message. Earlier Paul had appealed to the emperor rather than stand trial in Jerusalem (Acts 25:6-12).

In 63 C.E., while Agrippa was out of Jerusalem, excessive taxation by the Romans sparked riots. Agrippa returned immediately and both he and Berenice tried to quell the unrest. They were unsuccessful and the Roman authorities brutally crucified several leaders of the riot. As a result of this incident, Agrippa is said to have delivered an eloquent speech justifying and glorifying Roman rule. The speech was recorded by Josephus in his *Jewish War* 2.16.4.

Agrippa and his sister/queen Berenice supported the Roman authorities and moved in the government's social circles. Their association with their Roman overlords was strengthened when Berenice became Titus's mistress. Even when Titus conquered and leveled Jerusalem, including the magnificent Temple, Agrippa continued to serve for some twenty-five years. He was the last king of the dynasty of Herod the Great.

Eusebius) and to Josephus, at the order of the high priest Ananas and in defiance of Roman law, they killed James.

After the death of James, the relations between the Jews and the Romans and between the Jews and the rival groups among the Christian Jews continued to deteriorate. In time, the less rigid interpretations of Jesus' teaching, that is the interpretations of Paul and the Hellenized Christians, prevailed. For them, the fulfillment of the law was no longer the way to eternal life; instead, salvation was assured only in the eschatology revealed by Jesus, who was the new Messiah. Jesus had replaced Moses as the arbitrator of salvation, and his followers could claim that they had received their authority to make this claim as the gift of the spirit during baptism. The Hebrew-Christian church in Jerusalem faded precisely as Paul's mission to the gentiles and Hellenized Jews spread to Rome. Indeed, according to Paul, Jesus had made all things new (2 Cor 5:17).

FROM AN ANCIENT TEXT ❖ 2.7

Martyrdom of James, the Brother of Jesus Christ

There are two ancient accounts of the martyrdom of James, one by Hegesippus, a church historian c. 110–180 C.E. whose only extant works are quoted in the church history of Eusebius of Caesarea (c. 263–339 C.E.), and one by Josephus. This legendary account highlights James' righteousness and suggests that Hegesippus is a Jewish convert.

Hegesippus in Eusebius

Control of the Church passed to the apostles, together with the Lord's brother James, whom everyone from the Lord's time till our own has called the Righteous, for there were many Jameses, but this one was holy from his birth; he drank no wine or intoxicating liquor and ate no animal food; no razor came near his head; he did not smear himself with oil and took no baths. He alone was permitted to enter the Holy Place, for his garments were not of wool but of linen. He used to enter the Sanctuary alone, and was often found on his knees beseeching forgiveness for the people, so that his knees grew hard like a camel's from his continually bending them in worship of God and beseeching forgiveness for the people. Because of his unsurpassable righteousness he was called the Righteous and Oblias—in our own language "Bulwark of the People," and "Righteousness"—fulfilling the declarations of the prophets regarding him.

Representatives of the seven popular sects already described by me asked him what was meant by the "door of Jesus." He replied that Jesus was the Savior. Some of them came to believe that Jesus was the Christ: the sects mentioned above did not believe either in a resurrection or in One who is coming to give every man what his deeds deserve, but those who did come to believe did so because of James. Since therefore many even of the ruling class believed, there was uproar among the Jew and Scribes and Pharisees, who said there was a danger that the entire people would expect Jesus as the Christ. So they collected and said to James: "Be good enough to restrain the people, for they have gone astray after Jesus in the belief that he is the Christ. Be good enough to make the facts about Jesus clear to all who come for the Passover Day. We all accept what you say: we can vouch for it, and so can all the people, that you are a righteous man and take no one at his face value. So make it clear to the crowd that they must not go astray as regards Jesus: the whole people and all of us accept what you say. So take your stand on the Temple parapet, so that from that height you may be easily seen, and your words audible to the whole people. For because of the Passover all the tribes have forgathered, and the Gentiles too."

So the Scribes and Pharisees made James stand on the Sanctuary parapet and shouted to him: "Righteous one, whose word we are all obliged to accept, the people are going astray after

Jesus who was crucified; so tell us what is meant by the the door of Jesus." He replied as loudly as he could: "Why do you question me about the Son of Man? I tell you, He is sitting in heaven at the right hand of the Great Power, and He will come on the clouds of heaven." Many were convinced, and gloried in James' testimony, crying: "Hosanna to the Son of David!" Then again the Scribes and Pharisees said to each other: "We made a bad mistake in affording such testimony to Jesus. We had better go up and throw him down, so that they will be frightened and believe him." "Ho, ho!" they called out, "even the Righteous one has gone astray!"—fulfilling the prophecy of Isaiah 3.10: "Let us remove the Righteous one, for he is unprofitable to us. Therefore they shall eat the fruit of their works."

So they went up and threw down the Righteous one. Then they said to each other "Let us stone James the Righteous," and began to stone him, as in spite of his fall he was still alive. But he turned and knelt, uttering the words: "I beseech Thee, Lord God and Father, forgive them; they do not know what they are doing." While they pelted him with stones, one of the descendants of Rechab the son of Rachabim—the priestly family to which Jeremiah the Prophet bore witness, called out: "Stop! What are you doing? The Righteous one is praying for you." Then one of them, a fuller, took the club which he used to beat out the clothes, and brought it down on the head of the Righteous one. Such was his martyrdom. He was buried on the spot, by the Sanctuary, and his headstone is still there by the Sanctuary. He has proved a true witness to Jews and Gentiles alike that Jesus is the Christ.

Source: Eusebius, *Ecclesiastical History* 2.23 quoting the Christian Greek author Hegesippus (c. 110–180 C.E.) in *Eusebius: The History of the Church from Christ to Constantine,* tr. G. A. Williamson, rev. and ed. Andrew Louth (London: Penguin, 1965), pp. 59–60.

Josephus' shorter and legalistic account nonetheless illustrates the growing dissention among the factions in Jerusalem—Jewish, Christian, and Roman.

Josephus

And now Caesar, upon hearing of the death of Festus, sent Albinus into Judea, as procurator; but the king deprived Joseph of the high priesthood, and bestowed the succession to that dignity on the son of Ananus, who was also himself called Ananus. Now the report goes, that this elder Ananus proved a most fortunate man; for he had five sons, who had all performed the office of high priest to God, and he had himself enjoyed that dignity a long time formerly, which had never happened to any other of our high priests: but this younger Ananus, who, as we have told you already, took the high priesthood, was a bold man in his temper, and very insolent; he was also of the sect of the Sadducees who are very rigid in judging offenders, above all the rest of the Jews, as we have already observed; when, therefore, Ananus was of this disposition, he thought he had now a proper opportunity to exercise his authority. Festus was now dead, and Albinus was but upon the road; so he assembled the Sanhedrin of judges, and brought before them the brother of Jesus, who was called Christ, whose name was James, and some others; and when he had formed an accusation against them as breakers of the law, he delivered them to be stoned; but as for those who seemed the most equitable of the citizens, and such as were the most uneasy at the breach of the laws, they disliked what was done; they also sent to the king Agrippa, desiring him to send to Ananus that he should act so no more, for that what he had already done was not to be justified; nay, some of them went also to meet Albinus, as he was upon his journey form Alexandria, and informed him that it was not lawful for Ananus to assemble a Sanhedrin without his consent; whereupon Albinus complied with what they said, and wrote in anger to Ananus, and threatened that he would bring him to punishment for what he had done; on which king Agrippa took the high priesthood from him, when he had ruled but three months, and made Jesus, the son of Damneus, high priest.

Source: Josephus, *Jewish Antiquities* 20.9.1 in *The Works of Josephus*, tr. William Whiston (Peabody, Mass.: Hendrickson, 1987), pp. 537–538.

Conclusion

In this chapter we have considered the life of Jesus and the spread of his new religion, later called Christianity, against the political unrest in the territory ruled by Herod the Great and his successors, client kings of Rome. Their rise to power coincided with the birth of the Roman Empire and their appointments were solely at the discretion of the emperors, whose interests they obligingly served. Inevitably, the secular and political interests of the Romans whom they served conflicted with the religious priorities of the Jews whom they governed. Forced to negotiate between what was politically expedient and what was permissible under religious law, the Herods were often at odds with their Roman rulers or their Jewish constituents. The life and ministry of

Jesus, the self-proclaimed new Messiah, has implications for both sides of this conflict. As their long-awaited Messiah, the Jews hoped that Jesus would not only free the Jews from their Roman oppressors but also restore their nation to the golden days when devotion to Mosaic Law was unequivocal.

Jesus was born under Herod the Great. He was baptized, and he preached and taught in the territory of Herod's son Antipas. By order of the Roman procurator Pontius Pilate he was crucified. Evident in all the events of Jesus' life and in the reactions of the Herods and the Romans is the same tension between cultural secularism and religious orthodoxy that had characterized the conflict between the Maccabeans, the Jews, and their Hellenized rulers. Herod's extensive secular building program—"Roman" basilicas,

theatres, and colonnades—was balanced by
the construction of the most extravagant and
splendid Temple ever built in Jerusalem. Yet
the question of his orthodoxy always haunted
his title and surfaced anew during the succession intrigues among his heirs. His (fictitious)
order to slaughter all male children younger
than two years of age masked his fear that a
new King of the Jews with a stronger claim to
orthodoxy would claim his throne. Likewise,
when Antipas delivered the head of John the
Baptist to his stepdaughter Salome in gratitu-
ing for her graceful dance at the banquet celebrating his birthday, he was ensnared in a similar
struggle: whether to embrace the secularism
that would have sanctioned his marriage to
his brother's wife Herodias or the orthodoxy
that prohibited it.

During the reigns of the two Agrippas, the
same tension widened the divide between the
Hellenized Christian Jews and the Hebrew
Christian Jews in Jerusalem. One belonged
to the intellectual and cultural environment
of the Greco-Roman world, the synagogue,
and the Septuagint while the other thought
in terms of Jewish nationalism and a strict
devotion to Mosaic Law and Temple cult. The
persecutions under the Agrippas in these early
years of the church illustrate the increasing
resentment of the Jews who felt the oppressive hand of the Romans as they watched their
religious traditions transformed by these new
Christian Jewish sects.

More than any other cause, the shifting
balance between cultural secularism and religious orthodoxy among the Jews, Romans,
and Christians in Judea finally caused the
incipient church to separate from Judaism
and focus its missionary activities upon the
gentiles and beyond the borders of Palestine,
as far west as Rome.

STUDY QUESTIONS

1   When and under what circumstances did Judea first come under Roman control?

2   Briefly outline the career of Herod the Great and the history of the Jews in Jerusalem from 63 B.C.E.
    through the destruction of the Temple in 70 C.E. In what ways does this period echo the *pax Romana*?

3   Discuss the reigns of the two Agrippas. In what ways do their Roman rulers influence their political
    decisions, and in what ways do those decisions respond to their Jewish constituents?

4   Using the bibliographic resources provided at the end of this book, conduct further research into the
    conflicts among Jews, Christians, and Romans in the period from the death of Jesus to the death of
    James. Explain these conflicts in religious and political terms.

5   Paul has been called one of the great poets of history; he has also been called jealous, fanatic, and
    untrustworthy. Explain these characterizations in light of his missionary journeys, his arrest and trial,
    and his voyage to Rome to appeal to the emperor.

Chapter 3

ROMANS AND CHRISTIANS
Constantine's Christian Monotheism

He said that at midday, when the sun was sloping towards the west, he saw in the sky before his very eyes the triumphal sign of a cross, made of light. It was placed above the sun and had the following written upon it: "Conquer by means of this." At this sight both he and all the soldiers who were accompanying him on this march and who had also been witnesses of the miracle were astonished.

—Eusebius, *Life of Constantine* 1.28

In 312 C.E., on the eve of his battle against the usurper Maxentius, Constantine saw the vision Eusebius described above and "converted" to Christianity. This was a great turning point in the history of the early church. Until then, several Roman emperors—Domitian (96 C.E.),

Marcus Aurelius (177 C.E.), Septimius Severus (202 C.E.), Decius (249–251 C.E.), Valerian (253–260 C.E.), and Diocletian (303–313 C.E.)—had persecuted Christians, either sporadically or methodically. From this point on, however, Christianity was a *religio licita*, "legal religion." Before he was a Christian, Constantine was a tolerant monotheist, a worshipper of the sun god *Sol*. In 310 C.E., he had even experienced an apparition of this god. As a political leader, he trusted in the fundamental principle of ancient pagan religious practice: only the proper worship of the gods ensured the security and prosperity of the state. His Christian monotheism was thus an efficient combination of his earlier, personal devotion to *Sol* and the politically pragmatic view that a uniform

Personalities in Christianity 3.1
CONSTANTINE

Emperor from 306 C.E., Constantine (c. 273–337 C.E.) was the son of Constantius Chlorus, Diocletian's Caesar in the west, and Helena, the daughter of a stable keeper. Constantius Chlorus was a military general who had served with distinction under Aurelian. Like Aurelian, Constantius was a devoted follower of the sun god, *Sol Invictus*, and he may have influenced Constantine's devotion to that same god. As a youth, Constantine was sent to Diocletian's court in Nicomedia and remained there even after Diocletian and Maximian had abdicated in 305 C.E. When his father became ill, he left the court in stealth fearing that the new senior tetrarch, Galerius, would try to prevent him from going. According to legend, Constantine rode straight through to Britain only stopping to change horses, so that he could evade the soldiers Galerius had sent to pursue him. On July 25, 306 C.E., in York, England, his father's loyal troops proclaimed Constantine as the Augustus of the west. This left Severus, Constantius's former Caesar, in the odd position of official but unrecognized Augustus. Galerius resolved the problem by recognizing Severus as Augustus and Constantine as his Caesar. In 308 C.E., Galerius appointed his friend and fellow Illyrian Licinius to the position of Augustus in the west, to replace Severus. At a meeting of the tetrarchs in Carnuntum, Constantine was recognized only as Licinius's Caesar, even though his father's troops had proclaimed him Augustus. Although Licinius was the new Augustus of the west, Constantine remained a challenge to his authority by refusing to acknowledge him and continuing to call himself Augustus.

Constantine became sole emperor of the west after the Battle of the Milvian Bridge in 312 C.E., when he defeated Maxentius, the self-proclaimed ruler of Rome. His victory was preceded by a vision that instructed him to adopt the *labarum* (the chi-rho symbol of Christianity) and champion the cause of Christianity. Scholars debate whether or not he became a Christian as a result of the vision, but from then on he prohibited the persecution of Christians, restored their property, and gave legal sanction to their worship. In a monotheism that was reminiscent of Aurelian's (and his father's) syncretistic worship of *Sol Invictus*, Constantine united the empire in a single religious policy and intervened as the head of state and church in several doctrinal disputes.

Twice he convened a council of bishops to settle the Donatist controversy that was raging in North Africa, a dissension that arose during the persecutions and concerned the status of clergy who had "lapsed" (sacrificed to the gods of the state). He accompanied the decision of the councils with repressive measures against the Donatists, who insisted that no lapsed clergy could be readmitted to the church or deliver the sacraments. In the east, the Arian controversy surrounding the correct understanding of the relationship of the Father and the

Son was temporarily settled in favor of the orthodox (anti-Arian) position when Constantine convened the Council of Nicea in 325 C.E. Although the controversy continued to rage after his death, his intervention set a precedent for church-state relations that would be challenged in subsequent centuries. Constantine handled intrigue and dissent in his family in the same despotic way that he settled doctrinal disputes in the church. His wife Fausta and his son (by his first wife) Crispus, for example, were murdered on his order. Despite the brutality of his reign, Constantine is venerated as the "Thirteenth Apostle" in the east.

Constantine and Licinius clashed several times between the Edict of Milan, which they jointly promulgated in 313 C.E., and their final battle at Chrysopolis in 324 C.E. There Constantine defeated Licinius and ruled as sole emperor. In 330 C.E., he removed the capital of the empire to the city Byzantium (the modern Istanbul) and changed its name to Constantinople. Constantinople, the "new Rome," was adorned with a senate house, baths, a forum, and a circus for chariot races. Its splendid monuments and temples were made from columns, marble, statues, bronze, and various other public decorations that had been pilfered hastily from all over the empire.

The legend of the "Donation of Constantine" arose from a treatise erroneously dated to c. 750–800 C.E. which Constantine ostensibly authored to show his gratitude to Pope Sylvester for baptizing him and curing him of leprosy. In this treatise, Constantine bequeaths to Sylvester the Lateran Basilica and the symbols of imperial power: the diadem, tiara, collar, purple mantle, and crimson tunic. In addition, he decreed that Pope Sylvester and his successors would have supremacy over the four chief sees—Antioch, Alexandria, Constantinople, and Jerusalem—and jurisdiction over all ecclesiastical matters. Until the fifteenth century, when Lorenzo Valle proved by close philological investigation that the "Donation" was a forgery, it was invoked to lend authority to the pope's secular power.

Constantine was buried in the Church of the Holy Apostles in Constantinople and was succeeded by his three sons: Constantine II, Constantius II, and Constans.

empire-wide religious worship guaranteed the welfare of the state.

Long before Constantine's famous "conversion," the empire had been moving toward monotheism and away from polytheism. The ancient established tradition of the worship of *Sol*, which culminated in the reign of Aurelian (269/70–275 C.E.), had a long afterlife. In 321 C.E., nine years after his "conversion," Constantine recognized the *Dies Solis*, "Day of the Sun," as a holiday and established its celebration on the same day as the Christian celebration of the birth of Christ (December 25); and from the notations in the Codex-Calendar of 354 C.E., we know that the worship of *Sol* was still being celebrated with games and circuses in the fourth century C.E. Although the sweeping reforms of Diocletian (284–305 C.E.) saw a

FIGURE 3.1. *Constantine the Great. This marble head is from the colossal statue of Constantine, originally located in the Basilica of Maxentius and Constantine in fourth-century Rome.*

brief return to the ancient polytheistic worship of the gods of the state, the Christian monotheism of Constantine is here regarded, at least in part, as a continuum of the well-established monotheistic pagan worship of *Sol*.

Ancient Forms of Monotheism

The Supreme God of the Pantheon

Christianity developed in a world where most religious practices were primarily polytheistic. The term polytheism, however, when applied to the ancient world is misleading. Although Greek, Roman, Egyptian, and many Near Eastern peoples worshipped a pantheon of gods and goddesses, either there was one powerful god who ruled them all or these gods were conceived of as a plurality that acted by consensus or as aspects of a single supreme god who ruled all the other divinities. Either way we understand the ancient pantheon, at its base was a single divine leader who ruled other deities, variously called angels, demons, *numina*, "divine essences," or gods and goddesses.

The second-century writer Celsus whose work we know only from Origen's response to it, called the *Contra Celsum, Against Celsum,* perhaps summed up most succinctly the ancient concept of pagan monotheism when he argued (*Contra Celsum* 1.24) that it did not matter whether the god's name was Zeus or the Most High, or Zen, or Adonai, or Sabaoth, or the Egyptian Ammon, or the Scythian Papaeus. Whatever the name, he insisted, all these deities pointed to the concept of a single divinity, the supreme god or greatest sovereign.

Worship of *Sol*, the Sun God

Long before Constantine made Christianity the official state religion, the empire had been moving toward monotheism. There was an indigenous Roman sun god called *Sol Indiges*, an agricultural divinity that probably represented a widespread ancient belief that the sun was the single ruling principle and divine source of all life, the ruler of all other stars, and the moderating mind of the universe. The

TABLE 3.1

Roman Emperors

Julio-Claudians
Augustus ("Octavian") 27 B.C.E.–14 C.E.
Tiberius 14–37
Gaius ("Caligula") 37–41
Claudius 41–54
Nero 54–68

Year of the Four Emperors
Galba 68–69, Otho 69, Vitellius 69, Vespasian
69–79

Flavians
Vespasian 69–79
Titus 79–81
Domitian 81–96
Nerva 96–98
Trajan 98–117
Hadrian 117–138

Antonines
Antoninus Pius 138–161
Marcus Aurelius 161–180
Lucius Verus 161–169
Commodus 177–192

Severans
Septimius Severus 193–211
Caracalla 211–217
Geta 211–212
Macrinus 217–218
Elagabalus 218–222
Severus Alexander 222–235

Third Century
Maximinus ("Thrax") 235–238
Gordian III 238–244
Philip I ("the Arab") 244–249
Decius 249–251
Gallus 251–253
Valerian 253–260
Gallienus 253–268

Claudius II ("Gothicus") 268–270
Aurelian 270–275
Tacitus 275–276
Probus 276–282
Carus 282–283
Carinus 283–285 (Caesar 282–283)
Numerian 283–284

Tetrarchy
Diocletian 284–305
Maximian 286–305, 307–308
Constantius I ("Chlorus") (Caesar 293–305)
Galerius 305–311 (Caesar 293–305)
Flavius Severus 306–307 (Caesar 305–306)
Maximinus Daia 307–313
Licinius 307–324
Maxentius 307–312

House of Constantius
Constantius I (Augustus 305–306)
Constantine I ("the Great") 306–337
Constantine II 337–340
Constans 337–350
Constantius II 337–361
Julian ("the Apostate") 360–363 (Caesar
355–360)
Jovian 363–364

House of Valentinian
Valentinian I 364–375
Valens 364–378
Procopius 365–366
Gratian 367–383
Valentinian II 375–392

House of Theodosius
Theodosius I ("the Great") 379–395
Arcadius (eastern Emperor) 383–408
Honorius (western Emperor) 394–423

Personalities in Christianity 3.2
AURELIAN

Emperor from 270 C.E. and a military general in the campaigns against the Goths, Aurelian (c. 215–275 C.E.), along with so many other third-century emperors, was proclaimed emperor by his troops. After successful campaigns against the Vandals and the Alemanni, he built a twelve-mile wall around Rome to protect it from invasion. The wall was twenty-one feet high with intermittent towers. It was this wall that protected the usurper Maxentius against the third-century invasions of the tetrarchs before Constantine finally conquered him outside of the city. Aurelian quelled several uprisings in the east and it was to celebrate his victory in Palmyra that he established the worship of *Sol Invictus*, "Invincible Sun," in Rome. This syncretistic sun worship subsumed the attributes of all other deities and elevated monotheistic empire-wide worship above the traditional polytheism of the empire. In addition to the splendid temple he dedicated to *Sol* on the Palatine Hill, Aurelian established a College of Pontiffs *Dei Solis*, "of the god Sun." He was murdered en route to a military campaign in Persia and his death left the empire in chaos until the succession of Diocletian.

idea of a transcendent supreme divinity as an incorporeal and ethereal light or spirit may be traced back even further, to Plato and Aristotle. In the first century C.E., the great colossal statue of Nero was converted by Vespasion into a representation of *Sol*. In the second century, Hadrian's Pantheon, a temple dedicated to all the gods (from the Greek *pantheion*, "of all gods") was crowned with a dome that symbolized the heavens and its central opening was a representation of the solar orb, called *Helios*, the Greek word for "sun-god." In the third century, Aurelian, a devoted follower of the oriental sun god Ba'al, elevated this god, called *Sol Invictus*, "Invincible Sun," to the level of an imperial official state cult in gratitude for his military victory in Palmyra. In 274 C.E., he dedicated a temple (*Templum Solis*) in Rome to *Sol Invictus*. This was an enormous structure

richly fitted with jewel-encrusted metal, silver statues, and porphyry columns. According to some sources, Aurelian even intended to place in it a throne carved of solid ivory from the massive tusks of two elephants. Although Aurelian's reign marked a high point in the monotheistic worship of *Sol Invictus* in Rome, the third-century Severan dynasty (193–235 C.E.), beginning with Septimius Severus and his Syrian wife Julia Domna, had been characterized by a variation of *Sol* worship, called solar syncretism.

The Severan Heliogabalus or Elagabalus (218–222 C.E.) envisioned a universal religion that fused all beliefs into one system in which the sun (as a black conical stone) was the central object of worship. He wanted the religion of the Jews and Christians and all the mystery religions and cults to be transferred to the god

Heliogabalus, now enshrined on the Palatine Hill in the temple (*Templum Elagaballium*) he constructed in 221 C.E. His cousin and successor, Alexander Severus (222–235 C.E.), erected in his private oratory his own pantheon of statues, all of whom he considered manifestations of a single supreme solar deity: Abraham, Apollonius of Tyana, Orpheus, and even the Christian God, Jesus. His mother Julia Mamea also had Christian sympathies and included Jesus among the deities encompassed in her syncretistic worship of the sun. Eusebius tells us in his *Ecclesiastical History* (6.21.3) that when she was passing through Antioch, she sent a bodyguard of soldiers to summon to her court the Christian philosopher and theologian Origen (165–254 C.E.), to discuss the teachings of Jesus.

Mithraism

The old Indo-Iranian cult of the celestial deity of light led to the development of a widely popular solar mystery cult in the Roman Empire—Mithraism. The deity Mithras had been identified with the sun from at least the first century C.E. A personal but exclusively male religion, Mithraism flourished in the second and third centuries C.E. spreading rapidly through the military and among traveling merchants. Rome's port city Ostia was a major area of concentration and there are remains of some fifteen *mithrea*, "meeting places for the worship of Mithras," in the excavated portion (about one-half) of the town. The legendary Mithras was both

a hero and a model of honesty and morality. There is archaeological evidence that the *mithraeum* was usually situated in a cave, as a model of the Greco-Roman universe, and a strong iconographic tradition of Mithras slaughtering a bull and then dining with the sun god. The ubiquitous image, called the Tauroctony, is that of Mithras under a male sun and a female moon astride a bull and plunging a knife into its side. A shaft of wheat springs from the bull's tail and a scorpion, a dog, and a serpent appear near the wound. These figures form the basis of an astrological interpretation in which Mithras is the sun and the *mithraeum* the cosmos.

Christian Monotheism

To many pagans, Christianity seemed another manifestation of the same solar monotheism that had long been a presence in their religious culture. It shared features of mystery cults, like Mithraism, as well as of the monotheistic or syncretic worship of *Sol Invictus*. Initiates of these monotheistic religions shared as basic tenets a revealed doctrine, ritual initiations, and some sort of communion with the deity. But there were other, more obvious, similarities between the solar cults and Christianity: Christ, Mithras, and *Sol Invictus* were all believed to have been born on December 25, the winter solstice; Christians worshipped on the day of the sun (*sol*)—Sunday; and Christian churches were oriented to the east so that when congregants worshipped they faced the direction of the sun's rising. Thus, it was not the concept of monotheism that set Christians apart from non-Christians so

Personalities in Christianity 3.3
ELAGABALUS

Varius Avitus Bassianus (204–222 C.E.) who served as emperor from 217 C.E. and was known as Elagabalus, was infamous for his debauched behavior and because of his fanatical devotion to El Gabal (also called Baal), the oracular sun god of Emessa. Elagabalus became emperor through the machinations of his maternal grandmother Julia Maesa, who was Septimius Severus's sister-in-law and Caracalla's aunt. At the death of Caracalla, the young Elagabalus was serving as the high priest of the Syrian sun god. (The name Elagabalus is the Latin form of the god's name.) His grandmother Julia Maesa and his mother (her daughter) Julia Soaemias claimed that Elagabalus was really the bastard son of the former emperor Caracalla, his mother's cousin. This "filial" relationship endeared Elagabalus to Caracalla's troops who revolted against Macrinus and declared Elagabalus as their leader. At fourteen, the Roman senate confirmed him as emperor, but Elagabalus still seemed to consider his service to the sun god his primary duty. He brought the most sacred object of El Gabal's worship to Rome from Emessa—a black cone-shaped stone—and with great ceremony placed it in the Elagaballium, the temple on the Palatine Hill that he built especially to house the stone. He insisted that the Roman senators participate in the worship of El Gabal. This enforced worship coupled with the fact that the daily sacrifices were excessive caused outrage among some Romans, though the worship of the sun was popular in the military and would reemerge with a greater following in the guise of *Sol Invictus* under Aurelian and again under Constantine. The offenses of El Gabal's worship seem to have peaked when Elagabalus married a Vestal Virgin.

Vestal Virgins were priestesses who dedicated their lives to attending the sacred flame in the temple of the goddess Vesta. The Romans believed that the flame safeguarded Rome's prosperity and so could never be extinguished. Therefore, only patrician maidens could hold this high office, which was considered a great honor, and they could be buried alive for breaking their vow of chastity. When Elagabalus married the Vestal Virgin Aquilia Severa, he also "married" a statue of a female Roman goddess to El Gabal in imitation of his "divine" union. Yet he did not consider his marriage to a Vestal sacred; he married at least five times in his short reign. His religious fanaticism coupled with public sexual practices that offended many Romans hastened the plots that led to his murder.

In 221 C.E., as Elagabalus's behavior escalated into open orgiastic debauchery, his grandmother persuaded him to adopt his cousin, Alexander Severus. Shortly thereafter, in 222 C.E., troops murdered Elagabalus and his mother Julia Soesma. After dragging their bodies through the streets and tossing them into the Tiber River, they established Alexander Severus on the throne.

FIGURE 3.2. *A marble tauroctony (Mithras slaying the bull). From second-century* C.E. *Rome, this marble statue shows Mithras sitting astride the bull as the bull's blood drips down to the dog, snake, and scorpion, interpreted as signs of the zodiac in a symbolic representation of constellations.*

much as the Christians' unequivocal belief in the divinity of Jesus.

Christian doctrine taught that God the Father had sent his Son Jesus to redeem mankind by sacrificing himself on the cross. Through that sacrifice, Christians could anticipate eternal life, a blessed immortality. Unlike Jewish and other non-Christian religions, Christians could be saved by one act of faith—by believing that Jesus was the Son of God and that he had redeemed mankind by dying on the cross. Pagan monotheists did not reject the Christians' belief in a transcendent deity, nor the promise of eternal salvation in a blessed afterlife, but they did reject the idea of a deity who would take human form and suffer crucifixion, a means of death reserved for the lowest type of criminal.

Reign of Diocletian

Diocletian's Reforms

In the year 284 C.E., Diocles, the son of a freedman in Illyricum, took the name C. Aurelius Valerius Diocletianus and became the Roman emperor. Within a year, he had elevated a fellow Illyrian and former military comrade, Maximian, to the imperial honor of Caesar, a junior co-ruler, and within a year after that Maximian was made Augustus, a senior co-ruler. This new type of government was called a *diarchy*, or "rule by two." Diocletian and Maximian adopted the names *Iovius* (Jupiter), and *Herculius* (Hercules), to illustrate their patriarchal model of power. Diocletian was the representative on earth of *Iuppiter Optimus Maximus*, "Jupiter the Best and Greatest," the king of the gods; and Maximian was his heroic son, dedicated to performing labors on his behalf. In 293 C.E., after continuous warfare in many areas of the empire, they each raised another compatriot to the lesser rank of Caesar. This new type of government was called a tetrarchy, or "rule of four": Galerius became the Caesar of Diocletian and Constantius Chlorus (Constantine's father), the Caesar of Maximian. The *concordia,* or "harmony," of the tetrarchs ensured the empire's security, and a broad range of other reforms in the army and in the tax structure ensured the empire's stability. By 297 C.E., it was clear that Diocletian's tetrarchy had quelled the endless local rebellions and wars and also had set the stage for a smooth succession at his retirement.

Return to Polytheism

Old conservative religious values impelled Diocletian (284–305 C.E.) to reinstitute a more traditional polytheism. He may have hoped that by moving away from Aurelian's *Sol Invictus* cult and reinvigorating the worship of the traditional gods of the state that he could reverse the political turmoil that had thus far characterized the third century. If properly performed, the worship and ritual sacrifices to the revered gods of the state would ensure the gods' favor in return. But preserving the uniform traditional Roman religious practices meant that local religious activity had to be suppressed. Diocletian did not oppose this, as his harsh edict (quoted below) against the Manicheans in 296 C.E. illustrates. An ascetic Persian cult that followed the dualistic doctrine of the prophet Mani (216–276 C.E.), Manicheism was a syncretism of Judeo-Christian and Indo-Iranian doctrines that had spread throughout the empire and threatened to undermine Diocletian's religious reforms. Because their leaders had deserted the ancient worship of the Roman gods and goddesses, Diocletian ordered them to be burned alive with their scriptures and he ordered their followers to be killed by sword or sent to the mines. Many scholars see this edict as the beginning of the kinds of repressive tactics that characterized his later persecution of the Christians.

Diocletian's coinage also reflected his traditional religious morality. His new gold coins replaced depictions of the virtues with images of the Roman gods as guardians of the state. The silver coins featured the sacrifice to the gods and the virtues of loyalty and harmony. The ubiquitous bronze coins carried the inscription "To the Genius of the Roman People" and bore the figure of Jupiter holding a sacrificial dish in one hand and the cornucopia in the other. These numismatic images of peace and plenty in the hands of Jupiter were meant to invoke his earthly representative, Diocletian, under whose providence his worshippers would flourish.

Emperor Worship

Diocletian seems to have realized that the authority of the imperial court was dependent to some degree upon court ceremony. Once he had claimed divine status as Jupiter on earth, he demanded that his court adopt the court ceremonial of Hellenistic monarchs. He wore a diadem and in all official appearances he wore purple silk and gold embroidered vestments and stone-studded shoes. He insisted that his subjects approach him on their knees and kiss his purple imperial robe, a practice of eastern royal courts called the *adoratio purpurae*, "adoration of the purple." The emperor's arrival in a city was a great event, and people came from miles away to see his *adventus*, the spectacular procession of his pompous arrival in full imperial regalia. As *dominus et deus*, "lord and god," he imbued the office with an aura of sanctity that established the divine support of his dominion.

Under Diocletian we see the political transformation from Principate, the rule of the *princeps*, "first among equals," that had been established by Augustus, to Dominate, the authoritarian basis of the medieval divine right of kings. And we also see the shift of power away from Rome: not only had the tetrarchs not assumed their power at Rome, but their traveling courts no longer resided in the ancient imperial capital. In fact, it was only in 303 C.E., on the occasion of his *Vicennalia*, "twenty years of rule," that Diocletian finally appeared in Rome, although his monumental bath project—the Baths of Diocletian—had already been inaugurated there in 298 C.E.

Persecution of the Christians under Diocletian

After twenty years of a (mostly) peaceful tolerance, the persecution of the Christians by Diocletian seemed an inexplicable cruelty. It began in 298 C.E., when several Christian soldiers were seen making the sign of the cross in the presence of Diocletian, Galerius, and the *haruspices*, "priests who read the entrails of sacrificial animals," who were taking the auspices before a battle. Christians were blamed for interrupting the traditional rites by blessing themselves to ward off the demons of the pagans. Diocletian is reported to have been enraged by the Christians for interfering with this imperial religious ritual and to have ordered them to make a sacrifice to the pagan gods. The incident seems to have ended here, however, when the Christians either sacrificed or were discharged from the army.

No one is quite sure why, several years later, a series of edicts beginning on February 23, 303, were issued that led to a large-scale

Personalities in Christianity 3.4
DIOCLETIAN

Valerius (245–313 C.E.), who was Emperor Diocletian from 284 to 305 C.E., served with Constantius Chlorus in the army of Aurelian. When Carinus was murdered in 284 C.E., the army proclaimed Diocletian the new emperor. He changed the character of the monarchy in profound ways by endowing the title with an aura of divinity and reinstituting the worship of the state gods and the divinity of the emperor. Among his most dramatic reforms were the changes he made to the structure of the government. Although Diocletian no longer maintained his capital there, Rome still had some vestige of its political power as the seat of the senate. In addition to the senate, the Praetorian Guard was also still in residence at Rome. The city still enjoyed the privilege of being tax exempt, and its citizens still enjoyed subsidized games and free wheat. Tensions arose between the senate and the emperor when Diocletian did not seek the senate's cooperation in establishing the tetrarchy, "rule by four." For all the appointments to these new offices, he selected fellow officers, all from the Balkans, rather than Roman senators or aristocrats.

In 286 C.E., Diocletian appointed as co-Augustus the fellow Illyrian Maximian to rule in the west while he ruled in the east. In 292 C.E., each Augustus took a Caesar, called Hercules, to assist his Augustus, called Jupiter. In the west, Constantius Chlorus was Caesar to Maximian, and in the east, Galerius was Diocletian's Caesar. Diocletian governed in the east, Maximian, Italy and Africa, Constantius, Britain, Gaul, and Spain, and Galerius, Illyricum and the Danube basin. Their respective capitals were Nicomedia, Milan, Trier, and Sirmium.

In addition to settling the question of succession, Diocletian's tetrarchy initiated a broad range of other reforms in the army and in the tax structure, to ensure the empire's stability. A *comitatus*, "core court," traveled everywhere with the emperors. This meant that frontier troops were responsible for maintaining peace on the frontier but that when reinforcements were required, a tetrarch's army responded. This well-trained, well-equipped, and well-paid army answered only to the tetrarch, so that no local officers could build a power base strong enough to mount an imperial challenge. A new and complex bureaucracy developed around

imperial persecution of Christians. The patristic writer Lactantius dedicated an entire work, called *On the Deaths of the Persecutors* (*DMP*), to the persecution. In that work he suggested (*DMP* 11) that Galerius' mother, Romula, had instigated her son's hatred of the Christians. A superstitious woman, she was a priestess in Dacia and presided over religious rites there. She noticed that Christians often refused to attend her elaborate banquets and that when they did attend they would pray and fast rather than eat and drink to excess.

the *comitatus*: financial officers, military officers, officials with juridical powers, secretaries, civil servants, and provincial administrators all played a part in reorganizing the structure of the empire. The army was divided into small highly trained units each under a *dux*, "military commander," so that multiple operations could be carried out simultaneously. The provinces were reorganized into twelve larger units called dioceses, each of which was supervised by a vicar or deputy. The vicars reported to praetorian prefects who were the chief administrators for the tetrarchs. Provincial governors administered justice and collected taxes. To support the army and bureaucracy, Diocletian devised a new tax system that depended upon a census. He developed a system to assess the value of property or the wealth of an individual by reducing land and individuals into quantifiable units. Government officials then assessed the total value of property and people in a city, village, or province and collected the taxes. Historians estimate that to pay the army, supervise all the provinces, and collect taxes to defend the borders, required a bureaucracy of about 35,000 people.

For nineteen years of Diocletian's reign, the Christians were free to worship. There were even several Christians employed in the palace bureaucracy. In 303 C.E., however, at the instigation of Galerius and his mother Romula, a pagan priestess, the first of a series of repressive edicts against the Christians was issued. The edict was issued at Nicomedia and called for the destruction of Christian places of worship and for Christian books to be burned. The following two edicts called for harsh penalties for clerics who refused to turn over the scriptures. In some cases, Christians lost their legal rights or they were tortured or imprisoned and their property was confiscated. In the fourth edict, the laity had to sacrifice to the state gods and to the divinity of the emperor.

On May 1, 305 C.E., Diocletian formally abdicated at Nicomedia. His co-Augustus, Maximian, was forced to abdicate with him (although he came out of retirement a few years later) and the tetrarchy gave way to dynastic succession. In 308 C.E., Galerius urged Diocletian to resume power in the face of the dissolution of the tetrarchy, but he refused. He claimed that he cared only to tend to his vegetable garden. Diocletian spent a long retirement in his palace in Dalmatia, the modern Split, Croatia.

Moreover, Galerius had been very successful in his military operations and had even reconquered Persia (298 C.E.), a longstanding enemy of Rome. This would have earned him the good will and respect of Diocletian. Banking on the leverage he had earned by these military victories, Galerius approached Diocletian with buoyant confidence on the subject of the Christian menace. His objectives were to persuade Diocletian to consider Christians dangerous subversives and to take action against them. After consultations with

FROM AN ANCIENT TEXT ❖ 3.1

Edict of Diocletian against Manicheism

Manicheism was a Persian religion founded by the prophet Mani (216–276 C.E.) based on a dualistic doctrine of good and evil. Diocletian's ruling against the Manichees (296 C.E.) was an attempt to strengthen the traditional religion, and it defines the rejection of traditional Roman religion as a crime.

The Emperors Diocletian and Maximian, Augusti, and Constantius and Maximian, most noble Caesars, to Julianus, proconsul of Africa. Excessive idleness, my dear Julianus, sometimes drives people to join with others in devising certain superstitious doctrines of a most worthless and depraved kind. In so doing, they overstep the bounds imposed on humans. Moreover they lure on many others to accept the authority of their erroneous doctrine.

But the immortal gods in their providence have deigned to dispose and arrange matters so that good and true principles should be approved and fixed by the wisdom and constant deliberation of many good, eminent, and very wise men. These principles it is not right to oppose or resist, nor ought the age-old religion be disparaged by a new one. For it is the height of criminality to reexamine doctrines once and for all settled and fixed by the ancients, doctrines which hold and possess their recognized place and course. Wherefore it is our vigorous determination to punish the stubborn depraved minds of these most worthless people.

We take note that those men concerning whom Your Sagacity has reported to Our Serenity, namely the Manicheans, have set up new and unheard of sects in opposition to the older creeds, with the intent of driving out to the benefit of their depraved doctrine what was formerly granted to us by divine favor. We have heard that these men have but recently sprung up and advanced, like strange and unexpected portents, from the Persian people, our enemy, to this part of the world, where they are perpetrating many outrages, disturbing the tranquility of the peoples and also introducing the gravest harm to the communities. And it is to be feared that peradventure as usually happens, they may try, with the accursed customs and perverse laws of the Persians, to infect men of a more innocent nature, namely the temperate and tranquil Roman people, as well as our entire Empire with what one might call their malevolent poisons. And since, as Your Sagacity has set forth in your report on their religion, all types of offenses against the statutes have very plainly been devised and falsehoods contrived, we have accordingly established for these people afflictions and deserving and condign penalties.

Now, therefore, we order that the founders and heads be subjected to severe punishment; together with their abominable writings they are to be burned in the flames. We instruct that their followers, and particularly the fanatics, shall suffer a capital penalty, and we ordain that their property be confiscated for our fisc. But if indeed any office holders or persons of any rank or distinction have gone over to a hitherto unheard-of disgraceful and wholly infamous sect, particularly to the creed of the Persians, you shall cause their estates to be added to our fisc. . . .

In order, then, that this plague of iniquity may be extirpated by the roots from this most happy age of ours, Your Devotion shall carry out with dispatch the orders and enactments of Our Tranquility.

Given on March 31, at Alexandria.

Source: Naphtali Lewis and Meyer Reinhold, *Roman Civilization Sourcebook II: The Empire* (New York: Harper & Row, 1966), pp. 580–81.

his ministers, Diocletian agreed to send an *haruspex* to the oracle of Apollo at Didyma in Asia Minor to inquire about the allegations of Galerius (and his mother Romula) against the Christians. He received the reply that the "just" upon the earth were the cause of false oracles. Interpreting the "just" to mean the Christians, Diocletian finally issued the edict that Galerius had sought: Christians were required to give up their sacred books and scriptures; their worship was forbidden; and all churches were to be destroyed. The main Christian church in Nicomedia, opposite the imperial palace, was leveled in a day by axes and other iron tools as Diocletian and Galerius watched (*DMP* 12). On the next day, February 24, by a second edict, Christians who did not obey the first edict were deprived of their rank, which meant that they had no legal rights.

On November 20, 303 c.e., Diocletian was in Rome to celebrate his *Vicennalia*. Just after his arrival, he passed another edict, ordering the clergy to sacrifice and demanding the arrest of bishops and clergy who refused. When the jails were too full to hold them all, another edict

announced that they could be released on the condition that they apostatize by sacrificing to the pagan gods. This concession seems to have been at least partly motivated by the upcoming *vicennalia* celebration. In order to empty the prisons, bishops and clergy were tortured and bullied into making sacrifices, either by scattering incense on pagan altars or by eating sacrificial meat.

Galerius, who was now the lead tetrarch since Diocletian had become ill, issued the edict of 304 c.e., almost a year after the first edict had been issued. This edict decreed a universal sacrifice without distinction. Everyone—men, women and children—had to sacrifice or face death or hard labor in the mines. These edicts were no longer directed solely at the church leaders, but at all Christians. We have contemporary accounts of the persecution from the patristic period in the works of Lactantius and Eusebius and we have more modern iterations of the *passions*, "accounts of the trials and deaths," of the martyrs from the liturgical and literary traditions. We read in these accounts that lists were made of individuals who then had to come forward and sacrifice, and that

---

FROM AN ANCIENT TEXT ❖ 3.2

Martyrdom in the Persecution of Diocletian

According to these sources, the persecution of Christians who refused to participate in the universal sacrifice was horrific. This example is one of many that the ecclesiastical historian Eusebius records, but it is important to remember that the accuracy of all such accounts continue to be debated.

In the city named above, the rulers in question brought a certain man into a public place and commanded him to sacrifice. When he refused, he was ordered to be stripped, hoisted up naked, and his whole body torn with loaded whips till he gave in and carried out the command, however unwillingly. When in spite of these torments he remained as obstinate as ever, they next mixed vinegar with salt and poured it over the lacerated parts of his body, where the bones were already exposed. When he treated these agonies too with scorn, a lighted brazier was then brought forward, and as if it were edible meat for table, what was left of his body was consumed by the fire, not all at once, for fear his release would come to soon, but a little at a time; and those who placed him on the pyre were not permitted to stop till after such treatment he should signify his readiness to obey. But he stuck immovably to his determination, and victorious in the midst of his tortures, breathed his last.

Source: Eusebius, *Ecclesiastical History* 8.5 in Eusebius, *The History of the Church from Christ to Constantine*, tr. G. A. Williamson, rev. and ed. Andrew Louth (London: Penguin, 1965), pp. 261–62.

---

the penalties for not sacrificing were executed by local governors.

Diocletian's Abdication

Dissolution of the Tetrarchy

On May 1, 305 c.e., in the midst of the persecution, Diocletian abdicated, leaving his palace in Nicomedia to retire to his palace in the modern city of Split, in Croatia. At the same time, his co-Augustus Maximian abdicated (under pressure) in Milan. Maximian's Caesar in the west, Constantius, now became Augustus, and Diocletian's Caesar, Galerius, succeeded him as Augustus in the east. Diocletian acknowledged Galerius's primacy by granting him the exclusive privilege of appointing the new Caesars: the loyal officer Flavius Valerius Severus became Caesar of the west under Constantius; and Galerius's nephew, Gaius Galerius Valerius Daia, added Maximinus to his name and became his Caesar (Maximin Daia) in the east. Another fellow Illyrian, Valerius Licinianus Licinius, was also eager for power and would soon replace Severus. This marked the beginning of the dissolution of the tetrarchy that lasted only until the death of Constantius in July 306. Then, the stronger bonds of filial loyalty superseded Diocletian's plans for peaceful succession and resulted in the emergence of the new "Christian" monarchy of Constantine.

Flavius Valerius Constantinus (Constantine the Great) (c. 273–337 C.E.) was at Galerius's court in Nicomedia when the Augusti abdicated and the new Caesars were appointed. Soon after this, in July of 306 C.E., at Constantius's death, his father's loyal troops proclaimed Constantine the new Augustus of the west. Emboldened by Constantine's popular elevation to power at his father's death, Maxentius, also the son of a tetrarch (Maximian), made a bid for power. On October 28, 306 C.E., he had himself proclaimed emperor of Rome by the Praetorian Guard. The government was in chaos and in 308 C.E., the lead tetrarch, Galerius, called a conference at Carnuntum in Upper Pannonia, the modern Petronell, Austria. At that conference, after reaffirming his status as Augustus and that of Maximinus Daia as his Caesar, Galerius still had to contend with Maxentius, self-proclaimed emperor in Rome, and Constantine, who not only called himself Augustus, but also issued coins in his name depicting *Sol Invictus* rather than the tetrarchy's emblematic Jupiter and Hercules.

The End of the Persecution of the Christians

Although under the various leaders in the west (Severus, Constantine, Maximian, Maxentius, and Licinius) the persecution lost steam, it continued with fury in the east under Galerius

Personalities in Christianity 3.5
GALERIUS

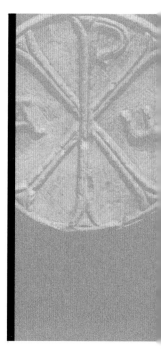

One of the several Illyrian generals who formed Diocletian's tetrarchy, Galerius (c. 250–311 C.E.) was appointed by Diocletian as the Caesar of the eastern empire in 293 C.E. By all accounts he was a fine general and his victories over the Germans and the Persians gained him enough political capital with Diocletian to persuade him to initiate a persecution of the Christians that lasted from 303 until 313 C.E. In 305 C.E., when Diocletian and Maximian abdicated, Galerius succeeded as Augustus of the east and appointed Maximinus Daia as his Caesar. Together they renewed the frenzy of the persecution of Christians in the east while Constantine and Maxentius, sons of the tetrarchs Constantius Chlorus and Maximian, contended with Galerius' appointments Severus and Licinius (308 C.E.) for control of the west. Galerius himself made an unsuccessful attempt to reclaim Rome from the usurper Maxentius, but he failed and withdrew to the east. It was not until he was on his deathbed in 311 C.E. that he issued his *Edict of Toleration* temporarily ending the persecution of the Christians. In that edict, he called for Christians to pray that he recover from the horrific disease of which he died shortly afterwards.

and Maximinus Daia. General sacrifices were ordered in 306 C.E. and in 308 C.E. Food for sale in public markets was sprinkled with libations to the gods and the baths were closed to anyone who would not sacrifice before entering. Those who refused were blinded in one eye or crippled, when they were not killed. The persecution only abated when Galerius became ill. In 311 C.E., he was in the final stages of what seems to have been an extremely painful cancer. His unbearable pain and ulcerous bleeding left him only intermittent periods of lucidity, and it was during one of these that he issued his edict of April 30, 311 C.E., sometimes called the Palinode of Galerius, which ended the persecution and granted tolerance to Christians on the condition that they pray for his recovery. The edict recognized that, despite earlier orders forbidding them to worship Jesus, the Christians had steadfastly refused to offer due religious observance to the pagan gods, and that, out of fear, they had even stopped worshipping their own God. In the hope that through the efficacy of the Christians' prayers to their own God he might recover, Galerius permitted Christians to resume their worship and to rebuild their meeting places.

This tenuous cessation of the persecution did not last. Within a few months of the edict of tolerance that Galerius had published just before his death, Maximinus Daia had renewed the attacks against Christians, purging whole cities and organizing pagan sacrifices. Priests performing the sacrifices had the right to arrest Christians who refused to participate and even have them put to death. To defend his severe anti-Christian policies, Maximinus

Daia made a show of attributing the plentiful harvests that year to the persecution of the Christians. It was not until his death, in 313 C.E., that the persecution finally ended.

The "Conversion" of Constantine

Constantine and *Sol Invictus*

In contrast to Diocletian, Constantine was a tolerant monotheist. He seems to have inherited from his father a membership in the sun-god cult of Helios and his first recorded religious act was to consult the oracle at the temple of Apollo, the Greek god of the sun, at Autun in 308 C.E. On his coins he was depicted as *Pontifex Maximus* with representations of the sun god. He consulted *haruspices* and pagan priests, yet, after conquering Maxentius at the Battle of the Milvian Bridge in 312 C.E., he also legalized Christian worship.

Constantine's devotion to a sun god was evident as early as 309 C.E. His bronze coinage of that year, for example, was exclusively dedicated to *Sol Invictus*. On these coins, the sun god was accompanied by the inscription *Soli Invicto Comiti*, which means "To the Sun, Invincible Companion." In 310 C.E., Constantine was celebrated in a panegyric that recounted his vision of a solar apparition and anticipated his famous "Christian" vision just before the Battle of the Milvian Bridge, in 312 C.E. By the time of the panegyric, Constantine controlled all the territory his father had controlled, he had forced his father-in-law and rival, Maximian, the popular Augustus of the west for twenty years, to commit suicide, he

FROM AN ANCIENT TEXT ❖ 3.3

Edict of Galerius on the Toleration of Christians

Extant both in its Latin original and in its Greek translation, this edict formally ended the persecution begun in 303 C.E. It was almost superfluous in the west, where the persecution had ceased by 306 C.E. under the tolerance of Constantine, but shortly after its publication Maximinus Daia resumed persecutions in his (eastern) provinces.

Among all the other arrangements which we are always making for the advantage and benefit of the state, we had earlier sought to set everything right in accordance with the ancient laws and public discipline of the Romans and to ensure that the Christians too, who had abandoned the way of life of their ancestors, should return to a sound frame of mind; for in some way such self-will had come upon these same Christians, such folly had taken hold of them, that they no longer followed those usages of the ancients which their own ancestors perhaps had first instituted, but, simply following their own judgment and pleasure, they were making up for themselves the laws which they were to observe and were gathering various groups of people together in different places. When finally our order was published that they should betake themselves to the practices of the ancients, many were subjected to danger, many too were struck down. Very many, however, persisted in their determination and we saw that these same people were neither offering worship and due religious observance to the gods nor practicing the worship of the God of the Christians. Bearing in mind therefore our own most gentle clemency and our perpetual habit of showing indulgent pardon to all men, we have taken the view that in the case of these people too we should extend our speediest indulgence, so that once more they may be Christians and put together their meeting places, provided they do nothing to disturb good order. We are moreover about to indicate in another letter to governors what conditions they ought to observe. Consequently, in accordance with this indulgence of ours, it will be their duty to pray for our safety and for the safety of the state and themselves, so that from every side the state may be kept unharmed and they may be able to live free of care in their own homes.

Source: Lactantius, *On the Deaths of the Persecutors* 34 in Lactantius, *De Mortibus Persecutorum*, ed. and tr. J. L. Creed (New York: Oxford University Press, 1984), p. 53. There is another version in Eusebius, *Ecclesiastical History* 8.17.6–10 in Eusebius, *The History of the Church from Christ to Constantine*, tr. G. A. Williamson, rev. and ed. Andrew Louth (London: Penguin, 1965), pp. 279–280.

had been admitted at last into the imperial college, and he had been elevated to the status of Augustus. (Maxentius, however, who had proclaimed himself emperor just after Constantine and who in the mean time had become Constantine's brother-in-law, was still considered a usurper by the tetrarch Galerius.) The panegyric defended Constantine's claim to the title of Augustus in two important ways: it put forth a new genealogy—that Constantine was descended from the much-loved emperor who had rescued the empire from the Gothic invasion, Claudius Gothicus (268–270 C.E.); and it described an epiphany of the sun god Apollo, who delivered personally his divine legitimatization to Constantine's still precarious reign.

According to the anonymous panegyrist, Constantine saw in a vision the god Apollo-*Helios-Sol* with the goddess Victory who was

---

FROM AN ANCIENT TEXT ❖ 3.4

Pagan "Vision" of Constantine

The subject of five contemporary Latin panegyrics (307–321 C.E.), this account of his "pagan vision" was delivered by an anonymous Gallic orator in the panegyric celebrating Constantine's Quinquennalia, "five years of rule." In the speech, Constantine is described as veering off on a military campaign to worship at the temple of Apollo Grannus at Grand (between Trier and Marseilles), where he saw a vision of Apollo-Helios-Sol promising long life and long rule over the whole world. Commentators upon this text argue that this vision and experience suggest a "religious conversion" to Sol, *the deity of his father and of the emperor Claudius Gothicus, from whom the panegyrist, in this same speech, claims Constantine is descended.*

Fortune herself so ordered this matter that the happy outcome of your affairs prompted you to convey to the immortal gods what you had vowed at that very spot where you had turned aside toward the most beautiful temple in the whole world, or rather, to the god present there, as you saw. For you saw, I believe, O Constantine, your Apollo, accompanied by Victory, offering you laurel wreaths, each one of which carries a promise of thirty years. For this is the number of human ages which are definitely owed to you—beyond the old age of Nestor. And—now why do I say I believe?—you saw, and recognized yourself in the likeness of him to whom the divine songs of the poets had proclaimed that rule over the kingdoms of the whole world was due. And this I think has now happened, since you are, O Emperor, just as he is, youthful, joyful, a bringer of health and very handsome.

Source: Panegyrici Latini 6.21.3–5 in In Praise of Later Roman Emperors: The Panegyrici Latini, tr. C.E.V. Nixon and Barbara Saylor Rodgers (Berkeley: University of California Press, 1994), pp. 248–251.

offering him laurel wreaths that were marked with numerals that indicated a sixty-year reign over the whole world. Constantine recognized himself in the god Apollo—a youthful, joyful, and handsome savior, a god manifest on earth. But in identifying Constantine with Apollo, the panegyrist also tacitly compared him with the first Roman emperor Augustus, who had favored Apollo. In the vision, the apparition of Apollo foretold that Constantine would soon rule alone (apart from the other tetrarchs) over the entire world. Hereafter, Claudius Gothicus appeared in other panegyrics to Constantine, and *Sol Invictus* appeared on so many coins between 310 and 313 C.E. that it seemed clear that Constantine had identified him as the "Highest Divinity." According to the panegyric, dynastic succession and an epiphany of the sun god Apollo separated Constantine from the other members of the tetrarchy. Moreover, just as Apollo was the representation of a universal monotheism centered around *Sol*, so was Constantine, through Apollo's divine patronage, the representative of universal monarchy.

Battle of the Milvian Bridge

After Galerius's death in 311 C.E., both Licinius and Maximin Daia raced to claim his territories. For different reasons—Licinius because he wanted Maximin Daia's territories and Constantine because he had no interest in the continued persecutions of Maximin Daia—Constantine and Licinius became allies. To cement their alliance, Licinius was betrothed to Constantine's half-sister Constantia. Mean-

while, Maxentius was losing control of Rome and had declared war on Constantine. The pretext was that he wanted to avenge the murder of his father Maximian, but in reality he had become more and more unpopular as his building program excessively taxed the Romans and the food shortages precipitated riots. He needed money, troops, and territory. He and Maximin Daia agreed to ally themselves against Constantine and Licinius. The tetrarchy had completely dissolved.

In the spring of 312 C.E., while Licinius and Maximin Daia remained in the east, Constantine crossed the Alps and took northern Italy in several difficult battles that required strategic acumen and daring leadership. Maxentius had remained fortified in Rome, which he had filled with supplies; to slow the approach of Constantine and his forces, he had cut all the bridges outside of the walls of Rome.

Complacent and overconfident, Maxentius was celebrating the anniversary of his accession when he received the news that Constantine was marching closer to Rome and could not be stopped. He ordered the Sibylline books to be consulted, to learn what the fortune of the day held: the *haruspex* read in the prophetic books that on that day the enemy of the Romans would perish. Interpreting the prediction of the *haruspex* to mean that Constantine was the enemy of Romans and would be defeated, Maxentius marched out to meet him. The date was October 28, 312 C.E., six years to the very day that Maxentius had proclaimed himself emperor.

The "Vision" of Constantine

On the eve of the battle, Constantine experienced another solar apparition. We have two accounts of his vision: Eusebius's *Life of Constantine*, 1.28, was written shortly after Constantine's death in 337 C.E., and Lactantius's *On the Deaths of the Persecutors* was written shortly after the event in 314 C.E. In the accounts, there are real distinctions between the exact form of the symbol that was revealed to Constantine. According to Lactantius, Constantine was directed in a dream to mark his soldiers' shields with the heavenly sign of God before engaging in battle. The sign was a letter X with a vertical line through it, the top of which was curved around. Some scholars have interpreted this as the symbol of the staurogram while others have identified this symbol as the Christogram. The staurogram was a common symbol for the cross already in use by the third century; the Christogram was the Christian emblem of

FIGURE 3.3. *Constantine's "vision" of the Cross. In the Raphael rooms of the Vatican Museum, there is an entire Hall of Constantine that includes this Vision of the Cross depicting the eve of the Battle of the Milvian Bridge with Constantine's "vision" of the chi rho with the Greek words* εν τούτω νίκα *("by this, conquer").*

FIGURE 3.4. *A chi rho symbol. From a panel of a Roman sarcophagus, ca. 350 C.E., this symbol, the interlocked chi and rho, the first two letters of the word "Christ" in Greek (χριστός), is said to have appeared to Constantine in a vision on the eve of his battle with Maxentius in 312 C.E. According to the account in Eusebius, Constantine ordered his soldiers to mark their shields with the image in order to ensure their victory in the battle.*

an interlocked *chi* and *rho*, the first two letters of the word "Christ" (χριστός) in Greek.

In Eusebius's account of the dramatic vision, Constantine was contemplating to which god he should pray to ensure his victory in the battle against Maxentius. He considered that those who worshipped many gods and propitiated them with sacrifices and dedications were often deceived; a multitude of gods could not protect them. He recalled, too, that his own father had condemned the error of worshipping a plurality of gods. Instead, Eusebius tells us in his *Life of Constantine* (1.28), his father had chosen to worship "the God who transcends the universe, the savior, and guardian of his empire." He prayed for aid to the god of his father and received a vision of a *labarum*, a tall pole with a horizontal bar forming a cross that was crowned with a wreath of precious stones; on it were two letters imitating the first two Greek characters of the name "Christ," the chi-rho symbol. According to Eusebius, it was the God of the Christians who promised Constantine victory in that vision, and in return he insisted that all the men in his army display on their shields the Christian emblem of the interlocked *chi* and *rho*.

Death of Maxentius

Maxentius met Constantine nine miles north of Rome at Saxa Rubra, the modern Malborghetto. As the forces of Maxentius were pushed back toward the city, they tried to cross the Tiber River on the flimsy bridge of boats and planks that they had hastily constructed. Maxentius, too, drove his horse across the planks, but there were so many troops rush-

ing to retreat that he was thrown into the river and was drowned by his heavy armor.

Carrying Maxentius's head on a spear, Constantine entered Rome the next day in a ceremonial *adventus* and set about obliterating the memory of Maxentius in what is called a *damnatio memoriae*, "obliteration of (someone's) memory." He spent three months in Rome and during that time he undertook the construction of several major Christian basilicas, including the Basilica of San Giovanni in Lateranoh and Basilica of San Pietro. He also issued several letters ordering that Christians who had lost property in the persecutions were to have it restored.

Edict of Milan

In February 313 C.E., Constantine went to Milan for the wedding of his half-sister Constantia and Licinius. There, Constantine and Licinius agreed to proclaim that the toleration of Christianity be extended into Licinius's territory. The so-called Edict of Milan was really a letter from Licinius to the governor in Nicomedia at the victory of Constantine and Licinius over Maximinus Daia in 313 C.E. It stated that Christians and all others were free to worship as they desired, so that whatever divinity was in heaven might be appeased and be propitious toward the empire's rulers and her citizens. The previous edicts ordering the persecution of Christians were nullified, all places of Christian worship were now to be restored, and all confiscated property was to be returned. In effect, the Edict of Milan granted the same policies of tolerance already practiced in the west and

FROM AN ANCIENT TEXT ❖ 3.5

Christian "Vision" of Constantine: Lactantius and Eusebius

There are two accounts of the famous Christian vision of Constantine, the divine epiphany and message he received just before the Battle of the Milvian Bridge on October 28, 312 C.E. The version of Lactantius written shortly after the event is considerably shorter than that of Eusebius written just after Constantine's death on May 22, 337 C.E., more than twenty-five years after the event.

Lactantius

Constantine was advised in a dream to mark the heavenly sign of God on the shields of his soldiers and then engage in battle. He did as he was commanded and by means of a slanted letter X with the top of its head bent around, he marked Christ on their shields. Armed with this sign, the army took up its weapons. The enemy came to meet them without their emperor and crossed the bridge. . . . Inspired by the prophecy to expect victory he [Maxentius] went forth and joined the battle. . . . The army of Maxentius was seized with terror, and he himself [Maxentius] fled in haste to the bridge which had been broken down; pressed by the mass of fugitives, he was hurtled into the Tiber. . . . Constantine was welcomed as emperor with great joy by the senate and the people of Rome.

Source: Lactantius, *On the Deaths of the Persecutors* 44 in Lactantius, *De Mortibus Persecutorum*, ed. and tr. J. L. Creed (New York: Oxford University Press, 1984), p. 63.

Eusebius

This God he began to invoke in prayer, beseeching and imploring him to show him who he was, and to stretch out his right hand and assist him in his plans. As he made these prayers and earnest supplications there appeared to the Emperor a most remarkable divine sign. If someone else had reported it, it would perhaps not be easy to accept; but since the victorious Emperor himself told the story to the present writer a long while after, when I was privileged with his acquaintance and company, and confirmed it with oaths, who could hesitate to believe the account, especially when the time which followed provided evidence for the truth of what he said? About the time of the midday sun, when the day was just turning, he said he saw with his own eyes, up in the sky and resting over the sun, a cross shaped trophy formed from light, and a text attached to it which said, "by this conquer" [εν τούτω νίκα]. Amazement at the spectacle seized both him and the whole company of soldiers, which was then accompanying him on a campaign he was conducting somewhere and witnessed the miracle.

He was, he said, wondering to himself what the manifestation must mean; then, while he meditated, and thought long and hard, night overtook him. Thereupon, as he slept, the Christ of God appeared to him with the sign, which had appeared in the sky, and urged him to make himself a copy of the sign, which had appeared in the sky, and to use this as protection against the attacks of the enemy. When day came he arose and recounted the mysterious communication to his friends. Then he summoned goldsmiths and jewelers, sat down among them, and explained the shape of the sign, and gave them instructions about copying it in gold and precious stones.

This was something that the Emperor himself once saw fit to let me also set my eyes on, God vouchsafing even this. It was constructed to the following design. A tall pole plated with gold had a transverse bar forming the shape of a cross. Up at the extreme top a wreath woven of precious stones and gold had been fastened. On it two letters, intimating by its first characters the name "Christ," formed the monogram of the Saviour's title, *rho* being intersected in the middle by *chi*. These letters the Emperor also used to wear upon his helmet in later times. From the transverse bar, which was bisected by the pole, hung suspended a cloth, an imperial tapestry covered with a pattern of precious stones fastened together, which glittered with shafts of light, and interwoven with much gold, producing an impression of indescribable beauty on those who saw it. This banner then, attached to the bar, was given equal dimensions of length and breadth. But the upright pole, which extended upwards a long way from its lower end, below the trophy of the cross and near the top of the tapestry delineated, carried the golden head-and-shoulders portrait of the Godbeloved Emperor, and likewise of his sons. This saving sign was always used by the Emperor for protection against every opposing and hostile force, and he commanded replicas of it to lead all his armies.

That was, however, somewhat later. At the time in question, stunned at the amazing vision, and determined to worship no other god than the one who had appeared, he summoned those expert in his words, and enquired who this god was, and what was the explanation of this vision which had appeared of the sign. They said that the god was the Onlybegotten Son of the one and only God, and that the sign which appeared was a token of immortality, and was an abiding trophy of the victory over death, which he had once won when he was present on earth. They began to teach him the reasons of his coming, explaining to him in detail the story of his self-accommodation to human conditions. He listened attentively to these accounts too, while he marveled at the divine manifestation that had been granted to his eyes; comparing the heavenly vision to the meaning of what was being said, he made up his mind, convinced that it was as God's own teaching that the knowledge of these things had come to him. He now decided personally to apply himself to the divinely inspired writings. Taking the priests of God as his advisors, he also deemed it right to honor the God who had appeared to him with all due rites. Thereafter, fortified by the good hopes in him, he finally set about extinguishing the menacing flames of tyranny.

Eusebius, *On the Life of the Blessed Emperor Constantine* 1.28–32 in *Eusebius, Life of Constantine*, tr. Averil Cameron and Stuart G. Hall (New York: Oxford University Press, 1999), pp. 80–82.

FIGURE 3.5. *The Battle of the Milvian Bridge. Raphael's fresco in the Vatican Museum captures the battle between the Roman emperors Constantine and Maxentius in 312 C.E., which resulted in the death of Maxentius and the establishing of Constantine as the sole ruler of Rome.*

in the territories of Galerius to the Christian subjects of the defeated Maximinus Daia.

It is important to notice that the edict neither sanctioned Christianity exclusively nor suppressed other non-Christian cults. It seemed clear that Constantine had embraced the widespread well-established monotheism of pagan religious tradition, but whether, or to what degree, Jesus was distinct from *Sol* is less clear. *Sol* maintained a prominent place as Constantine's patron divinity on coins

through 325 C.E. And on the arch erected by the Roman Senate in 315 C.E. to commemorate his victory over Maxentius and to celebrate his *Decennalia*, "ten years of rule," Constantine acknowledged his debt to the "inspiration of divinity" (*instinctu divinitatis*), but Jesus was not named as that divinity. In fact, the only depiction of divinities on the arch are in two medallions, one facing west and one facing east: facing west, *Luna*, "Moon," rides into the sea on her two-horse chariot; and facing east,

FROM AN ANCIENT TEXT ❖ 3.6

Edict of Milan of Constantine and Licinius

This letter to the governor in Nicomedia at the victory of Constantine and Licinius over Maximinus Daia in 313 C.E. grants the same policies of tolerance already practiced in the west and in the territories of Galerius to the Christian subjects of the defeated Maximinus Daia.

When I, Constantine Augustus, and I, Licinius Augustus, happily met at Milan and had under consideration all matters which concerned the public advantage and safety, we thought that, among all the other things that we saw would benefit the majority of men, the arrangements which above all needed to be made were those which ensured reverence for the Divinity, so that we might grant both to Christians and to all men freedom to follow whatever religion each one wished, in order that whatever divinity there is in the seat of heaven may be appeased and made propitious towards us and towards all who have been set under our power. We thought therefore that in accordance with salutary and most correct reasoning we ought to follow the policy of regarding this opportunity as one not to be denied to anyone at all, whether he wished to give his mind to the observances of the Christians or to that religion which he felt was most fitting to himself, so that the supreme Divinity, whose religion we obey with free minds, may be able to show in all matters His accustomed favor and benevolence towards us. For this reason we wish your Devotedness to know that we have resolved that, all the conditions which were contained in letters previously sent to your office about the Christian name being completely set aside, those measures should be repealed which seemed utterly inauspicious and foreign to our clemency, and that each individual one of those who share this same wish to observe the religion of the Christians should freely and straightforwardly hasten to do so without any anxiety or interference. We thought that this should be very fully communicated to your Solicitude, so that you should know that we have given a free and absolute permission to these same Christians to practice their religion. And when you perceive that this indulgence has been accorded by us to these people, your Devotedness understands that others too have been granted a similarly open and free permission to follow their own religion and worship as benefits the peacefulness of our times, so that each man may have a free opportunity to engage in whatever worship he has chosen. This we have done to ensure that no cult or religion may seem to have been impaired by us.

   We have also decided that we should decree as follows about the Christians as a body: if, during the period that had passed, any appear to have purchased either from our treasury or from anyone else those places in which the Christians had previously been accustomed to assemble, and about which before now a definite rule had been laid down in the letters that were sent to your office, they should now restore these same places to the Christians without receiving any money for them or making any request for payment, and without any question of obstruction or equivocation; those who received such places as a gift should return them in the same way but the more speedily to these same Christians; both those who bought them and those who received them as gifts should, if they seek something from our benevolence, make a request to the deputy for their interests to be consulted by our clemency. All these places must forthwith be handed over to the body of the Christians through your intervention and without any delay.

And since these same Christians are known to have possessed not only the places in which they had the habit of assembling but other property too which belongs by right to their body— that is, to the churches not to the individuals—you will order all this property, in accordance with the law we have explained above, to be given back without any equivocation or dispute at all to these same Christians, that is to their body and assemblies, preserving always the principle stated above, that those who restore the same property as we have enjoined without receiving a price for it may hope to secure indemnity from our benevolence. In all these matters you will be bound to offer the aforesaid body of Christians your most effective support so that our instructions can be more rapidly carried out and the interests of public tranquility thereby served in this matter too by our clemency. In this way it will come about, as we have explained above, that the divine favor towards us, which we have experienced in such important matters, will continue in all time to prosper our achievements along with the public well-being. Furthermore, so that the character of this ordinance and of our benevolence can be brought to the knowledge of all, it will be desirable for you to publish this document everywhere above a proclamation of your own, and to convey it to the attention of everyone, so that the ordaining of this benevolence of ours cannot remain hidden.

Source: Eusebius, *Ecclesiastical History* 10.5.2–14 in Eusebius, *The History of the Church from Christ to Constantine*, tr. G. A. Williamson, rev. and ed. Andrew Louth (London: Penguin, 1965), pp. 322–24. There is another version in Lactantius, *On the Death of the Persecutors* 48 in *De Mortibus Persecutorum*, ed. and tr. J. L. Creed (New York: Oxford, 1984), pp. 71–73. Both versions are substantially the same but for one line (. . . whose religion we obey with free minds), which is missing from the text in Eusebius.

FIGURE 3.6. *Basilica of San Lorenzo fuori le Mura. The Basilica of Saint Lawrence Outside the Walls was built by Constantine the Great in 330 C.E. Several alterations and additions took place in the sixth and eighth centuries. The Romanesque bell tower dates from the twelfth century and the portico, by Vassalletto, dates from 1220.*

Sol, in a four-horse chariot, rises from the sea, just above the scene of Constantine's *adventus* into Rome after the Battle at the Milvian Bridge in 312 C.E. As the empire moved toward a universal monarchy under the Christian God, the identity of that God, at least initially, was less important that the fact that Constantine was his divine representative on earth.

Conclusion

In this chapter, we have seen that the oriental god *Sol* was widely worshipped under Elagabalus and Aurelian and that under Constantine, at least for a while, *Sol* was jointly worshipped with Jesus. By the third century, in fact, the monotheistic worship of *Sol* or *Sol Invictus* had spread across much of the empire.

Diocletian hoped to reverse the tide of political, economic, and social chaos that he inherited when he became emperor in 284 C.E. by reintroducing the worship of the revered gods of the state. The result was a gradual weakening of the empire-wide worship of *Sol*. In addition to reestablishing the universal worship of the traditional gods, Diocletian also infused the worship of the emperor with a new aura of divinity. Moreover, he showed no tolerance for anyone who resisted his religious program. In 303 C.E., near the end of a twenty-year reign during which Christians and non-Christians had lived peaceably, he and his Caesar, Galerius, launched the most extensive

persecution of Christians in the history of the church.

To understand the persecution as an unpredictable aberration in an otherwise harmonious coexistence of Christians and non-Christians, however, is an oversimplification. For Diocletian and Galerius, as well as for many citizens, the Christians' refusal to participate in the official state religion, which was the only way to ensure the *pax deorum*, put the empire's survival at risk. All citizens were required to sacrifice to the traditional gods and also worship the emperor, in order to ensure the safety and prosperity of the state. Many considered it the fault of

FIGURE 3.7. *Arch of Constantine. Dedicated in 315 C.E., this Roman arch commemorates Constantine's victory over Maxentius at the Battle of the Milvian Bridge.*

FROM AN ANCIENT TEXT ❖ 3.7

Arch of Constantine

The Arch of Constantine, located between the Palatine and Caelian hills, is built of white and colored marbles and uses reliefs from other sculptures substituting the heads of Constantine and Licinius into the originals. The inscription is significant because there is no mention of Jesus or Christianity but rather a somewhat vague single divinity, one that would acknowledge Constantine's monotheism, even Christianity, but not offend the pagan senate.

To the Emperor Caesar Flavius Constantinus the greatest, dutiful and blessed, Augustus, the Senate and people of Rome dedicated this arch, marked with his victories, because, by the inspiration of divinity and by greatness of mind [*instinctu divinitatis mentis magnitudine*], he and his army avenged the state with righteous arms against both the tyrant and all of his followers at one and the same time. To the liberator of the city and the establisher of peace.

Source: The Latin is available in the *Corpus Inscriptionum Latinarum, Corpus of Latin Inscriptions* (Berlin, 1853–), 6.11139, p. 236, and there is a translation and discussion in A. D. Lee, *Pagans and Christians in Late Antiquity: A Sourcebook* (New York: Routledge, 2000), p. 83.

---

the Christians that the empire was crumbling internally. The constant wars and the continued threat of barbarian invasions only heightened the antagonism against those who refused to worship the state gods. More and more, people felt that the Christians had to be resisted and that traditional worship and traditional religious rituals had to be uniformly performed. The view of Diocletian and Galerius was that Christians were disrupting essential religious rituals and thereby provoking the anger of the gods against the empire. Thus, the persecution of 303 C.E., the most serious and sustained of all imperial anti-Christian persecutions, was the culmination of a steadily increasing intolerance of any worship that did not include prayers for the emperor and the due observance of the traditional gods of the state.

In contrast to Diocletian, Constantine was a tolerant monotheist. He primarily worshipped *Sol Invictus*. Even after his "conversion" at the Battle of the Milvian Bridge in 312 C.E., there is evidence that along with Jesus he continued to worship *Sol Invictus*. Thus, the supposition that when Constantine legalized Christianity a new Judeo-Christian monotheism triumphed over a worn-out polytheism is also an oversimplification. We need only think of the pagan worship of *Sol* or the Christian worship of the patron saints and martyrs (more than enough to fill an entire calendar!) to realize how the distinctions between the pagan pantheon and Christian monotheism blur. Just as

FIGURE 3.8. *Basilica of Sante Croce in Gerusalemme. The Basilica of the Holy Cross in Jerusalem have housed the passion relics brought from the Holy Land to Rome by Constantine's mother Saint Helena in the early fourth century.*

Sol shared many aspects with hundreds of deities, so were Christians able to find Jesus in the worship of hundreds of saints and martyrs. A powerful visual example of Constantine's unique Christian monotheism—an empire-wide syncretistic Jesus-*Sol* worship—is encapsulated in this detail: the last mention in the ancient sources of Aurelian's splendid temple to *Sol* relates that eight of its porphyry columns were removed to Constantinople, the modern Istanbul, Turkey, to adorn the grandest Christian building project in his new capital, the Basilica of Santa Sofia.

STUDY QUESTIONS

1 Long before Constantine "converted" to Christianity in 312 B.C.E., the Roman imperial court had begun to make the transition from polytheistic towards monotheistic worship. Discuss this trend citing specific examples of pagan monotheistic worship.

2 In what ways did Diocletian transform the Roman imperial court?

3 How did the Edict of Milan (313 C.E.) affect Christianity's status within the Roman Empire? What, if any, effect did it have on pagan worship throughout the empire?

4 Using the bibliographic resources provided at the end of this book, conduct further research into the cult of Mithras. How does your knowledge of Mithraism and of other mystery religions of the Near East and the Greco-Roman world affect your view of Christianity?

5 Why after almost twenty years of religious tolerance did Diocletian persecute Christians? Why did the persecution ultimately fail?

6 How is the climate of religious diversity and tolerance in the United States today like and unlike that in early Christian Rome?

Chapter 4

CHRISTIANS AND CHRISTIANS
Pope Damasus and the Christianization of Rome

All the temples of Rome are covered with soot and cobwebs, the city is shaken to its very foundations, and the people hurry past the crumbling shrines and surge out to visit the martyrs' graves.

—Jerome, *Epistula* 107.1

After Diocletian's persecution of the church and Constantine's "conversion" to a Christian monotheism, the process of Christianizing Rome began. One key factor in this transformation of the city was the new Christian building program that emphasized the commemoration of the martyrs at the holy shrines around their burial places, called in Latin *martyrium* or, in the plural, *martyria*. Since mar-

trydom was both a physical act that took place in a public space and a discourse, we will see that a second and complementary factor in the Christianization of Rome was the development of the related literary genres of hagiography and martyrology. Hagiographical texts are biographical accounts of the Christian martyrs and saints, while martyrologies detail the legendary accounts of their *passion* or "suffering." In this chapter, we will consider how the fourth-century Roman church leaders used these two important strategies, the construction of *martyria* and their related visual spectacles and the new Christian literary genre of martyrology, in their efforts to claim Rome's episcopal primacy as the *sedes Petri*, "seat of Peter."

Pope Damasus

The Struggle for the Papacy

After Constantine's "conversion," the future of the church was by no means secure. Heresies raged. The debates over Arianism were particularly virulent, the more so as they were played out among the dynastic successors of Constantine. Moreover, there were debates concerning church authority. When Constantine removed his capitol to Constantinople in 330 C.E., the apostolic authority of the church of Rome was threatened. Each of the four sees—Alexandria, Antioch, Rome, and Constantinople—sought to establish its primacy. The papacy of Pope Damasus (c. 304–384 C.E.) represented a new trend in church leadership. He embodied the single-minded goal of establishing Rome as the primate see of the Christian church, the capital of Christendom. His elevation to the papacy was difficult and he had to struggle to hold his power through his entire reign. In what may be loosely considered a Christian version of the Roman political *cursus honorum*, "sequence of offices," Damasus was first a deacon under Pope Liberius (352–366 C.E.) before moving up in the ranks of clergy. At Liberius's death, he began a fifteen-year struggle against his rival Ursinus to claim the papacy. Each was elected pope by his own group of followers, Ursinus in the Basilica of Santa Maria in Trastevere and Damasus in the Basilica of San Lorenzo in Lucina. In his *History* (27.3.12–13), the contemporary historian Ammianus Marcellinus (330–391 C.E.) described a bitter antagonism between the two rivals for the powerful office of pope. They were acrimoniously polarized in their views and their supporters brawled openly in the streets. In one day, Ammianus reports, there were 137 corpses after a deadly confrontation that caused Valentinian I to banish Ursinus to Cologne and recognize Damasus as pope. The same mob violence persisted, however, and Ursinus and his followers were relocated to northern Italy. Even from that remote location, they continued to dog Damasus through the end of his papacy.

Martyr Shrines and Basilicas

Under Pope Damasus's direction, the Christian building program inaugurated by Constantine flourished. In place of the great imperial complexes throughout the city—the imperial fora, circuses, baths, and temples—Christian basilicas and martyr shrines now formed a new and novel social network of meeting places. They served to connect the congregants of the imperially sanctioned, post-Constantinian church with those martyrs who had died rather than observe pagan religious rites. Scenes of martyrdoms appeared in decorative mosaics in new Christian basilicas, or verses detailing the passions of individual martyrs were carved in stone and placed above their burial places and shrines. The restoration of these burial places and shrines was at the center of the ambitious propagandizing efforts of Damasus. He was determined to reinvent Rome. The topography of the ancient cultural, social, and economic center of the empire, under the providence of his episcopacy, would be renewed in a Christian *renovatio urbis*, "renovation of the city."

Personalities in Christianity 4.1
DAMASUS

Damasus (c. 304–384 C.E.) became pope in 360 C.E., and during his reign the papacy was transformed into the supreme pontifical office and Rome was transformed into the primate see. Damasus served as a deacon in the church of Saint Lawrence in Rome under Pope Liberius. In the rivalry for the papacy after Liberius's death, Damasus and Ursinus with their unruly bands of supporters confronted each other in several places in the city. The riots and violent clashes continued until Valentinian I banished Ursinus to Cologne. Under Damasus's direction, pagan sacred spaces and holidays were transformed into martyr shrines and Christian holy days. He commissioned Jerome to translate the Bible into Latin, convened a council to establish the canon, worked to suppress Arianism and Donatism, the heresies that frustrated, respectively, the eastern and western churches, and sought to attract wealthy converts to the church. Damasus was declared the epitome of orthodoxy in an edict of Theodosius (380 C.E.). Together with the talented calligrapher Filocalus, Damasus produced a program of inscriptions to affix to the martyr tombs and shrines that he had erected or reconstituted around Rome. The inscriptions themselves are poetic verses composed by Damasus. The shrines and the inscriptions of the martyr shrines together with the festivities associated with their feast days attracted converts from the pagan aristocracy and strengthened the church in Rome, where the religious and cultural practices of classical antiquity were preserved in the conservative Roman senate.

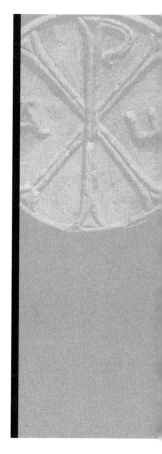

A new scale of extravagance characterized his restoration of the martyr shrines and, especially, the newly constructed basilicas. He completed three major churches and undertook work on two others, but the massive basilica dedicated to Saint Paul that he constructed on the road to Ostia, the port of Rome, was singularly remarkable. It was a magnificent structure that blended Christian and Roman architectural features. In the first century C.E., the site had housed a memorial to Paul. This was replaced by Constantine's modest longitudinal building on the same spot. Under Damasus, however, the concept of *concordia apostolorum*, "apostolic harmony," elevated Paul's stature. Now Peter and Paul shared an equal status as the apostolic founders of Christian Rome. The Basilica of Saint Paul had to match the grandeur of Constantine's Basilica of Saint Peter. An apsed transept covered Paul's tomb, at the end of a tall and wide nave lined with forty-two windows and forty elaborately carved Corinthian columns. The ceiling was lavishly gilded and the balanced, graceful proportions of the entire composition echoed its classical models. The splendor of this new basilica was considered proof that both Peter and Paul had suffered martyrdom in Rome. In turn, their twin martyrdoms legitimized the apostolic primacy of Rome.

Personalities in Christianity 4.2
ARIUS

Termed an heresiarch, or leader of an heretical movement (Arianism), Arius (c. 250–336 C.E.) had an early career as a priest before he became embroiled in the christological debate that defined the rest of his life. He disagreed with the teaching of Alexander, the Bishop of Alexandria and, in opposition, championed the teaching that the Son was not co-eternal with the Father but was subordinate to him (a heresy called "subordinationism"). There are only a few fragments of Arius's own writings, but his teaching can be traced to the Christian martyr Lucian of Antioch (died 312 C.E.) who directed a theological school in Antioch and under whom Arius studied.

For his dissenting christological views Bishop Alexander had Arius excommunicated and banished. Bishop Eusebius of Nicomedia (died 354 C.E.), however, Arius's fellow pupil under Lucian of Antioch, supported Arius's teaching. Since he was the priest who had baptized Constantine on his deathbed and then went on to join the ecclesiastic entourage of Constantius II, he eventually won imperial support for Arius's teaching, and it was through his influence Arius that was able to return from exile in 334 C.E.

Wealthy land-owning families who were attracted to Damasus' "Roman Christianity" converted in great numbers. To them, the social circuit of martyr commemorations and the pomp and luxury of the liturgical ceremonies invoked the spectacle of lavish pagan religious celebrations. We have a unique and invaluable record of those pagan celebrations in a fourth-century calendar called the Codex-Calendar of 354 C.E. After his appropriation of pagan monumental sacred space, it remained for Pope Damasus to appropriate sacred time. For this, the Codex-Calendar was vital.

The Codex-Calendar of 354 C.E.

For modern readers, the Codex-Calendar of 354 C.E. is an indispensable document for charting the growth of the Christian church in fourth-century Rome. It was also the fundamental calendrical model for Pope Damasus

as he developed a Christian cycle of festivals to support his claim that Rome was the *sedes Petri*, "episcopal seat of Peter," and the primate see of the Christian church.

The Codex was produced for a wealthy Roman Christian aristocrat named Valentinus by the talented Christian calligrapher Furius Dionysius Filocalus. Perhaps the most important pages in the Codex were those of the illustrated public Roman calendar of the year 354 C.E., which listed the pagan holidays (*ferialia*), rituals, and certain astrological phenomena. This is a principal source of fourth-century Roman pagan religious rituals. In addition to the calendar identifying the important pagan religious practices, the Codex also recorded chronologies and lists of secular and civic offices in the city. Among these, there are also three important Christian chronologies: (1) the *Depositions of Bishops*, a list of the burial dates of Roman bishops from 254–352 C.E.; (2) the *Depositions of Martyrs*, a list of commemorations for martyrs from Pope Callistus (222 C.E.) through the persecution of Diocletian in 305 C.E., including the feast of the Nativity of Christ and the Anniversary of the Chair of Peter; and (3) a list of bishops. These separate lists of Christian chronologies reveal the first attempts to name and recognize Christian bishops and martyrs.

The Codex-Calendar was made by and for a Christian. By the latter fourth century some Christian holidays were already a part of the fabric of daily life in Rome, yet Christian holidays were not included in the calendar. Instead, the calendar seems to have been important as a pagan Roman historical artifact. For Damasus, however, the imperial pagan past preserved in the Codex would guarantee Rome's *renovatio*, "rebirth," as a Christian capital. He simply applied Christian holy time to the pagan religious calendar to create a new calendrical cycle of Christian holy days.

The Roman "Popes": Damasus and Praetextatus

Damasus was worldly, wealthy, and resolute in his efforts to strengthen the power of his papacy and the dominance of the Roman church. The rival Ursinians were reported to have called him a *matronarum auriscalpius*, "an ear-scratcher of matrons," for his ability to persuade wealthy women to donate their worldly goods to the church. An edict of Valentinian I that forbade the practice of visiting wealthy matrons, widows, and orphans for the purpose of soliciting donations for the church may have been aimed at Damasus. By that edict, church leaders were forbidden to use their influence to appeal to wealthy Roman matrons for contributions, and any bequests they made were declared invalid. The scholar, churchman, and (later) saint, Jerome of Stridon, offers a contemporary comment upon Damasus's "ear-scratching" in a pamphlet entitled *Contra Ioannem Hierosolymitanum*, "Against John of Jerusalem," which he wrote in 397 C.E. In the pamphlet, Jerome described a meeting between the praetorian prefect of Rome, Vettius Agorius Praetextatus, and Pope Damasus. At the meeting, Jerome tells us, Praetextatus was so impressed by Damasus's urbanity and his imposing authority that he said, "Make me the Bishop of Rome and I will become a Christian immediately!"

Praetextatus and Damasus moved in the same social circles, one as a civil leader and one as a religious leader. Praetextatus supported Damasus against the rival Ursinians and was responsible for their exile, and Damasus supported Praetextatus in secular affairs. The praetorian prefect Praetextatus governed as a member of the traditional elite pagan Roman aristocracy. Pope Damasus was his Christian counterpart, who governed a Roman church that was a splendid Christian parallel to the elite social interactions of the pagan aristocracy. To many Roman aristocrats, the church's growing wealth, power, and social exclusivity appealed as much as any religious doctrine, and this status appeal accounted for the "religious" conversion of many Roman aristocrats. But Damasus' aim was not merely to swell the membership of the church. He wanted

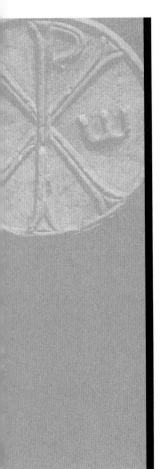

Personalities in Christianity 4.3
JEROME

One of the four doctors of the western church, Jerome (347–c. 420 C.E.) is considered one of its greatest (if most irascible) scholars. Born in Illyria, he straddled the theological issues and geographic centers of both the eastern and the western church. From about 360 C.E. until the end of his life, he was involved in church affairs as an historian, translator, and biblical scholar, as a principal in several doctrinal and political controversies (in Rome and in several centers of Christianity in the east), as a prolific correspondent, and as a monk in an ascetic community in Bethlehem. Jerome is best known for his Latin version of the Bible, called the *Vulgate*, which he began at the request of Pope Damasus (366–383 C.E.). Finding that the Septuagint (Greek) did not coincide exactly with the Hebrew scriptures, Jerome translated the New Testament from the Greek and the Old Testament from the Hebrew. In the Council of Trent in the sixteenth century, the Catholic Church endorsed Jerome's *Vulgate* as the authoritative Latin text. Catholics today still use a revised version of that text.

One of the earliest monastics, Jerome lived for over thirty years as head of a (western) monastery at Bethlehem. There the wealthy Roman matron Paula and her daughter Eustochium supported him. They had renounced their worldly goods to travel in the Holy Land and Jerome was eager to accompany them to escape his critics in Rome. It was during these years that Jerome produced his translations, commentaries, polemics, chronicles, historical compositions, hagiographies, and letters. Among the most important of these is the *De viris illustribus*, "On Illustrious Men," a collection of biographies of Christian authors.

to reinvent Rome as the primatial see of the church, a new Christian *caput mundi*, "head of the world." To accomplish this, he first needed to strengthen the office of the papacy.

Primacy of Rome

Strengthening the Papacy

It was during Damasus's papacy in 380 C.E. that an edict of Gratian and Theodosius upheld orthodox Christianity over the Arian per-

spective. Damasus was named as a model of the orthodox faith in Theodosius's edict. The edict, preserved in the *Codex Theodosianus* (16.1.2), required that everyone observe the religion handed down to the Romans by the apostle Peter. This orthodox apostolic religion, Theodosius claimed, was evident still in the practices of Pope Damasus.

Theodosius's imperial sanction may have emboldened Damasus to advance several initiatives to strengthen his papacy. First, he consistently referred to Rome as the "Apostolic

Jerome was a trained classicist and had read the works of Plautus and Terence, Sallust, Lucretius, Horace, and Virgil among others, and his own eloquent writing reflects that training. He comments in his letters that he found the early Christian authors somewhat crude compared to the classical models. In 384 c.e., in a letter (22) to Eustochium in which he extolled the virtues of a religious life consecrated to God, Jerome described a dream that he had while traveling to Bethlehem. This literary dream is an important source for scholars who assess the influence of the classical literary tradition upon Christian authors and texts.

According to the account in his letter, Jerome dreamed that he was traveling to his monastery in Bethlehem. En route he was reading Cicero and Plautus, because he had not been able to leave behind his library and could not completely put aside classical texts in favor of Christian authors. In the dream, he was brought before God who sat as a judge. Jerome was blinded by the glory of God's presence and could barely lift his eyes. When God asked whether or not he was a Christian, he answered that he was a Christian. God replied, "Where your treasure is, there is your heart." The divine tribunal judged him a Ciceronian rather than a Christian, for he could not discard his classical texts. This verdict caused Jerome to promise never to read secular texts again, but to read his Christian texts more zealously.

His collected corpus is filled with a range of political, historical, and theological views that provide modern readers with a unique view of the late fourth-century church as Rome was transformed from a pagan to a Christian capital. When he died, Jerome was buried in the Church of the Nativity in Bethlehem, but his remains have been since translated to the Basilica of Santa Maria Maggiore in Rome.

See," and made the point that it was the only see where two apostles, Peter and Paul, had ministered and were martyred, and where one of those martyrs, Peter, had been named by Jesus as his successor. As we saw earlier in this chapter, Damasus had already successfully adapted pagan festivals to a Christian calendar of celebrations. In turn, this new calendar of Christian holy days resulted in a spiritually important and economically advantageous enterprise—the pilgrimage to Rome. Damasus also restored several catacombs and constructed basilicas and shrines. He decorated the shrines with his own poetic verses, *Epigramata*, "Epigrams," which were engraved by the same Filocalus who wrote the Codex-Calendar of 354 c.e. Among all these initiatives, one of the most important was Damasus's charge to Jerome to produce a standardized, accessible Latin version of the Bible.

The *Vulgate* Version of the Bible
Together with his secretary Jerome, Damasus

initiated the series of translations from the Greek and Hebrew texts that would turn Latin into the liturgical language of the west. He commissioned Jerome to correct and trans- late the Old Latin version of the gospels by reading it against the Septuagint, or Greek, version and then reconciling the transla- tions. Ultimately, Jerome used not only the

Personalities in Christianity 4.4
THEODOSIUS

Theodosius's father seems to have died in disgrace after serving Valentinian I in Britain, Germany, and North Africa. From his father's death in 376 C.E. until 379 C.E., Theodosius (346–395 C.E.) lived in a self-imposed exile. At the defeat of Valens in 378 C.E., Gratian recalled him, appointed him general in the campaign against the Goths, and then named him co-Augustus in 379 C.E., to rule in the east. He signed treaties with the Goths (382 C.E.) to the north and the Persians (386 C.E.) to the east all the while battling internal disputes between rivaling Christianities.

One of his first acts as Augustus in the east was to grant imperial sanction to the orthodox Christianity practiced by Pope Damasus in Rome and to require (by his Edict of 380 C.E.) that the entire empire subscribe to Nicene orthodoxy. Theodosius did not legislate against pagan religious practices for another decade, but he did prohibit the practice of divination (predicting the future by reading the entrails of sacrificial animals) and magic. Theodosius first came to the west when the usurper Magnus Maximus attacked Italy in 387 C.E. Maximus had killed Gra- tian in 383 C.E. and had ruled the west in an uneasy partnership with Valentinian II since then. Theodosius moved west to defeat Maximus and secure Valentinian's reign, but also to secure his own role as lead Augustus. When he arrived to the court in Milan, Theodosius came into the orbit of Ambrose, then bishop of Milan and a sort of personal political/theological advisor to Valentinian. Ambrose and Theodosius seemed to want to achieve the same thing—mastery over the court of Valentinian to further their own ends. For Ambrose, this meant the suppres- sion of heresy and paganism; for Theodosius, empire-wide dominance.

His visit to the senate in Rome in 389 C.E. was calculated to achieve this goal. There he met with senators and in a show of clemency pardoned those who had aligned themselves with the usurper Maximus, most notably, Symmachus. He also took the opportunity to introduce to them his son Honorius. He did not, however, grant the senate's request to restore the altar of Victory to the *Curia.*

In 394 C.E., Theodosius was again called from the east, this time to put down the usurper Eugenius, a Christian rival for the throne. When he died a year later, his son Honorius succeeded him as emperor in the west and his son Arcadius succeeded him as emperor in the east.

Septuagint but also the Hebrew originals to produce his translation, which was called the *Vulgate.* The term "vulgate" is from the Latin *vulgus,* which means "common" or "of the people." When the term is used of the Bible, however, it means an agreed upon "common translation" rather than a "simple" or "popular" style. In fact, Jerome's translation reveals that he took great pains to reflect classical literary and stylistic conventions rather than a low or common style.

The *Vulgate* is, perhaps, the single most important text in western Christendom. Although it was not completed during Damasus's papacy, his plan to codify a canon of scripture in Latin that would be widely accessible to an educated Roman aristocracy is a prime example of his obdurate intention to increase the spiritual and political authority of the see of Rome. In some form or another, Damasus's intent to establish the primacy of the see of Rome was at the center of all his efforts to strengthen the papacy. And at the center of his intent to establish Rome's primacy were the apostles Peter and Paul.

Peter the "Rock"

Rome claimed its apostolic primacy from Peter to whom Jesus had given the keys to the kingdom of heaven and whom he had identified as the "rock" or foundation of the apostolic succession of popes. In Matt 16:18-19, Jesus called Peter a "rock" and announced that he was to become the very foundation of the church: *Tu es Petrus et super hanc petram aedificabo ecclesiam meam,* "You are Peter and upon this rock I will build my church." In the

text, there is an intentional play on the Latin words *Petrus* (Peter) and *petra* (rock). Though the forms are similar in the Latin, which is an accurate translation of the Greek, they would have been identical in the Aramaic original and would have allowed for the alternative translation, "You are the 'Rock' and upon this 'rock' I will build my church." By this simple sentence Jesus identified Peter as his successor and revealed that his successors would be popes, who, alone of the pastors of his church, would possess the keys to the kingdom of heaven. Because Jesus had declared Peter his successor, and because Peter was martyred in Rome, Damasus claimed Rome as the apostolic seat or primate see of the church. Yet, the last mention of Peter (Acts 15:7-11) in the New Testament finds him not at Rome but among the apostles at the Council of Jerusalem.

It is only in the Greek apocryphal *Acts of Peter,* written about 200 C.E. in Asia Minor, that we find an account of Peter in Rome leading a congregation of Christians when Paul arrives there. According to the *Acts,* Peter immediately set out to meet Paul when he learned that he had arrived, and as soon as they saw each other they wept with joy and embraced. This image, called the *concordia apostolorum,* "apostolic harmony," was widely applied to numerous fourth-century iconographic images of the apostles wherever they appeared together.

Concordia Apostolorum

These images of Peter and Paul, which suggest that they ruled in joint sovereignty, have been commonly termed *concordia apostolo-*

rum and are meant to recall Rome's other sets of twin founders—Romulus and Remus, Castor and Pollux, and Caesar and Augustus. Damasus applied the concept and imagery of *concordia apostolorum* to a broad artistic program as part of his propagandizing effort to promote Rome's apostolic primacy. Peter and Paul embracing each other in symmetric unity with their arms intertwined appeared in mosaics, paintings, the minor arts, and on inscriptions.

During the period of widespread conversion to Christianity and the legal suppression of paganism (380–480 C.E.), several Christian basilicas portray the image of Peter and Paul in an embrace that represented the *concordia apostolorum*. Among these is the Basilica of Santa Pudenziana, which is said to have been the first bishopric of Peter, the center of his life and ministry in Rome. Its singularly beautiful fourth-century mosaic depicts Peter and Paul on either side of Jesus, who sits among the apostles in an imperial Roman tunic, more like an emperor than the Messiah. Peter is represented with a full beard and thick white hair, a stout fisherman; Paul is swarthy, with a dark beard and receding hairline, a Pharisee. The setting is the heavenly Jerusalem, a sacred mount from which the rivers of paradise flow down. In the clouds above the scene are the symbols of the four evangelists—Matthew, the angel; Mark, the lion; Luke, the ox; and John, the eagle. This symbolism is called the *tetramorfo*, the four evangelists depicted together, which occurs here for the first time. The early church was often represented as the melding of two great traditions—Jews and

gentiles—and in this mosaic a woman symbolizing the *ecclesia ex gentibus,* "church of the gentiles," crowns Paul, and the female personification of the church of the *ecclesia ex circumcisione,* "church of the circumcision," crowns Peter. These respective missions—Paul to the gentiles and Peter to the Jews—are sometimes antagonistic when they are described in the New Testament. In Gal 2:11-14, for example, Paul complains that Peter has hypocritically disregarded the law by eating with gentiles. Yet, here, relocated from Jerusalem to Rome, the church is (re-)founded by Peter and Paul in perfect *concordia,* "harmony."

Damasus promoted the concept of Rome's apostolic primacy by other artistic expressions of *concordia apostolorum.* On sarcophagi, Peter and Paul appear in various scenes depicting their martyrdoms: Peter is portrayed carrying the cross en route to his own crucifixion, in imitation of Jesus, and Paul is shown opposite a soldier who is ready to strike him with an unsheathed sword. In some instances, the apostles are shown next to each other; in other instances they are on opposite sides of the scene and frame a central image. In almost all the examples of sarcophagi from the latter fourth century that include representations of Peter and Paul, however, it is easy to discern the quality of *concordia* between them.

The theme of the *concordia apostolorum* also appears in carved ivory and silver as well as in glass and bronze. Several ivory boxes and caskets produced at Rome contain scenes of Peter and Paul flanking Jesus. By their balanced portrayals they illustrate

FIGURE 4.1. *Basilica of Santa Pudenziana in Rome. Peter and Paul with other apostles flank Jesus in a heavenly Jerusalem in this mosaic from the fourth century. On the left, Peter, the "Apostle to the Jews," is crowned by a female figure that represents the converted Jews, and on the right, Paul, the "Apostle to the Gentiles," is crowned by a female figure that represents the converted gentiles. In the spirit of* concordia apostolorum *they are here represented as founders of the church of Rome.*

the mutual spirit of *concordia* between them. Such boxes were often commissioned by the Christianized Roman aristocracy to dedicate as *ex-voto* gifts, offerings that were promised beforehand (from the Latin, *ex voto suscepto*, "from the promise made") and then delivered when a prayer or request was granted. The glass medallions featuring the apostles facing each other in *concordia* (an image of joint sovereignty that was commonly used by the

tetrarchs) had similar uses and reflect a particularly Roman and local tradition. Found almost exclusively in the catacombs where they were offered for the dead, they were produced as souvenirs for pilgrims in Rome.

Damasus shrewdly marketed the claim for the primacy of Rome through the compelling imagery of the *concordia apostolorum*. He was resourceful in exporting it, too. The image appeared on portable glass cups and ivory boxes, articles pilgrims might purchase to use at one of the shrines as an *ex-voto* offering or to carry home as a souvenir. Damasus's program of propaganda was extensive, but his audience was limited. If he wanted to rule as pope of the primate see, he would also have to convince the church leaders of the other sees that this preeminent status belonged unequivocally to Rome.

Council of 382 C.E.

We have seen that Damasus worked with Gratian and Theodosius to suppress heresy and was named in their edict of 380 C.E. as a model of orthodoxy, and that in 377 C.E. he had commissioned Jerome's edition of the *Vulgate.* It remained for him to contest openly Rome's primacy with the two other major sees, Constantinople and Antioch. In 382 C.E., he convened a church council to produce a list of the canonical books of the Old and New Testaments. In the third part of the resulting *Decretum Damasi, Decree of Damasus,* he argued for the primacy of the see of Rome. Here, he appealed to the apocryphal *Acts of Peter,* which had portrayed Peter and Paul together ministering to the faithful in Rome. Later non-canonical texts drew upon the *Acts* to formalize the pictorial sequence encapsulated in the *concordia apostolorum*: Paul had arrived to Rome first and was ministering there; when he learned of Peter's arrival, he went out eagerly to meet him; the apostles embraced and embarked upon their joint mission of preaching, teaching, converting, and ministering to the faithful. The image of the apostles' embrace symbolized their joint

mission and also played into Damasus' claim for episcopal supremacy. By recalling similarly paired authority figures in the imperial history of Rome, such as Romulus and Remus, the image of the apostles represented a familiar hierarchical model. Pagan Rome, the ancient imperial capital founded by Romulus and Remus and ruled by the emperor, was now replaced by Christian Rome, the primate see, founded by the apostles Peter and Paul and ruled by the pope.

According to Damasus, Rome was *prima Petri apostoli sedis,* "the first see of the apostle Peter," above Alexandria, Antioch, and Constantinople (in that order), for three reasons: Jesus had called Peter the "rock" of the church and had given him the "keys" to the kingdom of heaven; Peter and Paul had come to Rome from the east and ministered in a harmonius *concordia apostolorum*; and both had suffered martyrdom there on the same day and at the same time under Nero. It was this last claim more than the others that authenticated the apostolic foundation of the Roman church. Among his other efforts to garner credibility for the papacy and to strengthen his claim for Rome's primacy, Damasus skillfully exploited the legendary and textual evidence for the martyrdoms of both Peter and Paul under Nero.

Martyrdoms of Peter and Paul, the "Roman Apostles"

Damasus must have learned the story of the concurrent martyrdoms of Peter and Paul under Nero from oral tradition and from the *Depositions of the Martyrs,* because these events are not reported in the *Acts of Peter*. According to the *Acts* (35), Jesus and Peter met on the Appian Way near the modern Basilica of San Sebastiano, during the persecution of Nero. Peter was fleeing the city at the urging of his congregation, which feared for his life. As Peter went out of the gate he saw Jesus entering Rome and asked him, in the lines made famous by the historical novel written by Henry Sienkiewicz and the 1951 film of the same name: "*Quo vadis, Domine?*," "Where are you going, Lord?" Jesus answered that he was going to Rome to be crucified. At this response, Peter suddenly realized that he should not be fleeing the persecutors in Rome but, instead, embracing his opportunity to imitate Jesus. He instantly returned to Rome, impatient to suffer martyrdom. At his own request he was crucified upside down to reflect his sinful state and so that his death would not be compared to that of Jesus. The narration in the *Acts* relates Peter's careful reasoning. He wanted to be crucified upside down, he explained, because it was a true reflection of man's sinful state. Jesus, however, had been crucified right side up to indicate his repentant state. The *Acts of Peter* include other events in Peter's life, but not the detail that both Peter and Paul were martyred in Rome on the same day and at the same time.

Many other accounts of their martyrdoms, however, have Peter and Paul martyred in Rome on the same day and at the same time but in different places: Peter was crucified upside down in the area of the modern Basilica of San Pietro, and Paul was beheaded (since he was a Roman citizen and therefore could not be crucified) in the area of the modern Basilica of San Paolo fuori le Mura, on the road to Ostia. The *Depositions of the Martyrs* records the date as June 29, during the reign of Nero. As early as 258 C.E., a *memoria apostolorum*, "shrine of the apostles," appeared on the Appian Way, dedicated to their cult. By the mid-third century, a cemetery basilica had been built for the apostles at the *memoria*, called the *Basilica Apostolorum in Catacumbas*, the "Basilica of the Apostles at the Catacombs." Based upon the evidence for the construction and location of this basilica, some scholars have suggested that the relics of Peter and Paul were transferred to the *memoria* in 258 C.E., after the Decian persecutions. Other scholars, however, argue that Peter never visited Rome and that the sources have been deliberately misread in an effort to lend apostolic authority to the monarchic episcopate that was establishing itself in this period.

The most famous inscription for Peter and Paul was composed and inscribed by the Damasus-Filocalus team sometime around 370 C.E. and placed in this Basilica of the Apostles on the Appian Way. The inscription underscores the argument Damasus made in the document from the church council in 382 C.E., that the primacy of Rome was legitimated by the martyrdoms of both apostles in Rome—*Petri pariter Paulique*, "Peter equal with Paul."

Cult of Peter and Paul

The cult of Peter and Paul reached its apex in the late fourth century when they were revered as the twin founders of the new Christian

FROM AN ANCIENT TEXT ❖ 4.1

Inscription of Peter and Paul

This inscription is one example of the kind of poetry Damasus wrote and Filocalus inscribed for the basilicas and shrines dedicated to martyrs, and it is significant for early claims that Rome was the primate see.

Whoever seeks the names of Peter together with
Paul should know that the saints once were here.
The East sent the disciples—that we readily admit.
On account of the merit of their blood, having
followed Christ through the stars they sought a
heavenly resting place and the kingdoms of the
pious. Rome most merits to claim them as her
citizens. Let Damasus tell these your praises,
you new stars.

 Source: Antonio Ferrua, *Epigrammata Damasiana* 20 (Vatican City: Pontificio Istituto di archeologia cristiana, 1942), pp. 139–144. Also printed in John Curran, *Pagan City and Christian Capital: Rome in the Fourth Century* (New York: Oxford University Press, 2000), p. 152 and n. 213.

Rome. Pope Damasus promoted the cult and dedicated the *memoria apostolorum* as a pilgrim site on the Appian Way to their commemoration. He marked the *memoria* with the inscription described above. By the late 380s, there were several feast days and a total of three sites of veneration for the "Apostles of Rome": the Basilica of the Apostles on the Appian Way, and the basilicas at the supposed sites of their martyrdoms—the Basilica of Saint Peter on the Vatican Hill, and the Basilica of Saint Paul Outside the Walls, on the road to Ostia (later greatly expanded by Leo the Great).

Damasus added a second feast dedicated to Saint Peter to the cycle of martyr commemorations that he had affixed to the pagan Codex-Calendar. The way he so cleverly blended the elements of the pagan into the Christian feast is an excellent illustration of his strategy for winning converts, strengthening his papacy, and convincing the world of the primacy of the see of Rome.

To the date of February 22, Damasus added the feast called the *Natale Petri de Cathedra*, the "Foundation of the Chair of Peter," the feast day of Peter's accession to the bishopric. In the Codex-Calendar, there was already a feast celebrated on February 22, the pagan feast called the *Caristia* or *Cara Cognitio*, which means "beloved family member." This feast was celebrated at a graveside where friends and family shared a meal and left a chair (*cathedra*) empty for the departed. The celebration took on new meaning when it was attached to the episcopate of Peter. Now it marked the day that he had assumed the episcopal *cathedra*, "chair," or the seat reserved for the bishop of Rome. This new holiday, the "Chair of Saint Peter," was one of the earliest Christian non-martyr holidays to enter the annual cycle of Christian celebrations. It demonstrates perfectly Damasus' practice of blending the classical pagan religious celebrations with Christian holy days.

A politically suave, aristocratic, and forceful pope, Damasus ensured that none of the pomp and spectacle of the pagan religious feasts was compromised in their Christian iterations. In the same way, the Christian authors eager to spread the new faith blended classical pagan forms and Christian themes in their new literary compositions. As we shall see in the next section, these Christian themes brought a new vitality to pagan literary forms.

Martyr Acts of Saint Agnes, Patron Saint of Rome

Christian Literary Propaganda

When Damasus joined Christian commemorations to the pagan feasts in the Codex-Calendar, the commemorations subsumed the essence of the original pagan feast. The result was a novel personal and communal religious experience. Just as the new feasts were a blend of pagan and Christian elements, the literary propagandizing texts of the same period also blended pagan and Christian elements. Their appeal relied upon the classical heritage common to Christians and pagans. Their poetic forms and intertextual references were directed to patricians and intellectuals in the church hierarchy who had been schooled in classical rhetoric. But they could also be adapted to sermons, liturgical ceremonies, and prayers that appealed to the wider congregation.

As the *martyria* became centers of pilgrimage, there was a corresponding embellishment and publication of the Roman martyrologies. These literary martyr acts were used in the service of conversion in the same way as the martyr shrines and the Christian calendar. In these martyr texts, certain common features appeared. First, the piety of the martyr was clearly established (young maidens zealous in their faith were typical protagonists) and the crowd that gathered to watch the struggle was characterized as both sympathetic and agitated. The martyrdom often was described as occurring in a trial-like setting. Finally, the martyr invariably exhibited an obstinate hostility toward the Romans. As we consider below the legends of Agnes, the virgin martyr and patron saint of Rome, we will discern all the elements typical of a martyrology.

The Story of Agnes

According to legend, as Constantine's daughter Constantina knelt at the tomb of Saint

Agnes and prayed for her leprosy to be healed, she heard the voice of the martyr herself. The voice told her to go forth "constant" (the word *constans*, "constant," in Latin is etymologically related to *Constantina*, a deliberate word play) in the faith of Jesus who, she promised, would heal her disease. Constantina was cured of her leprosy, and Constantine was so grateful that he built a basilica in honor of Saint Agnes on the Via Nomentana in Rome. Dating from the time of Constantine, Agnes was one of the oldest saints venerated in Rome; she was included in the Codex-Calendar of 354 C.E. on January 21. Although her acts and miracles have centuries of embellishments, we possess several fourth-century texts that allow us to reconstruct her early veneration. There is an account by Bishop Ambrose of Milan (374–397 C.E.) in his tract on virgins, called *De virginibus ad Marcellinam sororem, A Tract on Virgins to his Sister Marcellina*, in sections 2.5–9 and 4.19, a hymn to Agnes (*Agnes beatae virginis*) attributed to Ambrose, a verse inscription by Pope Damasus, and a poem by the Latin poet Prudentius (*Peristephanon* 14). By comparing these accounts, we can chart a growing popularity of the martyr cult of Saint Agnes, and we can see clearly the efforts of the papacy and the Christian aristocracy to use literary texts, a fusion of classical secular forms and Christian themes, to attract pagan aristocratic converts to the church.

Texts of Ambrose

According to all literary accounts Agnes was very young, only thirteen, when she was martyred. In his tract *On Virgins*, composed

FIGURE 4.2. *Saint Agnes. This charming depiction of Saint Agnes includes her most common attribute, the lamb, likely derived from the similarity of the name Agnes to the Latin word for "lamb,"* agnus.

about 377 C.E., Ambrose tells us that she was so young and slight that there was not enough flesh for her even to be struck by a sword, and that no chains were small enough to hold her delicate wrists. Yet she was brave. At the age when young brides should be led forth to marriage, she, instead, freely embraced her death, as a consecrated virgin bride of Christ. While everyone around her wept, Agnes did not shed a tear, but instead she embraced her martyrdom and challenged the executioner to kill her. She boldly bared her neck for him.

Ambrose emphasized Agnes' modesty and the importance of her virginity. At the conclusion of this tract, he tells us that Agnes obtained martyrdom and retained her virginity. In another work, *De officiis ministrorum, On the Duties of the Ministers* (1.41.203), he tells us that when she was forced to choose between her virginity and her safety she protected her virginity and exchanged her safety for immortality.

Later than his *On Virgins*, but also from the late fourth century, Ambrose's hymn to Agnes entitled *Agnes beatae virginis* relates details omitted in the tract *On Virgins*. Both

Personalities in Christianity 4.5
AMBROSE

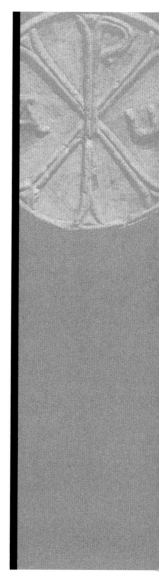

Ambrose (339–397 C.E.) served as bishop of Milan from 374 C.E. For his pivotal role in the political and doctrinal disputes of the fourth century, Ambrose, bishop of Milan from 374 C.E. until his death, is considered one of the four traditional doctors of the Latin church, along with Jerome (345–420 C.E.), Augustine (354–430 C.E.), and Gregory the Great (540–604 C.E.). He was born in *Augusta Treverorum*, the modern French city of Trier (sometimes called Trèves), which was then the imperial capital of the western empire. His father was the Roman governor in Gaul (Roman France) and his family was Christian. His brother Uranius Satyrus was his secretary, and in 353 C.E., Pope Liberius consecrated his sister, Marcellina, as a "virgin of God." Ambrose was a lawyer and provincial governor when he was called to Milan to oversee the election of a new bishop in a congregation divided on the christological issues under debate in the Arian controversy. He had not been baptized but was still a catechumen, "in training for baptism," when he was elected bishop by an Arian and Catholic consensus. In quick sequence he was baptized and consecrated. As the leading churchman in Milan, Ambrose instructed catechumens, including Augustine, wrote extensively on church matters, and convened episcopal councils to settle doctrinal debates. He was involved in ecclesiastical disputes (Arianism) and political intrigues in the imperial courts of Gratian, Valentinian II, and Theodosius and in the courts of the usurpers Maximus, Arbogast, and Eugenius. He wrote several treatises on the emerging ascetic movement among women (e.g., *On Virgins*), letters, hymns, and the well-known tract on Christian ethics (*On the Duties of Ecclesiastic Ministers*). His important correspondence over the altar of Victory is considered a factor in the Christianization of the Roman pagan aristocracy. He is buried in the Basilica of Sant Ambrogio in Milan, next to the relics of Gervasius and Protasius, martyrs under Nero, whose remains he had translated to the Basilica at its dedication in 386 C.E. His secretary, the deacon Paulinus, wrote a biography (at the behest of Augustine) called the *Life of Ambrose*, which is translated in the Fathers of the Church translation series, vol. 15 (1952).

FROM AN ANCIENT TEXT ❖ 4.2

Hymn of Saint Ambrose

Ambrose wrote this hymn in honor of Agnes, entitled Agnes beatae virginis, Of the Blessed Virgin Agnes, *after his tract* On Virgins, *which he wrote in 377 C.E. The hymn is significant as a literary tool for propagandizing the new faith among the educated non-Christian aristocracy.*

It is the feast day of the blessed
virgin Agnes, on which she was
consecrated by her holy blood
and restored her soul, owed to heaven.

She was old enough for martyrdom
though not yet old enough for marriage.
Faith wavered even among men
and even the elders, worn out, yielded.

Terrified by fear, her parents had
strengthened the lock on her purity.
That faith that knew no bonds
loosened the doors of guard.

Someone would think she went to her wedding
since she is being led out with such a glow,
bringing new wealth to her husband
endowed with the income of her blood.

She is forced to worship with torches
at the altar of the unholy god:
she responds, "Virgins of Christ
do not raise up such torches.

This fire extinguishes faith,
this flame steals the light.
Here! Strike here! Then I may
snuff out the fires with my blood."

When struck, she produced a great display,
for she covers herself entirely with a raiment.
She took care to respect decency,
so that no one would see her uncovered.

Even in death her modesty lived;
she had even covered her face with her hand.
She reached for the ground with her knee bent,
falling with a graceful glide.

Source: For the Latin text, see J. Fontaine, *Ambroise de Milan Hymnes* (Paris, 1992), pp. 377–379. English translation is the author's.

of Ambrose's texts describe Agnes as young, courageous, and willing to face the sword for her faith; and in both she defiantly refuses to sacrifice to the gods. Missing from *On Virgins*, however, is the hymn's description of her terrified parents who try to lock her up to keep her from martyrdom (vv. 9-12), and the elaborate praise for her modesty: she took care that no one might see her uncovered and even hid her face with her hand as she slid to the ground modestly (vv. 26-32). Here we see a clear example of the well-educated Christian Ambrose using the familiar Latin classical (pagan) models of Roman female virtue to give resonance to the Christian story.

The motif of a maiden dying by sword to protect her virtue was well known from the Roman legend of Lucretia. The historian Livy (59 B.C.E.–17 C.E.) narrates the story in his *History of Rome* (1.57.6–58). In his account, the last of the Etruscan kings, *Tarquinius Superbus*, "Tarquin the Proud," and several Roman nobles, were dining and drinking after a long day of hunting when they began to discuss the virtue of their wives. Collatinus, one of the nobles in the king's court, was so sure of his wife Lucretia's excellence that he challenged his companions to pay a surprise visit to Lucretia that very evening, to judge for themselves how virtuous she was. As he predicted, Lucretia was at home busily spinning with her maids instead of feasting with the other wives at a luxurious dinner party. Tarquin was so impressed by Lucretia—her virtue, her beauty, and her devotion to her husband—that he violated her in her own

home that very night. Lucretia was outraged and inconsolable. She confessed Tarquin's crime to her father and husband, then she killed herself in shame.

The Roman poet Ovid (43 B.C.E.–17 C.E.) wrote a version of the rape of Lucretia in his *Fasti* (2.685–834), a poem on the Roman calendar. He dramatically described Lucretia's shame as she confessed to her husband and father that Tarquin had raped her, and he then depicted her suicide before their eyes. Her last thought, he tells us, was that she had to guard her modesty even as she fell to the ground (vv. 833–34). Ambrose's treatment of the martyrdom of Agnes recalls the well-known story of Lucretia in Ovid's poem. Apart from the larger theme of female virtue and the courage of a delicate young woman in the face of death, the texts have unambiguous intertextual references. In both of his Agnes tracts—*On Virgins* and the *Agnes beatae virginis* hymn—Ambrose tells us that in the final moments before her death, Agnes was concerned more than anything that she fall to the ground with modesty. In vv. 26-28 of the hymn, Agnes covered herself with her cloak so that no one would see her uncovered, and in vv. 30-33, the poet offers an elaborately detailed description of how she covered her face with her hand and fell to the ground by carefully bending her knee so that she remained covered as she lay on the ground.

Inscription of Damasus

At the same time that Ambrose was composing his tract *On Virgins* and his hymn to Agnes, Damasus composed an inscription for

Agnes, which captures the pathos of her legend and allows us to observe the evolving tradition as details are added in these early texts. Damasus' inscription begins with the words *fama refert*, which means "legend has it." This suggests that he may have been working from an oral tradition rather than a written martyr tract. The references to Agnes's youth and her willingness to be martyred correspond with the works of Ambrose. Damasus writes (vv. 3-6) that she leapt from the lap of her nurse eager to burn in flames, despite her parents' attempt to protect her at home. Her delicacy and modesty (vv. 6-7) recall Ambrose's

hymn, but Damasus adds the detail that she conquered her fear with what strength such a delicate creature possessed and covered her nakedness with her hair. In the inscription, Agnes remains undaunted when she is threatened with death by fire (rather than a sword).

Poem of Prudentius

The Spanish poet Prudentius (348–c. 413 C.E.) has been called the greatest Christian poet of the late antique period. In his collection of martyr poems, he glorifies the cult of the martyrs and tells the stories of their tor-

---

FROM AN ANCIENT TEXT ❖ 4.3

Inscription of Damasus and Filocalus

Composed in the same time period that Ambrose wrote his hymn, Agnes beatae virginis, *and his treatise,* On Virgins *(c. 377 C.E.), the inscription rests today on Agnes' tomb in the basilica dedicated to her on the Via Nomentana in Rome.*

> Legend has it that her holy parents had just brought
> Agnes back when the trumpet sounded its mournful
> songs. Suddenly, the girl left the lap of her nurse and
> of her own free will stomped on the threats and the
> rage of the furious persecutor. When he had decided
> to burn her noble flesh with fire, she overcame a
> great fear with her small strength and let loose her
> hair to cover her naked limbs, so that as she perished
> her face would not look at the temple of the Lord.
> O guard of virginity and holy honor, revered by me,
> I pray that you will favor the prayers of Damasus,
> shining martyr.

Source: For the Latin, see Antonio Ferrua, *Epigrammata Damasiana* 37 (Vatican City: Pontificio Istituto di archeologia cristiana, 1942), pp. 175–178. The English translation is the author's.

tures and deaths without omitting any of the gory details. His collection of martyr poems is called the *Peristephanon, Crowns of Martyrs.* His hymn to Saint Agnes (*Peristephanon* 14) introduces well known elements of the legend not found in Ambrose's texts or in Damasus' inscription, perhaps gathered from an oral tradition while traveling in Rome in 402 C.E. However, it is also apparent that he knew the literary antecedents in Ambrose and Damasus.

While his account generally follows Ambrose's *On Virgins*, Prudentius introduces for the first time a component of the story that becomes central in subsequent texts—that Agnes's persecutor forced her into a brothel for refusing to sacrifice to Minerva (vv. 25-30): "Unless she lays her head on the altar and asks Minerva, the virgin goddess whom she scorns, I will put her into a public brothel. There all the young men will have her as a new slave of their sport."

FROM AN ANCIENT TEXT ❖ 4.4

Prudentius, *Peristephanon* 14, *Passion of Saint Agnes*

Prudentius wrote his Peristephanon, "Crowns of Martyrdom," to glorify the burgeoning fourth-and fifth-century cult of the martyrs.

In the home of Romulus is the grave of Agnes,
a brave girl and a glorious martyr.
Buried in sight of their towers, this maiden
guards the safety of the Roman citizens,
and she also protects strangers who pray with
a pure and faithful heart. A double crown of
martyrdom is offered to her virginity, untouched
by any crime; then the glory of a willing death.
They say that she was hardly ready
for marriage, a young girl, in her early
maidenhood, yet already aflame with the love
of Christ. She was brave enough to resist impious
orders to attach herself to religious idols and
desert her holy faith. Tempted by many arts,
now with the seductive persuasion of a smooth
judge, now with threats of rough physical abuse,
she remained firm with unbending strength and
offered her body to hard torture without resisting
death.

Then the cruel tyrant said: "Even if it is
easy to bear the torture and to overcome the pain,
even if her life is scorned, still the modesty of her
consecrated virginity is dear to her. I will toss her
into a public brothel if she does not put her head
to the altar and ask pardon of Minerva, the virgin
that she, also a virgin, continues to slight. A gang
of youths will rush to check out this new slave
of their wanton sport."
"No," Agnes says, "Christ is not so
forgetful of his followers that he would cause
our golden chastity to be lost or would desert us.
He is with the chaste and does not allow the gifts
of our sacred virginity to be polluted. You will
defile your sword with my blood if you wish
but you will not pollute my limbs with lust."
After she spoke, he orders the maiden to
stand in a public arcade in the square. The empathetic
crowd turned their faces and moved away so that
not anyone would look too rudely at her exposure.
One man does stare boldly at the girl as it happened
and does not shrink from looking at her holy form
with a lustful eye. Just then winged fire, vibrating
and burning like a lightning bolt, struck his eyes.
Blinded by the gleaming flash, he fell writhing
in the dust of the square. His companions lift him
half-dead from the ground and weep as those who
pronounce funeral rites.
The maiden triumphant continued singing
of God the Father and Christ in holy song because
beneath the unholy stain of danger, her virginity
was victorious: she found the brothel chaste and
unable to defile her. Some say that she was asked
to pray to God to return his vision to the youth
lying there, so she did. Then the youth's life

spirit was renewed and his vision restored.
But Agnes took this first step to the
celestial hall and soon a second ascent was
granted to her. For fury incited the wrath of her
blood-thirsty enemy. "I am conquered," he said
groaning. "Go, draw the sword, soldier, and carry
out the royal commands of our emperor." When
Agnes saw the cruel man with his sword unsheathed,
she became even happier and said, "I rejoice because
someone like this has come—a wild, dark, cruel
swordsman—rather than some languid and listless
and soft feminine type reeking of perfume, who
would destroy me by violating my honor. This lover,
this one, I confess, pleases me. I will go to meet
his onslaught and I will not restrain his hot desires.
I will have received the whole blade into my breast,
and then I will drag the force of his sword into the
depth of my chest. Thus as the bride of Christ, I will
leap over all the shadows of the sky, higher than the
atmosphere. Eternal ruler, open the doors of heaven
that were previously barred to the people of earth,
and call the soul that follows you, Christ, a virginal
sacrifice of the Father."
Saying this, she adores Christ, with her head
bowed as a suppliant, so that her bent neck might more
readily accept the wound. But he satisfied that great
hope with his hand: in one blow he cut off her head;
a swift death prevented any sensation of pain.
Now her loosened spirit shines forth and leaps
free into the airs. Angels surround her as she goes along
on the luminous pathway. She marvels at the world resting
beneath her feet. Climbing, she looks at the shadows
beneath and laughs at the orb of the sun as it circles,
at the whole world turning in on itself, at the black
vortex that contains life, and the vain preoccupations

of the fickle world: kings, tyrants, empires, and classes,
the arrogant pride of dignitaries; the power of silver and
gold which is sought by all with a thirsty greed, and by
every devious means; splendidly built residences; the
useless waste of embroidered clothing; anger, fear,
desires, dangers; the long sadness that alternates with
brief joy; the smoking torches of black jealousy that cause
the hope of men and their honor to become darkened;
and the foulest thing of all these evils, the black,
billowing clouds of paganism [*gentilitas.*] Agnes
tramples on these things and grinds them under
her foot, standing on and pressing the head of the
serpent with her heel, as he sprinkles all things of
the earth with venom and submerges them in hell.
Dominated as he is by the foot of the virgin Agnes,
he lowers the crests on his igneous head and now,
subdued, he does not dare to lift it.
Meanwhile God wreathes the forehead of
the unmarried martyr with two crowns. A reward
sixty times over issued from the eternal light and
comprises the one; a reward one hundred times over,
the other. O lucky virgin, o new glory, noble resident
in the celestial arc, turn your face and your dual diadems
from our muck, you, to whom alone the single parent
of us all has empowered to render even a brothel chaste.
If you should fill my core, I will be cleansed by the glow
of your welcoming countenance. Nothing is unchaste
which your piety deigns to look upon or your attendant
foot to touch.

Source: For the Latin, see *Prudentius,* tr. H. J. Thomson, Loeb Classical Library, 2 vols. (Cambridge, Mass.: Harvard University Press, 1961), vol. 2, *Crowns of Martyrdom,* pp. 338–345. The English translation is the author's.

According to Prudentius, when she was in the brothel, as she stood naked before a crowd of youths, all but one turned away, and the one who did not was blinded. In Christian kindness, Prudentius continues, Agnes then prayed for the youth's eyesight to be restored. Yet, for this, Agnes was accused of practicing magic.

The story of the brothel so dramatically developed in the Prudentius poem but missing from the accounts of Ambrose and Damasus, seems to be drawn from a Greek passion of Saint Agnes that was circulating in Rome about the time of Prudentius's visit. In this account, Agnes was brought before the prefect of the city and ordered to sacrifice or be enclosed in a brothel. She refused to sacrifice and was forced into a brothel where a youth who approached her was struck dead. When the prefect arrived to investigate the boy's death, Agnes told him that an angel from God in shining white garments had appeared and saved her from the young man by striking him dead. The prefect responded that they would all believe in God if, by her prayers, the young man was revived. Yet, when by the efficacy of Agnes's prayers the dead man was returned to life, the crowd accused her of practicing magic and called for her death. The scene in the brothel was central to the account in the Greek passion. In Prudentius's poem, however, the brothel scene was one of several incidents compiled from the tradition in the Greek passion and from the texts of Ambrose and Damasus. There are significant differences in the details. For example, instead of an angel of God, in Prudentius's poem a blinding flash of light struck the young man, and instead of dying by the sword as she did in Ambrose's poem, Agnes burned to death, as she had in the inscription of Damasus.

The Classical Literary Tradition in Prudentius's Text

Prudentius, like Ambrose, knew his classical literary texts well, and just as Ambrose's treatment of Agnes recalled the Lucretia episode in Ovid, Prudentius's treatment recalls another episode in Ovid, the death of the maiden Polyxena. Polyxena was one of the daughters of Troy's King Priam and Queen Hecuba. When the Greeks were unable to sail home from Troy because the winds were unfavorable, Neoptolemus, the son of Achilles, sacrificed Polyxena at his father's tomb. In Ovid's *Metamorphoses* (13.450–60), Polyxena was torn from the arms of her mother. Like Agnes she was young and fearless, and, like Agnes, when she saw her persecutor (Neoptolemus) standing before her ready to kill her with his sword, she made the bold gesture of calling for her own death: "Plunge your sword deep in my throat or breast!" (vv. 457-59). The scene is similar in the poem of Prudentius. There, when Agnes saw her executioner standing before her with an unsheathed sword, she, too, welcomed her death: "I shall welcome the whole length of his blade into my bosom, drawing the sword to the depths of my breast; and so as Christ's bride I shall leap over the darkness of the sky higher than the heaven" (vv. 77-80). Prudentius was well educated and trained in the schools of rhetoric and poetry. The echoes of Ovid are plain in the verbal reminiscences and in the overall setting of the maiden's sacrifice—a young Roman maiden was pit against a persecutor whom she faced boldly. To the educated ancient reader, Prudentius's poem on the martyrdom of Agnes artfully imitated and precisely recalled the sacrifice of Polyxena in Ovid's *Metamorphoses* (and would have reminded a Christian reader of the martyrdoms of Perpetua and Felicitas in Lyons in 203).

Another classical pagan reference, in Catullus, poem 34, the *Hymn to Diana,* also adumbrates the Prudentius poem. Catullus's poem to Diana recognized her primary attribute, her virginity, as well as two other attributes—as protectress of crossroads where strangers first enter a city (vv. 15-16) and as a guardian of the Roman people (vv. 22-24). Like Diana, Agnes guarded her consecrated virginity (v. 8), all strangers who prayed to her with pure heart (vv. 5-6), and the Roman people in general (v. 4). Prudentius's poem about Agnes, a Christian martyr, recalls (to the mind of the educated reader) the sacral poem of Catullus about Diana, which both anticipated the "divinity" of Agnes and conflated the attributes of the virgin goddess and virgin martyr. The imagery of the Catullus poem would have resonated in the minds of Prudentius' educated readers, as the pagan virgin goddess Diana was reborn as the Christian virgin martyr Agnes.

Later Literary Tradition of the Legend of Agnes

From these core texts, the cult of Saint Agnes continued to grow: in the fifth century, the legends were crystallized in the *Gesta* of Saint Agnes by an unknown author. In this account, several details of Agnes's passion are developed

from a pastiche of earlier texts and oral traditions of Ambrose, Damasus and Prudentus. For example, she acquired a suitor, the pagan fellow-aristocrat who was the son of the prefect who, in earlier accounts, had banished her to the brothel.

By the time we read of the martyrdom of Agnes in Jacob de Voragine's thirteenth-century *Golden Legend,* several miracles at her burial site were recorded as part of her acts, including the story of Constantina, the daughter of Constantine who was cured of leprosy while praying at Agnes's tomb. Despite its new accretions, the legend here still contains elements of the original fourth-century texts that Damasus, Ambrose, and Prudentius composed.

Agnes also appeared in the next great edition of saints' lives, that of Alban Butler. His four-volume *Lives of the Saints* was published in London between 1756 and 1759 after thirty years of research. It is based upon the *Golden Legend* and similar literary and oral traditions but, ultimately, has its origin in the *Deposition of Martyrs* extant in the Codex-Calendar of 354 C.E. It was then that Damasus first appropriated pagan sacred festivals and either transformed them into Christian celebrations or added Christian celebrations to the calendar. The original texts that we saw configured from literary and oral traditions in the fourth century have, in Butler's volumes, been regarded as historical documents. In this account, which included bibliography and scholarly comments, we also read of the ceremony connected to the lamb that was performed on Agnes's feast day—January 21. Two lambs were brought into her church on

FROM AN ANCIENT TEXT ❖ 4.5

Gesta of Saint Agnes

The fifth-century Gesta *of Saint Agnes by an unknown author (sometimes called Pseudo-Ambrose) illustrates how the medieval legends developed from earlier sources.*

In Rome, at an indeterminate time, the son of the Prefect of the city falls in love with Agnes, a maiden of thirteen years, as she is returning from school. He seeks out her family and asks to marry her. She repulses in horror the presents that he offers her in the hope of gaining her acceptance of him. In vain does he enlist the aid of friends. Agnes rejects him with insulting words. She is affianced to one nobler and more gracious than he; He has given her greater riches; her nuptial couch is already prepared; she has enjoyed His chaste embraces which harm not her virginity. In despair the youth falls ill. To the physicians who examine him he discloses the cause of the malady. His father, Symphronius by name, is acquainted with his unrequited love and he in his turn demands that the maiden marry his son. Agnes refuses and the Prefect threatens her and demands the name of the one to whom she is affianced. One of his satellites tells him that Agnes has been a Christian since infancy and that she calls Christ her spouse. The Prefect then has her appear before the judgment seat. First through promises, and then with threats he tries to win her over. She is neither seduced by his honied words nor influenced by fear. The Prefect enlists the aid of her parents. The next day the Prefect again tries to break down Agnes's will. Finally on the following day, he tells her of his decision to make her a Vestal virgin. Since she is so headstrong in her desire to remain a virgin, he will see that she be given the opportunity of doing so. She answers: "If I have refused for the love of Christ your son, a man endowed with reason, how shall I bow down before your dumb idols?" The Prefect excuses her rash words because of her tender years and begs her not to incur the wrath of the gods. Agnes replies that faith is not dependent on age and asks him to do his worst, for she will not accede to his wishes. Symphronius in anger offers her the alternative of becoming a Vestal virgin or of being brought to a house of shame and becoming the plaything of men. Agnes answers that she is not afraid, but that the angel of the Lord will protect her body from harm. The judge orders her disrobed and to be led to a brothel. A herald will precede her and announce her punishment because of her blasphemy. She is disrobed but immediately her hair grows to such length that her nakedness is perfectly covered. On her entrance into the place of shame, an angel appears at her side and a bright light encircles her so that she can neither be seen nor touched. As she prays, a white garment appears, a garment so perfectly fitted to her and of such dazzling whiteness that it must have been the work of angels. Thanking her Lord and Lover, she puts it on. The place of shame becomes a place of prayer and those who enter it remain to praise God and go forth purer than they had entered. The son of the Prefect appears surrounded by his companions, and determined to work his will upon the maiden. He reproaches with cowardice those who had entered and who had come out purified, in veneration and admiration of Agnes. He boldly enters and as he is about to lay hands on her, he is struck dead by the devil. One of his friends, wondering at his long stay, enters and finds his dead body. He shouts for help and cried that this infamous creature has killed the son of the Prefect by her magic. The Prefect hurries to the scene and inveighs against the holy virgin. Agnes justifies her actions and tells him of the behavior of his son and of his reward. The Prefect advises that she pray to that angel to raise his son to life in order that she may avoid all suspicion of being a magician. She agrees and through her prayers the youth is brought back to life. Immediately he confesses his faith in the true God and proclaims himself a Christian. The priests of the temple, in fear of her power and afraid that she will alienate the people from the service of the idols which provide their livelihood, take council. Entering among the people, they incite them against the magician. The Prefect does not dare to defend the virgin against the priests. Sadly he allows his vicar Aspasius to sit in judgment on Agnes. He orders that a great fire be lit, and that she be thrown therein. The flames are divided and turn upon those who stand by. Agnes is unharmed. As she prays in thanksgiving, the fires are extinguished. Aspasius to assuage the anger of the people orders that a sword be thrust through her throat. Thus does she become at the one and same time a virgin and martyr. Her parents joyfully bury her in a plot in their estate not far from the Via Nomentana.

Source: A. J. Denomy, C.S.B., *The Old French Lives of Saint Agnes and Other Vernacular Versions of the Middle Ages* (Cambridge, Mass.: Harvard University Press, 1938), pp. 25–27. Copyright © 1938 by the President and Fellows of Harvard College. Reprinted by permission of the publisher.

the Via Nomentana in separate baskets resting on expensive damask cushions. With their legs tied in blue and red ribbons, they were placed on the altar. The lambs were blessed while a choir sang an antiphonal hymn, and they were then presented to the pope at the Vatican. From there, the lambs were sent to the nuns at the convent of Santa Cecilia in Trastevere and at Easter they were shorn so that the fleece could be used to make the palliums, which are the special vestments worn by archbishops. Between 1926 and 1938, Herbert Thurston, S.J., published a revised and significantly rewritten edition of Butler's *Lives of the Saints.* In 1956, Donald Attwater published a second edition with considerable revisions.

Conclusion

The papacy of Damasus offers insight into some of the struggles among Christians as

FROM AN ANCIENT TEXT ❖ 4.6

The Martyrdom of Saint Agnes in the *Golden Legend*

The Golden Legend, *a popular collection of saints' lives, was composed between 1260 and 1275 by Jacob de Voragine. This collection was among the most frequently printed books in Europe and demonstrates the persistent attraction the cult of the martyrs enjoyed well into the late medieval period. In this text, we see that the life and martyrdom of Agnes has taken on new details from oral and literary traditions.*

The name Agnes comes from *agna*, a "lamb," because Agnes was as meek and humble as a lamb. Or her name comes from the Greek word *agnos*, "pious," because she was pious and compassionate; or from *agnoscendo*, "knowing," because she knew the way of the truth. Truth, according to Augustine, is opposed to vanity and falseness and doubting, all of which she avoided by the virtue of truth that was hers. Agnes was a virgin most sensible and wise, as Ambrose, who wrote the story of her martyrdom, attests. When she was thirteen years old, she lost death and found life. Childhood is computed in years, but in her immense wisdom she was old; she was a child in body but already aged in spirit. Her face was beautiful, her faith more beautiful.

One day she was on her way home from school when the prefect's son saw her and fell in love. He promised her jewels and great wealth if she consented to be his wife. Agnes answered: "Go away, you spark that lights the fire of sin, you fuel of wickedness, you food of death! I am already pledged to another lover!" She began to commend this lover and spouse for five things that the betrothed look for in the men they are betrothed to wed, namely, nobility of lineage, beauty of person, abundance of wealth, courage and the power to achieve, and love transcendent. She went on: "The one I love is far nobler than you, of more eminent descent. His mother is a virgin, his father knows no woman, he is served by angels; the sun and the moon wonder at his beauty; his wealth never lacks or lessens; his perfume brings the dead to life, his touch strengthens the feeble, his love is chastity itself, his touch holiness, union with him, virginity."

In support of these five claims, she said: "Is there anyone whose ancestry is more exalted, whose powers are more invincible, whose aspect is more beautiful, whose love more delightful, who is richer in every grace?" Then she enumerated five benefits that her spouse had conferred on her and confers on all his other spouses: he gives them a ring as an earnest of his fidelity, he clothes and adorns them with a multitude of virtues, he signs them with the blood of his passion and death, he binds them to himself with the bond of his love, and endows them with the treasures of eternal glory. "He has placed a wedding ring on my right hand," she said, "and a necklace of precious stones around my neck, gowned me with a robe woven with gold and jewels, placed a mark on my forehead to keep me from taking any lover but himself, and his blood has tinted my cheeks. Already his chaste embraces hold me close, he has united his body to mine, and he has shown me incomparable treasurers, and promised to give them to me if I remain true to him."

When the young man heard all this, he was beside himself and threw himself on his bed, and his deep sighs made it clear to his physicians that lovesickness was his trouble. His father sought out the maiden and told her of his son's condition, but she assured him that she could not violate her covenant with her betrothed. The prefect pressed her to say who this betrothed was, whose power over her she talked about. Someone else told him that it was Christ whom she called her spouse, and the prefect tried to win her over with soft words at first and then with dire threats. Agnes met this mixture of cajolery and menace with derision, and said: "Do whatever you like, but you will not obtain what you want from me." The prefect: "You have just two choices. Either you will sacrifice to the goddess Vesta with her virgins, since your virginity means so much to you, or you will be thrown in with harlots and handled as they are handled." Because she was of the nobility, the prefect could not bring force to bear upon her, so he raised the charge of her Christianity. Agnes said: "I will not sacrifice to your gods, and no one can sully my virtue because I have with me a guardian of my body, an angel of the Lord." The prefect had her stripped and taken nude to a brothel, but God made her hair grow so long that it covered her better than any clothing. When she entered the house of shame, she found an angel waiting for her. Thus, the brothel became a place of prayer; anyone who honored the light, came out cleaner than when he had entered.

The prefect's son now came with other young men, and invited them to go in and take their pleasure with her, but they were terrified by the miraculous light and hurried back to him. He scorned them as cowards and in a fury rushed in to force himself upon Agnes, but the same light engulfed him, and, since he has not honored God, the devil throttled him and he expired. When the prefect heard of this, he went to Agnes, weeping bitterly, and questioned her closely about the cause of his son's death. "The one whose will he wanted to carry out," she said, "thus got power over him and killed him, whereas his companions, frightened by the miracle they saw, retreated unharmed." The prefect persisted: "You can prove that you did not do this by some magical art, if you are able to bring him back to life by your prayer." So Agnes prayed, and the youth came to life and began to preach Christ publicly. At this the priests of the temples stirred up a tumult in the populace, shouting: "Away with the witch, away with the sorceress who turns people's heads and befuddles their wits!" On the other hand the prefect, impressed by the miracle, wished to set her free but fearing that he would be outlawed, put a deputy in charge and went away sadly.

The deputy, Aspasius by name, had Agnes thrown into a roaring fire, but the flames divided and burned up the hostile crowd on either side, leaving the maiden unscathed. Aspasius finally had a soldier thrust a dagger into her throat, and thus her heavenly spouse consecrated her as his bride and martyr. It is believed that she suffered in the reign of Constantine the Great, which began in A.D. 309. Her kinsmen and other Christians buried her joyfully and barely escaped the pagans who tried to stone them. . . .

Constance, Constantine's daughter and a virgin, was stricken with leprosy, and when she heard of the vision just described, she went to the saint's grave. While praying there she fell asleep and saw Saint Agnes, who said to her: "Be constant, Constance! If you believe in Christ, you will be freed of your disease." Awakening at the sound of the voice she found herself completely cured. She received baptism and had a basilica erected over the saint's grave. There she continued to live a virginal life and by her example gathered many virgins around her. . . .

And, from Ambrose's Preface: "Saint Agnes, disdaining the advantages of noble birth merited heavenly honors; caring nothing for what human society desires, she won the society of the eternal king; accepting a precious death for professing Christ, she at the same time was conformed to his likeness."

Source: William Granger Ryan, *Jacobus de Voragine The Golden Legend: Readings on the Saints,* vol. 1 (Princeton, N.J.: Princeton University Press, 1993), pp. 101–104. Copyright © 1993 Princeton University Press, 1995 paperback edition. Reprinted by permission of Princeton University Press.

they defined church hierarchy and doctrines. Damasus joined forces with the praetorian prefect Praetextatus, a fellow aristocrat, to overcome his rival for the papal throne. Once he was established as pope, he moved in aristocratic pagan and Christian circles to gain the financial patronage of wealthy converts. His hierarchical configuration of the church was modeled on the political structure of empire. The pope corresponded to the emperor, and Rome, as the primate see, was the Christian equivalent of the ancient imperial capital. For this reason, Damasus was particularly aggressive about asserting the primacy of the see of Rome. In 377 C.E., he commissioned Jerome's edition of the *Vulgate,* with the result that Latin became the liturgical language of the western church. He was the first pope to invoke the term *apostolica sedes,* "apostolic see," when referring to Rome. He worked with Gratian and Theodosius to suppress heresy and was named in their edict of 380 C.E. as a model of orthodoxy. Under his direction, the church council in 382 C.E. produced the first list of canonical works of the Old and New Testaments and a decree authenticating the non-canonical texts that reported the twin martyrdoms of Peter and Paul. By appropriating the existing Roman political and religious structure of public spectacle, he created a Christian calendar of martyr celebrations and a powerful cycle of images (*concordia apostolorum*) that underscored the

FROM AN ANCIENT TEXT ❖ 4.7

Butler's "Life of Saint Agnes"

In Butler's Lives of the Saints, *there are over 2,000 feasts of Catholic saints and martyrs listed for each day of the year. These accounts also include bibliography and scholarly comments.*

St. Agnes has always been looked upon in the church as a special patroness of bodily purity. She is one of the most popular of Christian saints, and her name is commemorated everyday in the canon of the Mass. Rome was the scene of her triumph, and Prudentius says that her tomb was shown within sight of that city. She suffered perhaps not long after the beginning of the persecution of Diocletian, whose cruel edicts were published in March in the year 303. We learn from St. Ambrose and St. Augustine that she was only thirteen years of age at the time of her glorious death. Her riches and beauty excited the young noblemen of the first families in Rome to contend as rivals for her hand. Agnes answered them all that she had consecrated her virginity to a heavenly husband, who could not be beheld by mortal eyes. Her suitors, finding her resolution unshakable, accused her to the governor as a Christian, not doubting that threats and torments would prove more effective with one of her tender years upon whom allurements could make no impression. The judge at first employed the mildest expressions and most seductive promises, to which Agnes paid no regard, repeating always that she could have no other spouse but Jesus Christ. He then made use of threats, but found her endowed with a masculine courage, and even eager to suffer torment and death. At last terrible fires were made, and iron hooks, racks and other instruments of torture displayed before her, with threats of immediate execution. The heroic child surveyed them undismayed, and made good cheer in the presence of the fierce and cruel executioners. She was so far from betraying the least symptom of terror that she even expressed her joy at the sight, and offered herself to the rack. She was then dragged before the idols and commanded to offer incense, but could, St. Ambrose tells us, by no means be compelled to move her hand, except to make the sign of the cross.

The governor, seeing his measure ineffectual, said he would send her to a house of prostitution, where what she prized so highly should be exposed to the insults of the brutal and licentious youth of Rome. Agnes answered that Jesus Christ was too jealous of the purity of His chosen ones to suffer it to be violated in such a manner, for He was their defender and protector. "You may," said she, "stain your sword with my blood, but you will never be able to profane my body, consecrated to Christ." The governor was so incensed at this that he ordered her to be immediately led to the place of shame with liberty to all to abuse her person at pleasure. Many young profligates ran thither, full of wicked desires, but were seized with such awe at the sight of the saint that they durst not approach her; one only excepted, who, attempting to be rude to her, was that very instant, by a flash as it were of lightning from Heaven, struck blind, and fell trembling to the ground. His companions, terrified, took him up and carried him to Agnes, who was singing hymns of praise to Christ, her protector. The virgin by prayer restored his sight and his health.

The chief accuser of the saint, who had at first sought to gratify his lust and avarice, now, in a spirit of vindictiveness, incited the judge against her, his passionate fondness being changed into fury. The governor needed no encouragement, for he was highly exasperated to see himself set at defiance by one of her tender age and sex. Being resolved therefore upon her death, he condemned her to be beheaded. Agnes filled with joy on hearing this sentence, "went to the place of execution more cheerfully," says St. Ambrose, "than others go to their wedding." Agnes remained constant; and having made a short prayer, bowed down her neck to receive the death stroke. The spectators shed tears to see this beautiful child loaded with fetters, and offering herself fearlessly to the sword of the executioner, who with trembling hand cut off her head at one stroke. Her body was buried at a short distance from Rome, beside the Nomentan road.

Source: Herbert J. Thurston, S. J. and Donald Attwater, eds., *Butler's Lives of the Saints*, vol. 1 (Westminster, Md.: Christian Classics, 1990), pp. 133–137.

joint Roman mission of the apostles Peter and Paul. Together with his fellow aristocrat Filocalus, he also produced a corpus of inscriptions dedicated to martyrs that were affixed to the *martyria* around the city.

The Agnes texts blended pagan and Christian motifs in the same way that Damasus's political and religious initiatives blended Roman and Christian institutions. Ambrose, Damasus, and the poet Prudentius skillfully drew upon classical literature in their new Christian compositions. Their texts fused accounts of a pagan heroine with the passion of Agnes. Relying as they did upon the shared classical heritage of pagans and Christians, their appropriation of the pagan culture of rhetoric was as effective as Damasus's appropriation of pagan Roman spectacle and political institutions in ensuring Rome's primacy as the *sedes Petri*, "episcopal seat of Peter."

STUDY QUESTIONS

1 What are martyrologies and *martyria*, and what role did they play in the Christianization of Rome?

2 Describe the process by which Pope Damasus appropriated sacred space and time for the Christian Church.

3 What does the Latin term *concordia apostolorum* refer to, and how did this concept fit within Pope Damasus' propaganda campaign to promote the supremacy of Rome?

4 How did Christian authors like Prudentius make use of classical texts when composing their own works?

5 Using the texts contained in this chapter and the bibliographic resources provided at the end of this book, conduct further research into the legend of Saint Agnes. What specific elements in the legend have their origins in the fourth century? Are there other modern literary texts about Agnes? How do these literary texts appropriate those of the early Christian writers?

Chapter 5

PAGANS AND CHRISTIANS
The Altar of Victory

Then Constantius, upon entering Rome [357 C.E.] the hearth of sovereignty and all excellence, . . . the most famous seat of power from ancient times, stood in amazement, overwhelmed by the wonderful sights which crowded upon him on all sides wherever he looked. . . . [*and*] having reviewed many amazing and awe-inspiring sights, the emperor complained that Rumor must be weak or spiteful because, while always exaggerating everything else, she is feeble when it comes to describing the wonders of Rome.

—Ammianus Marcellinus, *Res gestae*
16.10.13–17

The description of the emperor Constantius II's first visit to Rome excerpted above reveals the passion the city could evoke, for mighty emperors and humble pilgrims alike. Even though the centers of imperial power had shifted eastward under Constantine, the majestic splendor of Rome still held great appeal. Christian emperors exploited its symbolic significance to create an image of political solidarity and economic power. Moreover, the emperors needed the patronage of the Roman senatorial aristocracy. They sought the senate's goodwill in spite of the fact that this conservative patrician class was the very embodiment of Rome's pagan classical heritage.

The fourth-century shift from Rome to capitals more strategically located had allowed the Roman aristocracy opportunities to extend its powers. The senate gained prestige as its members assumed judicial and administrative duties. They assumed the role of the emperor in maintaining public monuments, providing spectacles and shows, and preserving public order in the city. At major public spectacles and civic events they perpetuated their "Roman" heritage, with all the trappings of the old religion. Public funds were used to finance traditional pagan religious ceremonies. Public funds financed the temple rituals, compensated the Vestal Virgins who guarded the temple fires, subsidized the priests, and

were used to pay for the extravagant and lavish spectacles themselves.

Christians came to resent this mixture of religion and tradition that characterized the public life of Rome. These Christians challenged the Roman aristocracy's insistence upon traditional pagan rites and ceremonies. In this chapter we will focus upon one of these conflicts between Christian and non-Christian patricians, the removal of the altar of Victory from the Roman *Curia*, "senate house." The Christian bishop Ambrose and the Roman senator Quintus Aurelius Symmachus presented

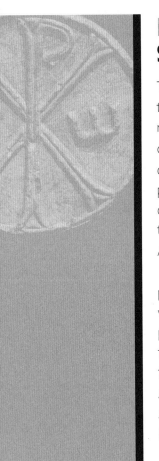

Personalities in Christianity 5.1
SYMMACHUS

The fourth-century patrician Quintus Aurelius Symmachus (c. 340–402 C.E.) was from a distinguished family, held a sequence of distinguished political offices, and brokered the senate's requests to the Christian imperial court for subsidies for pagan religion and for the restoration of the altar of Victory to the *Curia*. Symmachus represented the senate at the *Quinquennalia* ceremony of Valentinian I in 369–370 C.E., and while at court he delivered a total of three panegyrics. There he also met Ausonius, a Christian and fellow aristocrat who was brought to court as tutor to Valentinian's son, Gratian. Symmachus's collected letters offer a glimpse into the official and private life of an elite series of political and social appointments: proconsul of Africa (373 C.E.), prefect of Rome (383–384 C.E.), and consul (391 C.E.).

Three times in his career, Symmachus approached Christian emperors about support for pagan religious practices. The first request (382 C.E.) was directed to the young Gratian at whose accession the senate had become optimistic about the revival of traditional religious practices. He had been the pupil of the Christian scholar Ausonius, who was also a member of the complex web of aristocratic privilege and patronage to which Symmachus belonged. Gratian, however, was indebted to, and relied upon, Bishop Ambrose who opposed the subsidies. As a consequence, Gratian rejected the office of *Pontifex Maximus*, held by all emperors since Augustus, and began to legislate against paganism. He refused even to meet the delegation that Symmachus had led from the senate in 382 C.E.

In his *Relatio* ("Treatise") 3, addressed to Valentinian II, Symmachus again (384 C.E.) argued for the restoration of the altar of Victory to the *Curia*, this time as the urban prefect, the most their arguments in an exaggeratedly civil literary correspondence. Ambrose, the feisty and opinionated bishop of Milan, in northern Italy, argued against replacing the altar while Symmachus, the pagan patrician city prefect, presented the case for its return. For the senators, the issue was nothing less than the preservation of the revered cultural heritage of Rome—religious, literary, political, and artistic—that the altar had come to symbolize. For Ambrose and the Christians, the issue was the conversion of imperial Rome and its historic ruling aristocracy from an archaic pagan "superstition" to Christianity. We will see that the pagan and Christian aristocracy alike valued their shared cultural heritage even as Christianity emerged as the lawful religion of the empire and Rome emerged as its capital.

Roman Senate and Christian Court

The Goddess Victory in the Roman *Curia*

The goddess *Victoria*, "Victory," was a symbol of Rome's might and empire. Typically she

prestigious political appointment in Rome. Bishop Ambrose anticipated this second request (Pope Damasus had sent it to him in advance of the delegation's arrival) and in two letters (*Epistulae* 17 and 18) argued successfully against restoring the altar or subsidizing temple maintenance or temple rituals. Shortly after this second attempt to win subsidies from the Christian court, Symmachus's close friend and colleague, Vettius Agorius Praetextatus, the prefect of Italy, died and Symmachus resigned from his post as urban prefect.

When Theodosius visited Rome in 389 C.E., he made a great show of clemency toward all pagan senators who had supported the usurper Magnus Maximus. This included Symmachus. Despite the fact that he had supported Maximus and even delivered a panegyric in his honor (387 C.E.), Theodosius appointed Symmachus consul in 391 C.E. His friend and colleague, Nichomachus Flavianus, was made prefect of Italy. Once again, as consul, Symmachus led a delegation to Valentinian II in Gaul to request subsidies for pagan religious rites and to petition for the restoration of the altar to the *Curia*. The senate must have hoped that with Ambrose in Milan and Theodosius back in Constantinople Valentinian would see some advantage in allying himself with the Roman senate. Once again, however, the request was refused. The defeat of the usurper Eugenius by Theodosius in 394 C.E. and the subsequent suicide of his friend and colleague Nichomachus Flavianus left Symmachus politically indifferent and he died not long after in Ravenna.

Symmachus' son, the editor of his letters, married a granddaughter of Nichomachus Flavianius, and an ivory diptych celebrating the union of the two families is preserved in the Victoria and Albert Museum in London. It is an exquisite symbol of the late-fourth-century pagan Roman aristocracy that Symmachus embodied.

was represented as a woman with outstretched wings and bare feet; a long flowing garment stretched out behind her as though she was about to light. According to the third-century Roman historian Cassius Dio (*Roman History* 51.22.2), Augustus first set up the statue of Victory in the *Curia* in 29 B.C.E. to acknowledge her aid in conquering Egypt. He brought the statue from the south-Italian city of Tarentum and decorated it with the spoils from his victory over Cleopatra and Mark Antony. At the same time he also set up an altar to the deity *Victoria* right near the statue in the *Curia*. It was on this altar that senators offered incense and libations and allegiance to the emperor; it was on this altar that Roman religion and politics met. When Constantius II visited Rome in April 357 C.E., he ordered the altar removed in keeping with his legislation prohibiting sacrifices. This legislation had already required that temples be closed and sacrifices prohibited. The penalties for disobeying were harsh. We know, for example, from a law recorded in the *Codex Theodosianus*, "Theodosian Code" (16.10.4), from 356 C.E., that the property of anyone who sacrificed in the pagan temples could be confiscated for the imperial treasury.

Perhaps the emperor feared that if he were to speak in the *Curia* in the presence of the altar of Victory, he would be somehow defiled. Or, perhaps he ordered the altar's removal out of deference to Christian senators, so that they would not have to sacrifice upon it. In either case, besides the prohibition against sacrifices, there was no other legislation directed at pagan religious practices in Rome during

Constantius II's reign, and the altar did not remain removed for long. It was restored immediately, or soon, after the visit. It may even have been returned during the brief reign of Julian in 361–363 C.E., who restored other pagan altars. The altar remained in the *Curia* through the reigns of Jovian (363–364 C.E.) and Valentinian I (364–375 C.E.), even though there was a growing bitterness between the imperial Christian court and the Roman senators on the question of blood sacrifices, magic, and divination.

Outward Civility of the Christian Court and the Roman Senate

Valentinian I became emperor in 364 C.E. and ruled in the west from his capital Milan while his brother and co-emperor Valens ruled the east from his capital Constantinople. These emperors were military men and their courts were filled with a large professional class of bureaucrats who were ambitious and socially mobile. Their military character contrasted sharply with the Roman senatorial class. Although politically marginalized, Roman aristocrats enjoyed the leisure, wealth, and education reserved exclusively for their class. And the Roman senate still retained important ceremonial functions. Thus, in 367 C.E., a representative of the senate was summoned to the court to deliver a *laudatio*, "speech of praise," for Valentinian's *Quinquennalia*, the celebration of his first five years of rule.

The young noble Roman senator Quintus Aurelius Symmachus journeyed from Rome to the court in Trier to deliver the *laudatio* on behalf of the Roman senate. This was

Personalities in Christianity 5.2
JULIAN

Julian (331–363 C.E.) is called "the Apostate," which means someone who has renounced a religious belief. His brief reign is the only reversion to state-sponsored pagan religions after the "conversion" of Constantine in 312 C.E. In dynastic intrigues after the death of Constantine, Julian saw his father (Constantine's half-brother) and several other male members of his family murdered, to ensure that power settled into the hands of Constantine's three sons. We assume that Julian survived because he was too young to be a challenge to the court. Educated as a Christian in the family estate in Cappadocia, Julian nevertheless practiced a paganism founded in the philosophy of Neoplatonism.

In 355 C.E., Constantius II called Julian to court to serve as a military commander in Gaul and Britain. He was immediately successful and so instantly popular with the troops that he was proclaimed emperor. Constantius's death, soon after, allowed Julian to assume the throne without civil war.

As emperor, Julian made Neoplatonic philosophy and the worship of the sun god *Helios* a religion. His philosophy/religion was complicated and so did not hold the same broad appeal as traditional polytheism or Christianity. He believed in a single Supreme Being, the sun, who ruled all of creation in a divine philosophic harmony.

Julian ordered the pagan temples to be opened again, and he restored the ancient priesthoods. The Christian church no longer received state support and in his plan to marginalize Christianity he even forbade Christians to teach classical literature on the grounds that it was filled with the culture of ancient polytheistic religions. The only aspect of Christianity he did seem to admire was the social teaching and he emulated this by developing charitable practices modeled on the success of Christians. By lifting the ban on all exiled clerics and by rebuilding the Temple in Jerusalem, Julian hoped to dismantle the church. He refused to grant exemptions from any services to Christians and put great effort into restoring a widespread pre-Christian cultural and religious Hellenism.

Julian's writings reflect his personal piety and learning. His *Against the Galileans* is not complete but provides a thoughtful (and polemical) response to Christianity. He died in battle against the Persians in what may be seen as a military parallel that aimed to accomplish the same end as his religious initiatives. Just as he looked back to an empire unified under a cultural Hellenism, his battle against the Persians recalls the efforts of Alexander the Great to rule an empire unified by Hellenistic political ideals.

an important commission and reflected Symmachus's outstanding rhetorical skills as well as his tact: he was entrusted with the serious duty of forging diplomatic relations between the Roman senate and the imperial court. He also delivered from the senate the customary *aurum oblaticium*, "payment in gold," which the senate collected as a gesture of support for an emperor's fiscal agenda. In all, Symmachus was in Trier for a year. His time at court was so successful that he was invited by Valentinian to compose a second panegyric in honor of his third consulship in 370 C.E. Despite the exchange of goodwill between Symmachus and Valentinian, however, there were conflicts between the Christian court and the powerful and propertied Roman senators. Specifically, Valentinian's religious superstitions caused him to attack certain pagan religious practices.

Christian Emperor and Pagan Aristocracy

During the reign of Valentinian I (364–375 C.E.), charges were brought against several senators by one of his prefects. In 370 C.E., the senatorial class was purged for practicing magic arts, blood sacrifices, and divination. The ruthless investigations and brutal punishments reveal the deep distrust that must have existed between the senatorial overseers of pagan religion and a court that feared magic could be worked against it. Valentinian passed legislation (*Codex Theodosianus* 9.16.4) forbidding the ancient practices of consulting soothsayers, astrologers, diviners, augurs, or seers, something Constantine had already legislated against. Several senators were killed for employing magic potions in order to win favor, money, horse races, or, his great fear, to hurt the emperor. A delegation from the senate reacted and even visited the court to protest the charges and the punishments but Valentinian was unmoved.

Although he was merciless in suppressing their pagan religious practices and had directed violent attacks against them, Valentinian did not altogether reject the classical pagan heritage that the senators embodied. He retained the title, and presumably discharged the functions, of *Pontifex Maximus*, "Chief Priest," the highest office of the traditional state religion. (Every emperor since the time of Augustus had received this office together with its symbol, the pontifical robe, upon his succession to the throne.) Nor was it only the ceremonial trappings of Rome's classical heritage that he willingly assumed. The son of a military commander and himself a military general, he coveted for his son and future emperor, Gratian, the classical education that he had not received. Reserved exclusively for the senatorial class, a classical education still held the promise of wealth, leisure, property, and political influence, all advantages that the emperor wanted for his son Gratian. For this reason, he summoned the classically trained poet and Christian aristocrat Ausonius to his court to become his son's tutor.

Ausonius: A "Christian Aristocrat" at Court

Decimus Magnus Ausonius was trained in the rhetorical schools of Bordeaux. In 367 C.E., he arrived to Trier to become the private tutor of Gratian. While he was in residence at the imperial court, he wrote the didactic travel poem called the *Mosella*. Considered to be his masterpiece, the poem is a charming description of Trier and the surrounding area including the river Moselle. But the *Mosella* is not just a pretty frivolity. It is a fine example of the high status of Greco-Roman literary values in an imperial court that used literature to further its own political ends. In this case, Ausonius's idyllic description of the frontier in the *Mosella* conveyed the court's message that the emperor was preserving peace among the fractious barbarians on the empire's borders. Aristocrats to whom the poem was directed delighted as much in the message of

political security it conveyed as in the refined expression of that message. The poem had its intended consequence: wealthy aristocrats continued to support the emperor's military ventures.

The way Ausonius used the dignified classical poetic forms of Rome's literary golden age is similar to the way that the Roman senators appealed to the authority of Rome's imperial past to justify its traditional pagan religious practices. As members of the aristocracy, Christians and pagans had unique access to the classical education, which, in turn, guaranteed their political clout. It was an exclusive selective circle that religious considerations

Personalities in Christianity 5.3
GRATIAN

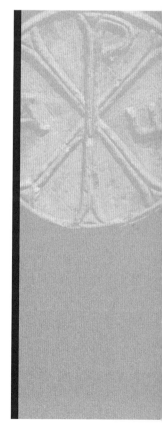

Gratian (359–383 C.E.) became emperor in 375 C.E. when his father (Valentinian I) died unexpectedly. His uncle Valens ruled in the east and his half-brother Valentinian II ruled, nominally, with him in the west. When Valens was killed in the Battle of Adrianopolis in 378 C.E., Gratian appointed Theodosius emperor in the east. Gratian was killed in a battle against Maximus, a general from Britain who had claimed the throne in 383 C.E.

Until Gratian, the fourth-century Christian emperors, like their pagan counterparts, were tolerant and religiously diverse. In these attitudes, pagan and Christian aristocrats had more in common with each other than with Christians or pagans of a different social class. By confiscating the temple revenues and withholding subsidies for traditional cult practices, and by removing the altar of Victory from the Roman *Curia*, Gratian changed the legal status of the old religions of Rome (most of which included prayers for the well-being of the emperor). Whether he had become a truly devout Christian, or, as many scholars think, he was politically overshadowed by Ambrose, or whether, as I have suggested in Chapter 4, he recognized in Ambrose a political efficiency that he did not wish to alienate, Gratian chose to issue edicts that unmoored the ancient pagan religions and with them the aristocratic civic culture of Rome. He even went so far as to refuse the pontifical robe that identified him as *Pontifex Maximus*, a revered and proprietary title of emperors since the reign of Augustus.

did not breach. Ausonius was no unassuming Christian professor. He was a professionally trained classical poet who had more in common with wealthy, privileged Roman senators like Symmachus than with the less-educated bureaucrats in the Christian court of Valentinian. Indeed, he and Symmachus met while Symmachus was at court in 368 C.E. and their correspondence reveals a complicated web of mutual acquaintances and reciprocal acts of patronage. Ausonius's actions at Valentinian's death (375 C.E.) further reveal his patrician, more than his Christian, sympathies and priorities. He was quick to join the group who purged the court of Valentinian's appointees. He seized the opportunity to replace them with his own family members and aristocratic friends, immaterial of whether or not they were Christians. For these he secured appointments, favors, and influence, and, for himself, the highest secular office in the government, the consulship of 379 C.E.

Doctrinal Debates

Eastern and Western Courts

At Valentinian I's death in 375 C.E., his son Valentinian II was made co-Augustus with his half-brother Gratian, who had been ruling as co-Augustus with his father since 367 C.E. Immediately upon their succession, the purge of the imperial courts led by Ausonius ousted most members of their father's court. Under the influence of Ausonius, Gratian replaced these career bureaucrats with landed gentry, literary scholars, and a propertied upper class—the old, pagan nobility. For the Roman senate the accession of Gratian was a cause for rejoicing. Valentinian I's henchmen who had persecuted the Roman senators for pagan religious practices were executed and the possibility of renewed political favors between the court and the senate offered itself. Indeed, the new Christian emperors still needed the support of the Roman pagan aristocracy. It was the emperor and the senate together who governed the Roman state. The Christian Ausonius and the non-Christian Symmachus were friends, correspondents, and, most importantly, fellow patricians, who supported each other to retain the privileges of their class. The link between the Christian court and the (mostly) pagan senatorial aristocracy was strong. To the Roman aristocracy, the spirit of tolerance exhibited by the successors to Constantius II seemed assured in Gratian and there was no reason to expect that the altar of Victory and all that it symbolized were in jeopardy. The military catastrophe of 378 C.E. was the beginning of a turning point, however, in these comfortable relations between the Christian and non-Christian aristocrats in the imperial court and the Roman senate.

In 378 C.E., when the Visigoths won the battle against Valens, the brother of Valentinian and the emperor of the eastern empire, at Hadrianople in Thrace, events happened quickly: Gratian, at sixteen, became the senior Augustus and his five-year-old brother Valentinian II, his co-ruler. Theodosius, a loyal military commander under Valentinian I, was recalled from Spain and replaced Valens as emperor in the east. Early in his reign he set about establishing western ortho-dox Catholicism throughout his areas of jurisdiction.

The Arian Heresy and the Council of Nicea

In 380 C.E., the very year he arrived in Constantinople to assume power, Theodosius issued an edict at Thessalonica hoping to quell a longstanding doctrinal debate over christology, called the Arian Controversy. The sum of the edict (*Codex Theodosianus* 16.5.5) was that all the people of Constantinople were to accept the doctrines handed down from the apostle Peter and practiced by Pope Damasus of Rome. These and only these were orthodox. Without mentioning him by name, Theodosius had denounced Arius and his her-esy, called Arianism.

Arius (256–336 C.E.) had been a presbyter, or church leader, in the city of Alexandria. He openly disagreed with his bishop's teaching on the relationship between God the Father and his Son Jesus. His bishop, Alexander, taught that Jesus, the Son of God, was begotten from eternity of the same essence as the Father. The Greek term for this relationship is *homoousios*, meaning "of the same substance." Arius, how-ever, disagreed. He wrote to Alexander out-lining his position. To Arius, the Son was the offspring of God the Father but not co-eternal with him, which meant that he had a begin-ning and that there was a time when he did not exist. He was subordinate to the Father, of a similar but not the same substance as the Father. The Greek term for this relationship is *homoiousios*, "of a similar substance." Arius also postulated that there was a time when

God was not a Father and that his Word (his Son) did not exist from eternity and therefore was mutable. Alexander was furious, and in a letter to several bishops he excommunicated Arius.

Arius immediately fled to Nicomedia where his teachings were approved by a synod, a council of church members. Further, his doc-trine was declared orthodox, "correct," which meant that there could be no other understand-ing of the relationship between the Father and the Son except as Arius had expressed it. As the controversy festered, bishops and church-men on both sides sought to promote one or the other of these doctrines, either *homoou-sios* or *homoiousios*. Constantine wanted to settle the dispute. To him, these matters were almost frivolous and they obstructed his plan for a universal and unanimous empire-wide worship. He urged reconciliation between Alexander and Arius. When the situation con-tinued to deteriorate, however, Constantine convened an ecumenical council to meet at Nicea in Asia Minor in 325 C.E., when Arius was already close to seventy years old. An imperial postal service was put at their dis-posal and over 250 bishops met from all over the east and west. Under considerable pres-sure from Constantine, they (almost unani-mously) repudiated Arius and his teaching. They formally declared that God the Father and his Son were *homoousios*, that is, "of the same substance," rather than *homoiousios*, "of a similar substance." This doctrine has come to be called the Nicene Creed.

The decision taken at the Council of Nicea lasted only until Constantine's death, in

337 C.E. As his sons divided the empire and promoted different doctrines, the debate raged anew. Constans (337–350 C.E.), in the west, was orthodox, and Constantius II (337–61 C.E.), in the east, was Arian. Add to the mix the politically unscrupulous and doctrinally single-minded Athanasius (300–373 C.E.), the new bishop of Alexandria, an inflexible supporter of the decision of the Council of Nicea, and we have some idea of how unsettled the debate remained. During his forty-five year reign, Athanasius was exiled from his see for a total of almost sixteen years, but during the ten-year period between 346 and 356 C.E. he was the undisputed leader of the church in the east. During that time, Arianism was reduced to a minority and Athanasius and the Niceans prevailed. In 355 C.E., Constantius II convened councils at Arles (353 C.E.) and Milan (355 C.E.) hoping to overturn the decision taken at Nicea and to displace Athanasius. In 356 C.E., the emperor's troops surrounded Athanasius's church to find that their attack had been anticipated and that Athanasius already was safely lodged among the remote monasteries in the deserts outside of Alexandria. For the moment the Arians had won.

The pagan Julian (363 C.E.) assumed the throne at the death of Constantius II and immediately recalled all exiled ecclesiastics from both sides of the argument, even as he actively promoted a revitalization of the pagan cults and temples. While his pardon may seem to have been motivated by a spirit of toleration, in fact, it allowed the various factions to regroup and take up old hostilities. Athanasius convened a council in 362 C.E. at which some

twenty-one bishops condemned Arianism, and the Nicenes were again ascendant. Under the religiously tolerant Valentinian I (364 C.E.), however, strong Arian bishops in the west were not ousted, although when they died they were replaced with Nicenes; in the east, the doctrine of consubstantiality was extended to include not just God the Father and his Son but also the Holy Spirit.

With the accession of Gratian (375 C.E.) and Theodosius (379 C.E.), there were still a number of different christologies that co-existed all over the empire. As a consequence, their attempts to eradicate Arianism met with only limited success, at least until 382 C.E., when two things happened. In the east, Theodosius secured peace with the Visigoths after long years of constant warfare. In the west, Gratian removed the western imperial court from Trier to Milan. It was then that Gratian and, soon after him, Theodosius fell under the opinionated and politically astute Bishop Ambrose of Milan, with grave consequences for the religious traditions and pagan heritage of Rome.

A Holy Alliance: Bishop Ambrose and the Emperor Gratian

In the administrative and military milieu of northern Italy in the fourth century, Aurelius Ambrose (337 or 339–397 C.E.) had held office as an imperial governor in several regions of northern Italy before being acclaimed the new bishop of Milan in 374 C.E. His hagiographer Paulinus, a *vir ecclesiasticus,* or "deacon," of the church of Milan, recorded the event. He tells us that Ambrose, as governor, had been summoned to Milan at the death of the Arian bishop Auxentius to keep order during the contentious election of a new bishop. Although Ambrose himself was only a catechumen, that is, "under religious instruction," a child in the crowd is said to have shouted "Bishop Ambrose!" as the governor entered the cathedral. According to Paulinus, a throng of voices, Arians and Catholics, quickly took up the chant. His elevation was endorsed immediately, both by the clergy and the emperor Valentinian I. Within a week he was baptized and consecrated as bishop. Ambrose's family was aristocratic, Roman, and Christian:

his father, also named Ambrose, was Prefect of Gaul, and in 353 C.E., when the family had returned to Rome from Gaul at his death, Ambrose's sister, Marcellina, was consecrated as a virgin dedicated to God (something very like a modern nun) by Pope Liberius.

When Ambrose became bishop of Milan in 374 C.E., the city was part Arian and part Catholic. In the first years of his episcopacy, he was largely preoccupied with what he considered the Arian problem, and he intervened in several bishoprics to ensure that Catholic bishops replaced Arian bishops. In order to

Personalities in Christianity 5.4
ATHANASIUS

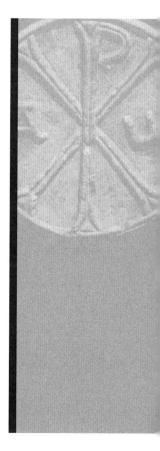

The secretary to Alexander, Bishop of Alexandria, Athanasius (c. 296–373 C.E.) attended the Council of Nicea in 325 C.E. and was the archenemy of Arius and the Arian cause. He is counted as one of the four great doctors of the eastern church, with Basil (330–379 C.E.), Gregory Nazianus (330–390 C.E.), and John Chrysostom (345–407 C.E.). When he became Bishop of Alexandria in 328 C.E., he began a long career resisting Arianism. He was deposed in 336 C.E., exiled in 339 C.E. to Rome, recalled in 346 C.E., exiled again in 356 C.E., recalled and exiled in 361–362 C.E., and recalled again in 366 C.E. Until he died, Athanasius ardently defended orthodoxy through the treatises he wrote explicating orthodox christology, that God the Father and his Son are co-eternal. As bishop, he worked through political channels (sometimes using very violent and ethically questionable means) to win adherents to the orthodox/Nicene view. He directed the Council of Alexandria (362 C.E.) where the terms *homoousios*, which means "of the same substance," and *homoiousios*, "of a like substance," were again debated, and he was the first to identify the canonical twenty-seven books of the New Testament. He battled other heresies besides Arianism and supported the growing monastic movement in Egypt by writing a biography of Anthony (251–356 C.E.), the eremitic monk who organized the first community of hermits in the Egyptian desert under a monastic rule that anticipated a much more structured medieval monasticism.

instruct the emperor Gratian in the orthodox faith and thereby win his allegiance in
these doctrinal battles, Ambrose dedicated his
anti-Arian work called the *De fide* (380 C.E.),
On Faith, to him. In this work, the emper-
or's impending military campaign against
the Goths along the Danube in the Illyrian
provinces was likened to a crusade against
heresy, that is, the religion of the Arian barbarians. The emperor should avoid defeat,
Ambrose advised, by championing the Nicene
orthodoxy of the west. Subduing the Arian
heresy, according to Ambrose, would ensure
military victory. This clever (if transparent)
analogy and its sophisticated rhetorical treatment made the work appealing to the literate
Ausonians at court even as it established the
west's political theology for the upcoming
council of bishops at Aquileia.

In 380 C.E., Gratian planned to remove his
court to Milan from Trier, a move calculated
to ease the military hardship of traveling such
great distances to the Illyrian front. By March
of 381 C.E., now in Milan, he planned to con-
vene a grand council of bishops from the east
and the west at Aquileia in the coming summer. Undoubtedly, he hoped to establish an
ecclesiastical hierarchy loyal to him as the
senior Augustus and to ensure that orthodoxy
prevailed. However, his co-Augustus in the
east, Theodosius, beat him to it. Theodosius
convened a meeting of the eastern bishops in
Constantinople in May of 381 C.E., in advance
of the larger council Gratian had planned for
the summer. Gratian must have been embar-
rassed. Not only had Theodosius undermined
his imperial authority as senior Augustus but

he had also staked a pre-emptive claim to the
loyalty of those eastern bishops. Gratian's plan
to establish the primacy of the west in the
realm of theological doctrine had been superseded by Theodosius's council, and it would
be difficult for him to reassert his authority.

Ambrose's immediate reaction—to proceed
with the council but to include only the western bishops—had effective political outcomes.
He convincingly advocated Nicene orthodoxy,
he restored credibility to Gratian's senior status, and he acquired political clout. After the
meeting in Aquileia, in a letter to Theodosius
(*Epistlula* 14), Ambrose rewrote the sequence
of events to his own advantage. He thanked
Theodosius for convening the eastern bishops
to address the unrest in the east and he made
it plain that there was no similar unrest in
the west where the true champions of orthodoxy—Ambrose and Gratian—already had
defeated the Arian heretics. For his diplomatic
victory in this imperial struggle between the
two emperors, Ambrose had won the gratitude of Gratian. For his part, Gratian was
clever enough to recognize the advantage of
relocating his court from Trier to Milan. In
Ambrose, he had found a politically astute,
cultured, and resourceful ally.

Ambrose dominated the court at Milan.
Rhetorician, diplomat, and bishop, he was the
consummate Roman Christian patrician, a
politician at the center of imperial court society. In one stroke, he had trumped Theodosius
in the affair with the bishops and reclaimed the
pre-eminence of the western court. Gratian
was under his sway. Whether he feigned a new
and more orthodox Catholicism or whether

he was genuinely converted, Gratian's new and more severe policies against heretics and anti-Catholics (to the benefit of the imperial treasury) defined his final years as emperor.

Ambrose, Gratian, and the Altar of Victory

Gratian's Edicts against Ancient Religions

In 382 C.E., Gratian issued various edicts that severely restricted pagan religious practices. Although his edicts are not extant, we can reconstruct them from several sources, including the letters of Ambrose, the treatises of Symmachus, and an important law—*Codex Theodosianus* 16.10.20. Unequivocal in his efforts to contain pagan religious practices, Gratian withdrew funding for the traditional pagan cults at Rome and confiscated the revenues and properties for maintaining cult practices and ceremonies, diverted into the treasury revenues from the pagan temples, including those of Vestal Virgins, and stripped pagan religious officials of their exemptions from any other public service. Finally, he ordered that the altar of Victory be removed from the *Curia*. The unchecked euphoria that had spread through the senate when Gratian came to power had passed. Even after the repressive measures of Valentinian I, these measures seemed harsh and inflammatory.

The Delegation of Symmachus

When a delegation led by Symmachus arrived from Rome to protest against the measures, Gratian refused them an audience. This must have been a staggering blow to Symmachus's pride, apart from its clear political implications; it was as much a rejection of the senatorial aristocrat himself as of the senators' ancient, revered pagan religious practices. In addition, members of the delegation had with them the pontifical robes, to remind Gratian

---

FROM AN ANCIENT TEXT ❖ 5.1

Codex Theodosianus on Gratian's Edict (382 C.E.)

Though issued in 415 C.E. by Emperor Honorius, this law refers to Gratian's Edict of 382 C.E. and illustrates his escalating hostility directed at pagan religious practices, perhaps as a result of Bishop Ambrose's influence.

Also, all the places that the error of the ancients allotted as sacred, in agreement with the edicts of our divine Gratian, we order confiscated for the state so that from this time when public money can no longer be used for that foulest of superstitions revenues may be exacted from the priests.

Source: Clyde Pharr, *The Theodosian Code and Novels, and the Sirmondian Constitutions* (Westport, Conn.: Greenwood, 1969), p. 475.

that as *Pontifex Maximus* he was to protect the traditional shrines, priesthoods, and cults, not cut off their support. In a dramatic gesture, Gratian refused the pontifical robe. He was the last Roman emperor to hold the title, for the college of Pontiffs was abolished under Theodosius in 395 C.E. Why Gratian, heretofore eager to promote good relations with the Roman senate, refused to see the powerful delegation of senators from Rome and why he refused to acknowledge his duties as *Pontifex Maximus*, even going so far as to spurn the title and the robes, may be traced to the influence of Ambrose. Before the delegation from Rome arrived in Milan, Ambrose had already presented the emperor with a protest signed by Christian senators. They claimed that they were not in support of the delegation of senators and that they would resign from the senate if Gratian's policies were reversed. Pope Damasus (366–384 C.E.) himself, the primate of the church in Rome, had forwarded the protest to Ambrose.

The Revolt of Magnus Maximus

During this same period (late 382 to early 383 C.E.), Magnus Maximus, the commander of the army in Britain, revolted and established a second western court. By mid-383 C.E. he had crossed the channel to Paris and forced a confrontation. Gratian redirected his campaign away from the Alemanni nation on the German frontier and headed toward Paris. For a variety of reasons, his army defected to Maximus, and by August 383 C.E., Gratian had been murdered. To some Roman senators, no doubt, Gratian's defeat seemed like divine justice for his abandoning of the traditional Roman gods.

The boldness of Magnus Maximus in revolting against Gratian was, at least in part, due to Theodosius' independence. Remember that in the spring of 381 C.E. he had convened the bishops in the east in anticipation of the bishops' council in Aquileia that Gratian had announced. And, as Magnus Maximus must have anticipated, he did not immediately respond to Gratian's murder by moving west to confront the usurper. In addition, already in January of 383 C.E., Theodosius had proclaimed his son Arcadius, then only five, as his co-Augustus. With good reason Ambrose feared that with Gratian dead his own power would be compromised if the center of power shifted east to Theodosius' court. Together with the Roman aristocracy, who above all wanted the center of imperial power to remain in Italy to ensure the benefits of their patronage, Ambrose joined the machinations that led to the accession of Valentinian II.

The Court of Ambrose

Immediately after Gratian's death, Ambrose went to the court of Magnus Maximus at Trier and began negotiations on behalf of Valentinian II. For sinister reasons, Maximus asked Ambrose to persuade Valentinian II to come to Trier. He promised to accept him as his own son, but Ambrose saw through the deceit. In response, he made excuses to delay such a meeting. He argued that it was too long a journey, the winter was too harsh, and that Valentinian II was too young to travel without his mother. Maximus grew impatient with the delaying tactics and dispatched Ambrose to Milan insisting that he try to work out the details of a conference. But while Ambrose had been purposefully impeding the negotiations with Maximus, Valentinian II had established his court in Milan and rallied his supporters, including Theodosius. Though he did not rush to avenge Gratian's murder, Theodosius reckoned rightly that he could only profit by supporting Valentinian II, a weak and younger co-ruler. Before he could set out from Constantinople, however, Valentinian II and Maximus reached an accord and subsequently ruled together, if uneasily, for three years. Though he led Maximus to believe that the young Valentinian II would come to Trier and assume the role of the lesser Augustus, Ambrose knew otherwise. He was working on behalf of Valentinian II and, foremost, he was looking to his own interests: he may have abhorred the murder of Gratian who had lately become a devout ally, but he also abhorred Justina, the Arian mother of Valentinian II. To Ambrose, Magnus Maximus, a Nicene Catholic, was the lesser of two evils. At least, he would promote orthodoxy.

Above all, Ambrose hoped to avoid alienating either ruler and keep the court in Milan, where he could continue to rule as an episcopal demagogue. The Roman senators also hoped to keep the court in Milan rather than Trier, to safeguard their own interests. Whether that court was ruled by Magnus Maximus or Valentinian II was less important than that the aristocrats, both pagan senators and Christian bishop, retained their respective influence.

Ambrose, Valentinian II, and the Altar of Victory

The Second Delegation of Symmachus

In July 384 C.E., Valentinian II appointed Quintus Aurelius Symmachus prefect of Rome and his good friend Vettius Agorius Praetextatus praetorian prefect of Italy, Illyricum, and Africa. These appointments ranked among the most important in the administration and represent the *Realpolitik* of the western court. Valentinian was young, inexperienced, and no match for the military might of Magnus Maximus' court at Trier. This was no time to alienate the Roman senate. Moreover, the conflict between Valentinian's Arian mother Justina and the staunchly orthodox Ambrose led the senators to believe that Ambrose was out of favor and that this might be a good opportunity to renew their protest against Gratian's edicts, particularly the removal of the altar of Victory. Symmachus must have felt confident leading another embassy to Milan, where Valentinian, the twelve-year-old half-brother of Gratian, was presiding over a weakened court.

Among his *Relationes, State Papers*, Symmachus presented a petition to Valentinian for the reinstatement of funds for state cults and for the restoration of the altar of Victory. In *Relatio* 3.7, Symmachus invoked the actions of Constantius II to argue that even when he had ordered the altar of Victory removed in 357 C.E., he did not repudiate his obligations as *Pontifex Maximus* but continued to fund the state cults and their priesthoods. We may infer that a similar argument had been presented to

Gratian at the time of the anti-pagan legislation he promulgated and that it was then, in 382–383 C.E., that he refused the pontifical robe and the role of *Pontifex Maximus.* By all standards, Symmachus's document was a rhetorical triumph: it deployed all the persuasive logic and linguistic precision of the oratorical training that was at the heart of classical pagan education. He argued that the state needed the altar to protect it from barbarian invasions, and that the ancestral rites had always been venerated and should continue to be respected. It was by sanctioning varied religious practices, he continued, that the emperor revealed his own philosophical spirit and erudition. For Symmachus, the altar of Victory was a symbol of Rome's glorious imperial past. Each time the senators (pagans and Christians alike) passed it upon entering the *Curia,* they were reminded of the sentiment so often expressed by the classical writers—that as long as she revered the gods, Rome would continue to rule. Symmachus did not challenge the Christians (indeed, he argued for tolerance of all religious practices), and he never pleaded for the exclusive religious practices of the traditional cults, only that the emperor continue to support the ancestral gods, so that the gods would continue to support the state. Nonetheless, the arguments of Symmachus' *Relatio* fell on deaf ears.

Letters of Ambrose

Before he even knew the details of the petition, Ambrose wrote a letter (*Epistula* 17) to Valentinian opposing the senators' request. He argued that Valentinian would be endorsing paganism and persecuting Christian senators if he returned the altar of Victory. He threatened that he would not be received in a Christian church and would even meet with an unforgiving God if he yielded to the demands to restore funds and property for pagan rituals. How could the emperor grant revenues and property to Vestal Virgins, he asked, when Christian virgins dedicated to Jesus did not receive the same support? Above all, Ambrose demanded a copy of the *Relatio* so that he could write a pointed response. When he finally read the *Relatio* himself, Ambrose wrote a second letter (*Epistula* 18) in response, with detailed refutations of Symmachus' arguments. Certainly, his responses were no more eloquent or logical than the arguments of Symmachus; nor were the requests of Symmachus as threatening as he claimed. Yet, Ambrose prevailed and neither the altar nor the subsidies were restored.

The key to Valentinian's decision may rest with the fact that he was indebted to Ambrose for his diplomatic intervention with Maximus. Just as Ambrose had intervened in the court rivalry over the bishops' councils—the one convened by Gratian at Aquileia in summer 381 C.E. and the one convened by Theodosius in spring 381 C.E. at Constantinople—and saved Gratian from considerable embarrassment, so now had his embassy to the court of Maximus provided Valentinian an interval of time to safely establish his court in Milan. While Ambrose equivocated in Trier, Valentinian consolidated his power base in Milan. Ambrose had shown himself to be an indispensable ambassador of the court and

FROM AN ANCIENT TEXT ❖ 5.2

Symmachus, *Relatio III*

In elegant prose, Symmachus argued that the altar symbolized Rome as empire and that the same traditional worship that had always safeguarded the empire would only be ensured if traditional sacrifices continued. Symmachus did not ask that other religious practices be suppressed in favor of those associated with the altar; he argued, in fact, that all forms of worship should be respected. The selections here illustrate the tact and discretion with which Symmachus approached the emperor and represented the senate.

It is the honor of the times which has most to gain from our defense of our traditional institutions, of our country's rights and destinies; and that honor is all the greater at this moment because you understand that you have no power to do anything contrary to the precedents set by your parents.

That is why we ask you to give us back our religious institutions as they used to be when for so long they were of value to the state. Of course, we can list Emperors of either faith and either conviction: the earlier Emperors venerated our ancestral religious rites, the later did not abolish them. If the religious attitude of the earlier Emperors did not set a precedent, let the policy of the blind eye adopted by more recent Emperors set a precedent! We are not on such good terms with the barbarians that we can do without an Altar of Victory! We are cautious in our attitude to the future and we avoid the portents incidental to change. If honor is refused to the divinity herself, at any rate let it be duly given to the divine name. Your Eternities owe much to victory and will owe more. Let those reject her powerful aid who have never received a benefit from it; do you refuse to abandon a patronage so ready to bring you triumphs! Everyone prays for power of that kind; no one should deny that such power is to be venerated if he admits that it is desirable. . . .

Grant, I beg you, that what in our youth we took over from our fathers, we may in our old age hand on to posterity. The love of established practice is a powerful sentiment; the action of the late Emperor Constantius quite rightly did not stand good for long. You should not adopt any precedent which you have discovered to have been quickly set aside. We are safeguarding the perpetuity of your good name, ensuring that future ages will not find it necessary to reverse your measures.

Where else are we to take the oath of allegiance to your laws and ordinances? What religious sanction is going to deter the treacherous from giving false evidence? Admittedly everywhere is full of God and nowhere is safe for perjurers; but to have it borne in upon you that you are in the presence of a divine being is a powerful influence to make you fear to do wrong. That altar holds together the harmony of all as a group and that same altar makes its appeal to the good faith of each separately, and nothing gives more authority to the proceedings of the senate than the feeling that all its measures are passed by a body of men acting, as it were, on oath. Is a perjured witness to have ready access to a place no longer consecrated, and to such a measure will my noble Emperors give their considered approval who are themselves protected by a general oath of loyalty? . . .

Let your Eternities accept the other acts of this same Emperor Constantius and adopt them into practice, and so earn greater respect. He stripped away nothing from the privileges of the Vestal Virgins; he filled priesthoods with men of noble birth, he allowed the cost of Roman ceremonies; he followed an overjoyed senate through all the streets of the Eternal City and, with no sign of disapproval in his face, he saw its shrines, he read the inscriptions giving the names of the gods on pediments; he put questions about the origins of the temples; he showed his admiration for their founders; though he himself followed other rites, he preserved established rites for the Empire.

Everyone has his own customs, his own religious practices; the divine mind has assigned to different cities different religions to be their guardians. Each man is given at birth a separate soul; in the same way each people is given its own special genius to take care of its destiny. To this line of thought must be added the argument derived from "benefits conferred," for herein rests the most emphatic proof to man of the existence of the gods. Man's reason moves entirely in the dark; his knowledge of divine influences can be drawn from no better source than from the recollection and the evidences of good fortune received from them. If long passage of time lends validity to religious observances, we ought to keep faith with so many centuries, we ought to follow our forefathers who followed their forefathers and were blessed in so doing.

Let us imagine that Rome herself stands in your presence and pleads with you thus, "Best of emperors, fathers of your country, respect my length of years won for me by the dutiful observance of rite, let me continue to practice my ancient ceremonies, for I do not regret them. Let me live in my own way, for I am free. This worship of mine brought the whole world under the rule of my laws, these sacred rites drove back Hannibal from my walls and the Senones from the Capitol. Is it true that I have been kept alive solely for the purpose of being reprimanded at my age?

I will see what kind of changes I think should be set on foot, but reformation of old age comes rather late and is humiliating."

And so we ask for peace for the gods of our fathers, for the gods of our native land. It is reasonable that whatever each of us worships is really to be considered one and the same. We gaze up at the same stars; the sky covers us all; the same universe compasses us. What does it matter what practical system we adopt in our search for the truth? Not by one avenue only can we arrive at so tremendous a secret. But this is the kind of case for men to put with time on their hands; at the moment it is prayers that we present to you, not debating arguments. . . .

Source: R. H. Barrow, *Prefect and Emperor: The* Relationes *of Symmachus A.D. 384* (Oxford: Clarendon, 1973), pp. 34–47. By permission of Oxford University Press.

FROM AN ANCIENT TEXT ❖ 5.3

The Altar of Victory Debate

Even before Symmachus and his delegation from the senate arrived to Valentinian's court to request that subsidies for pagan religious rituals be restored and that the altar of Victory be returned to the Curia, Ambrose wrote Epistula *17 arguing (1) that Christian senators were not in favor of the delegation's requests and (2) that to acquiesce to the requests of the delegation would invoke God's wrath.*

Ambrose, *Epistula* 17

Since, then, most Christian emperor, you should bear witness of your faith to the true God, along with enthusiasm for that faith, care and devotion, I am surprised that certain people have come to harbor expectations that by imperial edict you might restore to the pagans' gods their altars and also provide funds for the celebration of pagan sacrifices. These funds, which have for some time been vindicated to the public and private treasuries, you will appear rather to be donating from your own purse than restoring from theirs. They who never spared our blood, who overturned the very buildings of the Church from their foundations, complain about expenses. They ask too that you confer privileges on them, although they denied us the right of speaking and teaching, which is common to all, in the law of Julian not so long ago. Those privileges were ones by which even Christians were often led astray; for they hoped to ensnare some by exploiting those privileges, some through their foolishness, some through the wish to avoid the trouble of expenditure on public needs; and because not everyone shows themselves to be brave, a substantial number lapsed, even under Christian emperors. Yet had these privileges not already been removed, I would have sanctioned their removal at your command. Although these rites have been curtailed and forbidden throughout the world by many previous emperors, at Rome, however, they were abolished and made things of the past by the rescripts of Your Merciful Highness's brother, Gratian of august memory, following the principle of true faith. I ask you not to destroy what your brother in his faith established, nor go back on your brother's precedent. In secular business no one believes there is any need to fear that a decision once made may be reversed—yet is a principle of religion to be trampled underfoot? Do not let anyone cheat you because of your youth; if the man making this demand of you is a pagan, he should not entangle your mind in the chains of his superstition but rather he should instruct and advise you by his own zeal as how you should pursue the true faith instead of defending empty vanities with such violations of truth. I, too, urge you to respect the high character of senators; but beyond doubt, God is to be put first, before all others. . . .

One cannot avoid sacrilege in the passing of this decree; therefore I request that you do not pass it, promulgate it, or lend your name to any decrees of this king. I, as priest of Christ, call your faith to account. All we bishops would agree with this, if people had not heard without warning the otherwise unbelievable tale that some such measure was being put forward in our consistory or requested by the senate. Yet far be it from the senate to be described as asking such a thing; a few pagans are exploiting the name of the whole assembly. For about two years ago at the time they were trying to put forward this request, the holy Damasus, Bishop of the Roman Church, appointed by the will of God, sent me a document drawn up by a numerous body of Christian senators, protesting that they had not made any such demand, did not concur with the pagans' petitions of this kind and did not give their consent to them. They also complained, publicly and privately, that they would boycott meetings of the senate if such a resolution were to be passed. Is it worthy of your times, Christian times that is, that Christian senators should be dishonoured so that pagans' unsanctified pleasure should be put into effect? This document I forwarded to Your Clemency's brother Gratian whereby it was proved that it was not the senate as a whole who charged its representatives with any mandate about the financing of superstition. But someone may object, "Why did they not attend the senate while this resolution was under discussion?" My answer is that they spoke their wishes clearly enough by not being present; their words were clear enough when they spoke before the emperor. Yet are we surprised that they rob individuals at Rome of the power of resistance, seeing that they deny your freedom to refuse to swear by what you do not approve or to hold by what you believe? . . .

Therefore, Emperor, now that you perceive it would be an injustice, first to God, and then to your father and brother, should you pass any such decree, I request that you act in the manner you realize is conducive to your salvation before God.

Source: The Latin text is found in Otto J. Faller, *Epistularum libri I–VI*, Corpus Scriptorum Ecclesiasticorum Latinorum 82 (Vienna: Austrian Academy of Sciences, 1968) and the full English translation in Brian Croke and Jill Harries, *Religious Conflict in Fourth-Century Rome* (Sydney: Sydney University Press, 1982), pp. 30–35. Only select passages that correspond to the points discussed in Chapter 5 are quoted here.

that he could achieve in diplomatic negotiations what the Roman senate could not. Moreover, in *Epistula 17*, he did not hesitate to remind Valentinian of the debt he owed to him for his successful embassy to Maximus on his behalf.

This was the second unsuccessful delegation from the Roman senate to the Christian court to request the restoration of public subsidies for religious rites and to request that the altar of Victory, the very symbol of imperial Rome and her classical heritage, be returned to the *Curia*. Valentinian did not refuse because of any deep-seated doctrinal or faith-based objection. He refused because it was politically expedient to refuse, in order

FROM AN ANCIENT TEXT ❖ 5.4

Ambrose, *Epistula* 18

These selections from Epistula 18 *illustrate Ambrose's religious position regarding pagan subsidies, his political clout over Valentinian, and his very fine command of the persuasive rhetoric emblematic of the educated aristocracy.*

The most distinguished Symmachus, Prefect of the City, has petitioned Your Clemency that the altar which was removed from the senate-house in the city of Rome should be restored to its place. You, emperor, although still in your earliest years, fresh in the flower of your youth but experienced in the worth of faith, must not support the petitions of the pagans. I offered a small treatise against this as soon as I found out, raising the points, which seemed necessary to the general drift, as far as I could understand it. Nevertheless, I demanded to be given a copy of the Prefect's petition.

Thus, while not doubting your faith but exercising the foresight of caution, although assured of your devout purpose, I reply to the argument of the Prefect's document with this work, asking only this: that you should make up your mind to expect not eloquence of language but the plain force of factual argument. For, as holy scripture teaches us, the tongue of the wise man learned in letters is golden, it is armed with all the weaponry of speech, it flashes with the splendor of glorious eloquence like the sheen of the precious metal, it captures the eyes of the mind with its beautiful appearance and holds men fast by its look. But if you test this gold carefully with your hand, it is valuable on the surface but beneath it is dross. I ask you to turn over and test with the hammer the pagans' sect. They ring with a sonorous grandeur, as if of value, but defend things devoid of the gold of truth; they speak of God but worship an image.

In his petition as Prefect of the City, the distinguished senator puts forward three propositions where he thinks he has a good case: that Rome, as he says, needs to have back her own ancient cults; that payment should be offered to their priests and Vestal Virgins; that because you denied the priests their stipends a general famine followed.

On the first point, Rome wept for herself with a tearful complaint and she asked the return of her ceremonial cults, ancient, as she said. These holy objects, she argued, drove Hannibal from the walls and the Senones from the Capitol. Thus, while she asserted the power of the sacred objects, their real weakness was betrayed. For, by this, Hannibal had so effectively defied the sacred objects of Rome and her gods who fought against him that his conquering course had brought him right up to the city walls. How could men whose gods were fighting, armed, at their side have allowed themselves to be besieged at all?

As regards to the Senones, what can I say? The Roman sacred relics would not have driven them off once they had penetrated the secret ways of the Capitol, if a goose had not betrayed them by squawking in a panic. See the kinds of guardians the temples of Rome possess! Where was Jupiter then? Was he speaking through the mouth of a goose?

Why should I deny that the sacred rites fought on the Romans' side? Yet Hannibal too worshipped the same gods. So they chose, then, the side they preferred? If the holy things on the Romans' side won, the Carthaginians were thereby overcome; if the Carthaginian rites triumphed, their gods could not then be any help to the Romans.

So let the Roman people hush that unhelpful complaint. Rome herself did not authorize it. She interrupts them with different words, "Why do you stain me every day with the blood of innocent beasts? Trophies of victory are not to be found in the sinews of cattle but the strength of warriors. I conquered the world through a different discipline. Camillus went to war and brought back the standards taken from the Capitol, taking those who had vaunted their triumph on the Tarpeian rock; his military prowess overthrew men whom superstition had failed to dislodge. I need not mention Attilius *Regulus* who fought with death itself. Scipio Africanus won his triumph not among the altars of the Capitol but the battle-lines of Hannibal.

Why do you throw historical precedents at me? I hate the rites of Nero. Why mention the emperors of two months whose reigns ended almost as soon as they had begun? Or perhaps it has never happened before that barbarians left their own territories? Surely they were not Christians, those who set a new, disastrous example, the one emperor a prisoner himself, the other making the world his prisoner, when omens promising victory deceived them and betrayed their own rites? Perhaps there was no altar of Victory at that time either?

Their failure makes them regretful: the grey hair of old age has brought a blush of shame to the cheek. I do not blush at Rome's conversion after a long life, along with the whole world. There can be no doubt that no age is too old for learning. Let the senate blush because it cannot mend its ways. It is the grey hairs, not of old age, but of good character which win praise. There is no reproach in improvement. The only thing I had in common with barbarians was that previously I did not know God.

Your sacrifice is a rite of splashing yourselves with the blood of animals. Why do you look for the voice of God in dead cattle? Come, and learn the service of heaven on earth; we live here but serve there. Let God himself who established it teach me the secret of Heaven—not man who does not know even himself. Whom should I trust more on the subject of God than God himself? How can I have confidence in you pagans who admit you are ignorant of what you worship?

He says, "Man cannot come to so profound a mystery by one road alone." The object of your ignorance we know well from the voice of God. What you seek through vague hints, we have found through the real wisdom and truth of God. Your situation, therefore, bears no relation with ours. You beg from the emperor peace for your gods; we ask Christ for peace for the emperor himself. You worship the work of your hands; we regard it as offensive that anything that can be made should be considered God. God refuses to be worshipped in stones. Besides, your own philosophers themselves laughed at those practices of yours.

You deny that Christ is God, because you do not accept that he died—you deny that his death was of the flesh alone not of his divinity, and by his death none, now, of those who believe in him shall ever die. How unwise of you, to worship in an insulting way and criticize with an honorable reproach! You think your God is of wood—what abusive respect! And you believe Christ could not die—what an honorable obstinacy!

He says that their old altars should be restored to the images, and their ornaments to the shrines. Let them be demanded by a partner in superstition. The Christian emperor has learned to honor the altar of Christ alone. Why do they force the hands of the God-fearing, the mouths of the faithful priests, to be associated with their sacrilege? Let the voice of our emperor ring with Christ, and let him speak only of the one he knows; for "the king's heart is in the hand of the Lord." Did any pagan emperor ever raise an altar to Christ? While they demand back what previously existed, they state an opinion on the basis of their own past actions on how much Christian emperors should defer to respect for the religions that they follow—seeing that then the pagans assigned all resources to their own superstitions.

Our beginning was recent and already the gods they follow are shut out. We boast of our blood, they are motivated by expense. We see this as a victory, they regard it as an injury. Never did they do us greater service than when they ordered Christians to be flogged, proscribed and killed. Religious fervor made a reward out of what they, in their delusion, thought was punishment. Look at those noble souls. Through injury, through poverty, through punishment, we grew; the pagans have no confidence in survival of their rites without subsidies.

He says, "Let the Vestal Virgins keep their exemption." This can only be said by those incapable of believing in the power of chastity without reward: let those who lack confidence in their virtue make an issue out of money. Yet how many virgins have the promised rewards created? Barely seven girls have been accepted as Vestals. See the whole number attracted together by the sacred headbands, the purple-dyed dresses, the processions on their litters surrounded by their escort of priests, the enormous privileges, the huge salary and, finally, the prescribed period of chastity.

Let them raise their vision, both of body and mind, and see a populace of modesty, a nation of uprightness, a council of chastity. Their heads are not adorned with headbands but with a veil poor in its material but noble through purity. The allurements of beauty are not sought out by them but renounced. They have no ornaments of purple, no charming luxuries, but instead the practice of fasting: no privileges, no rewards of money. In short, all their way of life is such as you might imagine would, in the performance of its duties, deter from practicing such a vocation. Yet, while their tasks are being carried out, their enthusiasm is strengthened. Purity increases by its own rewards. It is not a chastity purchased for a price but not preserved through any passion for virtue; it is not uprightness that can be sold off for money to the highest bidder. Purity's first victory is the conquest of the desire for worldly goods. Greed for money undermines the resistance of purity to temptation. Let us, nonetheless, lay down a generous sum to be doled out to virgins. What rewards can the Christians gain? What treasury is rich enough to supply such wealth? Or, if they feel the Vestals alone should be granted it, have they no shame that, although they claimed everything for themselves under pagan emperors, yet under Christian rulers these same do not believe we should have the same advantages as they?

They also complain that their own priests and sacred officials are not getting the public subsidies due to them. What a noisy protest erupted from them on this score! But we, on the other hand, were denied even the proceeds of inheritance from private individuals by recent laws, yet nobody complained; we did not consider it an injury because we do not resent financial loss. If a priest sought the privilege of being exempt from curial duty, he would have to surrender the lands of his father and grandfather and all worldly possessions. How the pagans would exaggerate that grievance, if they had it, that a priest buys his regalia for the loss of his whole patrimony, purchasing his use of public indulgence for the sacrifice of all his comforts as an individual. While observing his vigils for the general good, he may console himself with the reward of his personal poverty, because he has not sold his office but stored up grace for himself.

Compare our positions. You are prepared to exempt the decurion, although you may not exempt the priest of the Church. Wills are drawn up to benefit the ministers of the temples, no irreligious man is debarred from the right to inherit, no one of the lowest condition, no one who squanders his reputation. The cleric alone of all men is shut out from the right all have and he alone, who joins with others in prayers for the public good, is denied the public right. No bequests are allowed, even from dignified widows, and no gift. Though no stain can be found on their character, yet they are penalized for their office and their right is denied them. The legacy left by a Christian widow to priests of the pagan temple is honored; that left to the priests of God is not. I have included this point not by way of complaint but so that they should understand why I do not complain. I prefer that we should be poorer in money than poorer in grace.

Yet they maintain that gifts and legacies to the Church were not interfered with. Let them tell us for themselves which temples had their endowments confiscated, as happened to the Christians. If that had been done to the pagans, it would have been inflicting injury by way of retaliation rather than an injustice. Is it only now that they cite justice in their defense and demand fair treatment? Where was that resoluteness of theirs when all Christians were robbed of their goods, when they grudged them the bare breath of life, when they denied the dead their due and put obstacles in the way of their achieving final burial. Those whom the pagans hurled into the sea, the sea restored. The victory of the faith is this, that the pagans themselves feed on the deeds of their ancestors whose actions they condemn. Yet, alas, is it not a strange principle, to request the payments granted to those whose deeds they reject?

No one, however, has refused the shrines their gifts, or the augurs their legacies. They are only being deprived of their estates because, although they defend them on grounds of religion, they do not make use of them in a religious fashion. They exploit the parallel with us, but why not the religious function as well? The Church possesses nothing of her own except the faith. This is its revenue, this is its fruits. The property of the Church resides in the maintenance of the needy. Let the pagans list the prisoners ransomed by the temples, the sustenance they have offered to the poor, the exiles to whom they have supplied a means of livelihood. It is only their estates, therefore, that are taken from them, not their rights. . . .

Finally, emperor, there remains the most important question of all, as to whether you should restore the subsidies that have helped your own position: for he says, "Let them protect you while being worshipped by us." It is this, most faithful of emperors, that I cannot tolerate, that they make us liable to the reproach incurred by their prayer to their gods in your name, and commit a heinous impiety without your sanction, mistaking your tolerance for agreement. Let them keep their guardians for themselves. Let them protect their own followers, if they can. For, if they cannot help those by whom they are worshipped, how can they protect you who do them no honor at all?

"But," he says, "we must preserve the rites of our ancestors." . . .

Let them, therefore, say that everything should stay as it was in the beginning; they object that the world is freed from darkness because the glory of the sun has shone upon it. How much more welcome is it to dispel the darkness of the mind than of the body, for the ray of the faith to shine out than the ray of the sun? So the youth of the world, as of all things, has grown hesitant, so that the honorable old age of the faith, with its grey hair, may follow. Let those who object to this blame the harvest because its abundance comes late; let them criticize the grapes for ripening in the waning of the year; let them criticize the olive for coming last of all. . . .

They seek to set up an altar of this victory in the senate-house of the city of Rome, that is, where a substantial number of Christians meet. There are altars in all the temples, there is also an altar in the temple of the Victories. Because they get pleasure out of numbers, they perform their sacrifices all over the place. What is it but an insult to our faith to lay claim to the sacrifice of one altar? Can it be endured for a pagan to sacrifice in the presence of a Christian? Let them, he says, let them inhale the smoke through their eyes, even against their will, hear the sound of the music in their ears, feel the ash in their throats, the incense in their nostrils and let the ashes from our hearths scatter over their faces even though they turn their heads away. Is it not enough for him that his baths, his porticoes, his public squares are crowded with images? Is there to be no equality of status in that shared assembly? Shall the Christian part of the senate be choked with the cries of those calling their gods to witness, the pledges of men swearing such a faith? If he refuses to swear, he will appear to wish to lie; if he agrees, he associates himself with a sacrilege.

"Where," he asks, "shall we swear loyalty to your law and utterances?" Shall your mind, therefore, which is bound up with the laws, receive its vote and accept the guarantee of loyalty with pagan ceremonies? Now the faith not only of those present but those absent and, what is more serious, your own, emperor, is under attack; if you compel them, if you so order it. Constantius of august memory, when not yet baptized into the sacred mystery, thought that he was polluted were he to set eyes on that altar. He ordered its removal, he did not order its restoration. The former course has the weight of his action, the latter lacks that of his command. . . .

I have replied to those who attack me as though I have not been attacked. My concern has been to refute the State Paper, not to expose their superstition. But, emperor, let the State Paper itself put you on your guard. For when he constructed an argument about previous emperors, he said the earlier ones of their number worshipped with the ceremonies of their fathers and the later did not abolish them; and even added that, if the religious practice of the former did not form a precedent, the toleration of the more recent should do so. In so arguing, he has clearly taught that your duty to your faith is that you should not follow the precedent of pagan ritual, and to your family that you should not contradict your brother's decrees. For if they cited in support of their own argument the tolerance of emperors who, although Christian, did very little about abolishing pagans' decrees, how much more should you show respect for the love of your brother in not abrogating his decrees, since you should conceal disapproval even though you might happen not to approve? Thus you should now hold by the course, which in your judgment accords both with your faith and our relationship with your brother.

Source: The Latin text is found in Otto J. Faller, *Epistularum libri I–VI*, Corpus Scriptorum Ecclesiasticorum Latinorum 82 (Vienna: Austrian Academy of Sciences, 1968), and a full English translation in Brian Croke and Jill Harries, *Religious Conflict in Fourth-Century Rome* (Sydney: Sydney University Press, 1982), pp. 40–51.

to return the debt owed to Ambrose for his critical diplomacy. It is the great irony of the situation that the very system of aristocratic political patronage that Valentinian honors in refusing the senate's request, is the system that the senate was defending.

Praetextatus unexpectedly died shortly after Valentinian refused the senators' petition. Symmachus was inconsolable at the loss of his long-time friend and in grief he resigned his post as prefect. But there were to be more deputations to restore state subsidies for pagan religious practices and to restore the altar of Victory.

Ambrose, Theodosius, and the Altar of Victory

Theodosius at the Court of Milan: The Synagogue in Callinicum

In the summer of 388 C.E., Theodosius finally came to the aid of Valentinian against Maximus. After sending Valentinian with his mother Justina to Italy by sea, Theodosius traveled through Illyricum by land to meet Maximus at Aquileia. Theodosius had never been to Italy and had not been in the west for ten years. To celebrate his victory over Maximus, Valentinian and the metropolitan Ambrose must have staged a grand reception for him in Milan. Theodosius seems to have understood that this was an opportunity for him to extend his power over the weak and younger Valentinian, who was technically his senior Augustus. To that end, he was willing to

participate in the flamboyant public piety of Ambrose and to court the favor of the Roman senate.

Theodosius's grand victory reception in Milan had already turned sour by the end of 388 C.E. Only a few months after he arrived, he found himself in a no-win situation with the perspicacious Ambrose, who had no intention of losing his widespread influence regardless of who ruled as emperor. On the order of their local bishop, a group of Christians had burned a synagogue in Callinicum in Mesopotamia. When Theodosius ordered the synagogue to be rebuilt at the bishop's expense, Ambrose advised (*Epistula* 40) the emperor that it would be sacrilege to resurrect "a house of impiety, a shelter of madness under the damnation of God Himself." Ambrose had an opportunity to preach on the topic in his own cathedral in Milan. He did not waste it. The sermon is mentioned in a letter to his sister (*Epistula* 41) in which he explained that he had obliquely addressed the situation in Callinicum with the emperor in the congregation. When he came down from the pulpit, Ambrose wrote, Theodosius asked if it were he about whom Ambrose had just spoken. He then openly admitted there and then to Ambrose that he had been too harsh in his decision about the bishop's repairing the synagogue. Ambrose acknowledged that his sermon had been directed at the emperor, and he then offered to make a solemn sacrifice on his behalf. Theodosius accepted and then agreed to withdraw the edict. It was a prudent decision on the part of the emperor, but he had not yet fallen completely into the orbit of Ambrose.

Theodosius Courts the Roman Senate

In the summer of 389 C.E., eager to secure a power base in Rome, Theodosius visited the city where he presented his young son Honorius to the leading Roman senators. He showed clemency to any of the aristocratic families who had (albeit briefly) supported Maximus (including Symmachus, who had traveled to Milan to deliver a panegyric in his honor). While he was in residence at Rome, Theodosius also appointed Nicomachus Flavianus and Symmachus as praetorian prefect and consul, respectively, for the following year. It had been a congenial visit and the senators seem to have concluded from it that they could anticipate a sympathetic hearing for their request for the reinstitution of subsidies for religious cults. So, in 390 C.E., they sent another deputation to Theodosius, who was back in Milan (and perhaps still smarting from Ambrose's victory over the incident at Callinicum). Again, subsidies for the traditional pagan religious cults were refused, but this time Ambrose had been explicitly excluded from the deliberations. Theodosius's decision was not antagonistic and not motivated by any political obligation to Ambrose, but consistent with legislation prohibiting sacrifice.

Theodosius at the Court of Milan: The Massacre at Thessalonica

There were other minor battles between Ambrose and Theodosius while he main-tained his court at Milan, but the massacre at Thessalonica in the summer of 390 C.E. irrevocably changed the balance of power between them. In that incident, a Gothic leader named Butheric, a general of one of the garrisons in Thessalonica, had arrested a favored charioteer and the charioteer's fans were furious. Butheric and several generals were killed and their corpses mutilated as they were dragged through the streets. Theodosius's order for reparations may have been botched, but whether he ordered it or not Butheric's troops locked the gates of the hippodrome where some 7,000 people had thronged for the races and then slaughtered them all. Ambrose excommunicated Theodosius for his order to avenge his general and insisted that he perform public penance before he could enter the church and receive the sacraments. Theodosius accepted the penance and was received into the church on Christmas day in 390 C.E. (with great ceremony we may imagine). Whether under the influence of Ambrose or whether the emperor had his own religious or political motivations, shortly after this incident, Theodosius published several edicts that harshly curbed the traditional pagan religious practices. To add insult to injury, it was the urban prefect Ceionius Rufius Albinus, pagan senator and aristocrat, who had to enforce these new laws contravening the ancient religion. The growth of Christianity not withstanding, Rome had, until now, held its position as the conservator of traditional pagan cults.

Despite the harsh legislation, however, the senate did not yield. Perhaps sensing tension

FIGURE 5.1. *Ambrose and Theodosius. Saint Ambrose forbids Emperor Theodosius to enter the church in this painting by Antony van Dyck (1599–1641), now in the National Gallery in London.*

between Theodosius and his weaker and younger co-Augustus, they again mounted a deputation to Valentinian II, who was now in Gaul, to request subsidies for pagan religious practices. Once again, Symmachus, who was consul in 391 C.E., headed the deputation. With

Theodosius headed back to his court in the east and their nemesis Ambrose in Milan, the senate must have felt confident that Valentinian would see the advantage of strengthening his alliance with Rome. However, even though his German protector and co-ruler Arbogast was

FROM AN ANCIENT TEXT ❖ 5.5

Codex Theodosianus on Pagan Practices (391 C.E.)

Issued by Theodosius, this was the most comprehensive of all edicts limiting pagan practices. In a law of February 391 C.E. (Codex Theodosianus 16.10.10), he completely forbade pagan cults, public and private, prohibited access to temples, and meted out fines for judges who exercised their religious practices while serving in an official capacity.

Let no one pollute himself with sacrifices, let no one slaughter a mute victim, let no one approach shrines, wander through temples, or worship statues made with mortal work lest he become guilty by divine and human sanctions.

Source: Clyde Pharr, *The Theodosian Code and Novels and the Sirmondian Constitutions* (Westport, Conn.: Greenwood, 1969), pp. 472–473.

---

in favor of granting the subsidies, Valentinian again refused.

Eugenius and the Altar of Victory

Restoration of Public Subsidies

In May of 392 C.E., the twenty-year-old Valentinian II was hanged at his court in Gaul and Arbogast raised Flavius Eugenius to the throne. Eugenius immediately sought the support of Ambrose and Theodosius, who was by now back in his court in the east. Theodosius's response was to appoint his own son Honorius as his Augustus in the west and declare Eugenius a usurper; Ambrose's response was to leave Milan. Honorius was not recognized in the west, however, and Eugenius, by political necessity and by aristocratic disposition, allied himself with a willing Roman senate. Although he was himself a Christian, Eugenius was a rhetorician, trained in classical texts and educated in an aristocratic culture. Knowing that reconciliation with Theodosius was hopeless, he did not want to alienate either his Christian supporters or the pagan senators, so he attempted a compromise solution on the question of subsidies for pagan cults. He agreed to funnel funds from his own resources to individual senators so that they could finance traditional cult practices. Upon receiving the funds, Virius Nicomachus Flavianus, prefect of Italy, with his son Nicomachus Flavianus, prefect of Rome, immediately undertook the construction of numerous temples and shrines and the restoration of their priesthoods and cult practices. Other pagan practices were also resurrected: several festivals, including that of Attis and Cybele, and the grand Megalensian Games were celebrated in Rome in the spring of 394 C.E., despite the fact that Theodosius had removed all pagan festivals from the calendar during his visit to Rome in 389 C.E.

(*Codex Theodosianus* 2.8.19). Symmachus himself in this exhilarating atmosphere of renewed pagan festivals sponsored public games in honor of his son's quaestorship.

The Statue of Winged Victory Restored

In 394 C.E., Theodosius defeated Eugenius in what some have called the last great pagan battle. All along the battle line on the Frigidus River in northern Italy, Flavianus had set up statues to the Roman gods, especially Jupiter, and the army carried images of Hercules among its standards. If Eugenius had restored the altar of Victory when he restored the subsidies for pagan religious rites, Theodosius must have removed it again when he defeated

FIGURE 5.2. *Diptych of the Nicomachi and Symmachi. Commissioned by Symmachus, this fourth-century ivory diptych recalls the brief revival of Roman religion under Eugenius. The panels are located in the Musée de Cluny and the Victoria and Albert Museum respectively.*

Eugenius. Of this, however, we cannot be sure: in 404 C.E., the court poet Claudius Claudianus in his poem on the sixth consulship of Honorius (vv. 597–602) wrote of Honorius's triumphal entry into Rome. He described a statue of a winged victory, which he called Rome's guardian, in her temple (presumably the *Curia*) with her golden wings stretched out in protection.

Although Claudian may have been speaking here only of the statue of Victory, it is tempting to wonder whether he considered the two—the statue of Victory and her altar—as one and the same. When Claudian wrote of the statue of Victory he might have intended his readers also to understand the altar of Victory, whose vicissitudes under the late-fourth century Christian emperors we have tracked in this chapter. Whether or not the altar of Victory was in the *Curia*, Claudian had the Christian Honorius pay homage to her *numen*, "divinity." By this period, such homage transcended religious factions. The *numina* of the Roman gods and goddesses had moved into the realm of the shared cultural traditions of the late antique pagan senatorial aristocracy and their Christian rulers. *Roma aeterna* was no longer a viable political idea so much as a faded ideal.

Conclusion

This chapter began with Ammianus Marcellinus's description of Constantius II's first visit to Rome in 357 C.E. Constantius was dazzled by the pagan splendor of ancient Rome and to commemorate his visit he dedicated an ancient (pagan) obelisk in the Circus Maximus. Yet, he had also passed legislation against pagan religious practices and closed pagan temples. Imperial subsidies for the traditional religions were withdrawn, and he even removed the altar of Victory from the Roman *Curia*.

A focused study of the important literary exchange concerning the removal of the altar of Victory forms the core of this chapter. In this exchange, the Christian bishop Ambrose and the Roman senator Symmachus presented written arguments to successive emperors over whether to return the altar of Victory to the Roman *Curia*. In their smooth eloquence Ambrose and Symmachus compete not so much for the cause of religion as imperial favor, and they both rely upon the same classical literary training that was at the center of the pagan heritage that the altar of Victory represented. After each delegation from the senate, the emperors decided in favor of Ambrose and refused to subsidize pagan religious celebrations or return the altar of Victory. More than any religious impetus, what persuaded the emperors Gratian and then Valentinian II to bow to the demands of the Christian bishop Ambrose rather than the pagan Symmachus had more to do with the weakness of the imperial court in the face of political revolt.

Ambrose had proved himself to be an effective benefactor and indispensable patron of the court. He was himself a member of the well-educated senatorial aristocracy. In several critical situations, he used his power and patronage and his privileged classical education on behalf of the emperors. In turn, the emperors gave him leave to use that same power and education to suppress the traditional religious cults practiced by his fellow (pagan) aristocrats in Rome. It is ironic that the very same rhetorical training that Symmachus deployed in his arguments to restore the altar, Ambrose also deployed to oppose its restoration. They shared alike in the classical heritage that the altar symbolized.

STUDY QUESTIONS

1   What were the basic tenets of Arianism and how did these conflict with the principles espoused by "orthodox" Christianity?

2   Based on what we know from sources such as Ambrose, Symmachus, and the *Codex Theodosianus*, what policies did Gratian enact to weaken and marginalize Rome's pagan senatorial aristocracy?

3   Briefly outline the events surrounding the altar of Victory controversy, beginning with the reign of Constantius II and ending with the reign of Theodosius. Why was the altar a source of tension between pagans and Christians?

4   Using the texts contained in this chapter and the bibliographic resources provided at the end of the book, conduct further research into the various arguments which Symmachus and Ambrose raise in favor of, and against, keeping the altar of Victory in the *Curia*. Which arguments do you find to be more convincing?

5   Using the bibliographic resources provided at the end of this book, conduct further research into the "last great pagan battle" between Eugenius and Theodosius. Discuss its symbolic, political, and religious importance as a turning point in the ascendancy of Christianity.

Chapter 6

CONCLUSION
The Christian Church through the Centuries— Conflict and Accommodation

The Apostolic Church through the Edict of Theodosius in 391 C.E.

In these five chapters we have traced the foundation and spread of Christianity, which began in the first century C.E. as a small sect of Jewish followers of Jesus, considered the Messiah. Jesus was born in the early years of the Roman Empire in Judea, where the Herods ruled as client kings of Rome. The Jews resented their Roman overlords and the Herods, their puppet client kings, and that resentment festered into open conflict. A growing divide between the new Christian sect and the more traditional Jews exacerbated the antagonism between the Jews and the Romans. Many Jews considered the Christian Jews heretical, especially as their

sect began to accept converts from among the gentiles who did not have the same devotion to the Torah and Mosaic Law. Paul, a Pharisee who was originally one of the traditionalist Jews who had persecuted the Christian Jews, was converted dramatically (he believed that he experienced a theophany) to Christianity while traveling on the road to Damascus from Jerusalem. From that time, Paul began to preach the word of Jesus. He has been called the "apostle to the gentiles" because he extended his mission beyond the Jews in and around Jerusalem and traveled to synagogues all over the empire. These kinds of antagonisms and open confrontations between Christians and non-Christians have resurfaced many times in subsequent centuries of church history, most significantly in the wars between Muslims and Christians, and in the hostilities between Jews and Christians and among rivaling Christianities.

By the end of the first century C.E., the church had spread throughout the Roman Empire and beyond. It had definitively split from Judaism and, according to legend, the apostles Peter and Paul had traveled to Rome where they jointly ministered and preached the new religion of Christianity. Christians were monotheists who believed that Jesus was the Messiah sent by God the Father to die for their sins; they could worship no other god. Their long period of struggle with, and persecution by, the Romans stems from this belief. Christian doctrine forbade them to worship the gods of the state that, according to Roman religious belief, safeguarded the state's and the emperor's well-being. These struggles between the Romans and the Christians resulted in sporadic and systematic persecution, especially under Diocletian from 303–313 C.E. Similar confrontations and religious persecutions in the church have re-emerged since that time, and, in some cases, these "holy wars" have engendered similar violence.

In 313 C.E., Constantine, the first "Christian" emperor, issued the Edict of Milan, which legalized Christianity. Almost immediately, doctrinal controversies plagued the church. One of the earliest of these controversies was called Arianism after the presbyter Arius who argued that the Father had created the Son and that, therefore, the Son was not co-eternal with the Father. This teaching was antithetical to the orthodox belief that the Father and Son were of the same substance and co-eternal. When Theodosius assumed the throne in 379 C.E., his first edict unequivocally required that the entire empire practice orthodox Catholicism as it had been defined at the Council of Nicea in 325 C.E. He pointed to Pope Damasus of Rome, the apostolic see of Peter and Paul, as an example of this orthodoxy. Theodosius's unilateral legislation in church matters set the stage for the medieval and modern conflicts concerning the separation of church and state. Moreover, his claim that the Christianity of Rome in the person of the pope was the only orthodox practice anticipated debates concerning the primacy of Rome and the infallibility of the pope that still confront the church hierarchy.

By the time Theodosius gave legal sanction to Christianity in 391 C.E., Rome was the episcopal see of the new Christian capital and the polytheistic religions of antiquity were cultural rather than religious phenomena. In the historical period called the Renaissance, the Christian church appropriated the classical pagan heritage into a program of didactic Christian art. This blending of pagan and Christian iconography when coupled with the church's political and religious dominance recalled the fourth-century controversy between the pagan and Christian aristocracy and anticipated the Protestant Reformation.

Indeed, these same controversies that we have traced in these chapters—conflicts between Christians and other religious groups, competing theological doctrines among different Christian sects, tensions between the church and secular rulers, the primacy of Rome, and the cultural heritage of antiquity—survive in various ways in the late antique, medieval, and modern church. This chapter will consider some of the consequences of these early conflicts as they re-emerge in the medieval and modern church.

The Church in Late Antiquity

Islam and Christianity

In the late antique period of the church, Justinian (482–565 C.E.) ruled the Byzantine or eastern Roman Empire, reasserting an imperial dominion that rivaled that of the ancient empire. He subdued Germanic tribes in the west, especially in North Africa and Italy, and in the east was able to conclude a long-lasting peace with the Persians. His famous Latin compilation of all Roman law, called the *Corpus iuris civilis*, "Corpus of Civil Law," contained statutes requiring universal orthodox Christian worship and the suppression of all religious rituals associated with paganism. Judaism was also suppressed. Jews were forbidden to use Hebrew in the synagogues and those who did not comply were forced to convert. His insistence upon orthodoxy led to attacks against heretics and extended privileges for the clergy and monastic communities. Justinian was despotic in his attempts to ensure harmony between the eastern and western bishops, but in the end the fractious Christian sects were more concerned with the growing strength of Islam as the Muslims conquered more and more territory.

Islam (from the Arabic word for "surrender") is the monotheistic Abrahamic religion that developed in the seventh century and was based upon the teaching of Muhammad (570–632 C.E.), whom the Muslims claim is the final prophet (after Abraham, Moses, and Jesus) of God, and the one to whom he revealed his teachings in the Islamic holy book called the Qu'ran. As God's prophet, Muhammad united several tribes under Islamic law, and by the time of his death Islam had spread over the entire Arabian Peninsula, the area that comprises the modern Arab Gulf States. Islam continued to spread, both by violence and by peaceful proselytizing, but when the Muslims gained the territory of the Holy Land and had spread deep into Christian Europe, Pope Urban II (1088–1099 C.E.) convened the Council of Clermont (1095 C.E.) to respond to this territorial aggression. At that council he called for all the "knights of Christendom" to defend the Holy Land and stop the "pagans" and "infidels" who had attacked their fellow Christians, the Greeks. Pope Urban called this march a pilgrimage and promised that whoever made a vow to God and wore a sign of the cross on his forehead or breast and took up this cause would have his sins forgiven and would enjoy eternal life. These military crusades were carried on between 1095 and 1291 C.E., but they were not restricted to aggressions against Muslims. En route to the Holy Land, the crusaders also killed Jews and eastern Christians whom they considered schismatic. In 1202 C.E., Innocent III launched the Fourth Crusade. The crusaders never reached the Holy Land but instead sacked Constantinople, the capital of the Byzantine Empire, and established the Latin empire of Constantinople. This violent offensive left a legacy of distrust and contempt for the western church throughout much of the eastern empire.

Medieval Christianity

East-West Schism

The sack of Constantinople was the ultimate outrage in a series of political and doctrinal disputes that ended in the division of eastern and western Christendom into two separate Christianities—the Roman Catholic Church and the Eastern Orthodox Church. The east and the west had been separating since the fall of the western empire in the fifth century. When the west fell to barbarian invaders, the Byzantine Empire had continued to flourish. This political separation was soon strengthened by a linguistic separation: the *lingua franca* of the east was Greek, and that of the west, Latin. In the ninth century, after the pope intervened in a dispute between rival patriarchs in the east, the political schism intensified. In the eleventh century, when Pope Leo IX (1049–1054 C.E.) replaced the eastern bishops ministering in southern Italy with western bishops, Patriarch Cerularius responded by closing all western churches in Constantinople. Pope Leo had also demanded that the patriarch insert the word *filioque*, "and the son," into the Nicene Creed, to harmonize their discrepant doctrines of the Holy Spirit—the eastern church did not believe that the Holy Spirit came from the father and the

son (*filioque*). By the time a papal legate from Pope Leo excommunicated the patriarch of Constantinople in 1054 C.E., the rift had already become irreparable. Added to this series of indignations, the sack of Constantinople was an unforgiveable transgression.

Although there were attempts to reunite the two churches, in the Second Council of Lyon (1274 C.E.) and in the Council of Florence (1439 C.E.), the two sides could not overcome the centuries of ill will and mutual slights. Today, the eastern (Holy Oriental Orthodox Apostolic Church, usually called the Orthodox or Oriental) church and the western (Roman Catholic) church share most doctrinal canons, as well as the Nicene Creed (except for the word *filioque*). Moreover, the Orthodox Church shares many practices and conventions with the Catholic Church. The eastern church has a rich tradition of Mariolatry, Marian worship, although its members do not believe in the Immaculate Conception proclaimed as dogma in 1854 C.E.; they believe in the saints, whose images (but not statues) they worship, and they venerate relics; they require good works as a justification of faith; they teach the same seven sacraments; they share baptismal regeneration; and they believe in transubstantiation (that the consecrated bread and wine truly becomes the body and blood of Christ during the Mass) and the efficacy of prayers for the dead. However, they do not believe in the universal authority and infallibility of the pope. We have seen that this issue had its origins in the late fourth-century papacy of Damasus, who claimed apostolic primacy for the see of Rome and, by extension, the papacy.

Since that time, in different periods and in various circumstances the authority of the pope has continued to be a source of friction in east-west relations as well as in relations between the pope and secular leaders.

Investiture Controversy

The most important medieval example of the separation of the powers of church and state is the eleventh-century Investiture Controversy, sometimes called the Lay Investiture Controversy. "Investiture" is the ritual of appointing church officials. The term is derived from the Latin *investire*, "to clothe," because the bishop was invested with the mitre (ceremonial headdress) and the crozier (pastoral staff), as symbols of his episcopacy. The German king and Holy Roman Emperor Henry IV (1050–1108 C.E.) and Pope Gregory VII (c. 1020–1085 C.E.) disagreed over who would invest, or ceremonially appoint, bishops. At stake were the proceeds from the bishoprics. If the king appointed the bishops then he controlled the lands of the bishopric and could even claim the proceeds from those lands in the event of a vacant bishopric. The church wanted to ensure that the papacy had control of the lands of the bishopric and the proceeds from the land even when the bishopric was vacant. The church also wanted to curb simony (the purchase of ecclesiastical offices), something that lay investiture encouraged.

Gregory maintained that papal power was received from God directly and that no one but the pope had the authority to appoint churchmen. In 1075 C.E., he asserted in an edict (*Dictatus Papae*) that only the pope could appoint or depose bishops. He forbade investiture by laymen. But from the early medieval period, it had been the king's right to invest churchmen with their office. Henry's reaction (1075 C.E.), therefore, was to depose Gregory. Gregory immediately (1076 C.E.) responded in kind and excommunicated Henry. For complex political reasons, Henry backed down. In his famous "Walk to Canossa," Henry received absolution after a public penance: he walked barefoot in snow wearing only a hairshirt.

The controversy over lay investiture continued for over fifty years and resulted in a diminution of imperial power in favor of papal authority. This medieval controversy changed the equilibrium that the secular and ecclesiastical powers had established by relying upon the same justification the western bishops had used against Constantius II, when he insisted that they accept an Arian christology—the separation of church and state—with the same outcome.

Inquisitions

By the thirteenth century, the heresy of Catharism, a sect similar to Manicheism, had spread across Europe. In response, the church appointed special councils, called Inquisitions, to investigate all offenses against the church, but especially to root out heresies like Catharism, and punish them. Heretics convicted by an Inquisition could confess and spend time in prison or remain obstinate and be burned at the stake. In the latter case, the secular authorities stepped in to carry out the sentence.

The Spanish Inquisition was separate from the more general papal Inquisitions. In Spain, there were violent persecutions of Jews and Muslims, who were forced to convert to Catholicism in large numbers. In 1492, King Ferdinand and Queen Isabella issued the Alhambra decree that ordered all of some 40,000 Jews to convert or leave their kingdom. Once they had converted, they might be accused of having pretended to convert for political expediency when in reality they were continuing to practice their own religions. These false converts were called *conversos*, "new Christians." The Inquisition set about identifying the *conversos* by compiling a list of signs. These signs, such as refusing to prepare food on Saturday, the Jewish Sabbath, indicated which *conversos* had lapsed back into Judaism. Like the Jews, Muslims were exiled or forced to convert, and like the Jews, if they did convert they were regarded with great suspicion. By some estimate the number of Muslims and Jews forced to migrate was more than a million.

In 1542, the pope established the Congregation for the Doctrine of Faith to supervise the Inquisitions. It was this body that censured Copernicus for his heliocentric theory (that the earth is one of a group of planets that revolves around the sun) and, in 1633, banned Galileo's works on suspicion of heresy. Pope John Paul II, in 1992, publicly apologized for the Inquisition's condemnation of Galileo, but, as we have seen, violent persecution and martyrdom were regrettable signifiers even of the early church, from the Maccabees to Diocletian.

Reformation and Counter-Reformation

Martin Luther

The year 1517 was a great turning point in the history of the church. On October 31 in that year, Martin Luther (1483–1546), a German Augustinian monk, posted his *Ninety-Five Theses on the Power of Indulgences* on the door of Castle Church in Wittenburg, Germany, to protest the corruption of the papacy. He was reacting to Pope Leo X's promulgation of indulgences (an official pardon for a sin committed) for building the Basilica of San Pietro in Rome. He and other restorers protested against a variety of frustrations including the primacy of the pope, abuses like simony and nepotism, and the secularism of the papacy, especially with regard to art. Luther also advocated the dissolution of the monasteries. Monasticism was one of the most important developments in the early and medieval church. It emphasized spirituality and asceticism, the renunciation of worldly pursuits in either an eremitical, "desert" or "solitary," community or a cenobitic, "in common," community. Luther felt that these religious communities were corrupt corporate entities more concerned with financial gain than with the virtues that the monastic life was supposed to enhance: poverty, chastity, and obedience. Above all, Luther and the other reformers wanted to restore the church to the "true gospel," to what they considered the singular and unique truth—the Bible. They sought to substitute the authority of the scriptures for the authority of the pope and all his councils. For this reason, Protestantism has been termed "evangelical" Christianity, because it looks back to the *evangelion*, the "good news" of the gospel.

Two Branches of Western Christendom

We can characterize these two branches of Christianity by contrasts. In general, the Catholic Church was conservative and the Protestant progressive. The Catholic Church was hierarchical and the Protestant more democratic and spiritual, with direct access to the Bible, the word of God, without any mediators. One achieved by ascetic and monastic models what the other achieved by a secular social morality. The Catholic Church incorporated oral tradition and extra-doctrinal teaching; Protestantism insisted upon the gospel alone. The Protestant reformers also rejected the lavish ceremonial trappings of the Catholic Church, all the splendid displays of pomp and wealth that attended Catholic rituals and worship, and, especially, the theatricality of papal processions. The legacy of the pagan classical triumphal processions and emperor worship that the church hierarchy had appropriated as early as the reign of Constantine was repudiated in favor of a more simple worship.

Protestantism spread quickly, which was perhaps as indicative of the widespread dissatisfaction with the Catholic Church as of the appeal of the new Christianity. From Germany it spread to northern and eastern Europe and had reached England, Scotland, and then the Americas by the seventeenth century. The invention of printing aided the dissemination of Protestant teaching, and it also made more widely available the Greek Bible so that wor-

shippers could approach the text to form their own spiritual relationship with God, separate from the church hierarchy. Within the movement, several separate traditions formed, like the Calvinist, Lutheran, and the Anglican, which has been called a reformed Catholic rather than a Protestant church.

The Reformation in England was at first staunchly repudiated by King Henry VIII, who defended the papacy. Yet, he defied the authority of the papacy when Pope Clement VII refused (for political reasons more than theological) to annul his marriage to Catherine of Aragon so that he could marry Anne Boleyn. Without papal sanction, Henry VIII was powerless to remarry. His dispute led to the creation of the Anglican (from the Latin *Anglia*, "England") Church in 1531 with the King at its head. Not long after (1540), Henry exercised his power as the head of the Church of England to dissolve the monasteries. He confiscated the lands and wealth of centuries—manuscripts, silver, gold, precious vestments, relics, and gems—and distributed much of it among the nobility, to ensure their support.

Erasmus

In his *Theses*, Luther put forth the germ of a personal spiritual reformation. His contemporary, the Dutchman Desiderius Erasmus of Rotterdam (1466–1536), saw this as the particular competence of education. Erasmus represented the epitome of liberal reform based upon classical and patristic scholarship. He was devoted to the ideals of the humanist traditions and sought to extend the publication of classical texts to include a critical edition of the Greek New Testament (1516). He also produced an accompanying copy of Jerome's *Vulgate*, so that scholars could read the two side by side and observe errors, many of which had been uncontested since the first appearance of Jerome's *Vulgate*. Erasmus remained a Catholic all of his life, even while criticizing the excesses of the church. An itinerant and independent scholar, he sought to liberalize the church through literature and satire rather than by doctrinal debates. His best-known work is the *Praise of Folly*, a satire that pokes fun at its traditions and excesses but does not openly criticize the Catholic Church or call for its reform. Erasmus was not a Protestant reformer, nor was he entirely a secular humanist, but he seemed to straddle those movements in ways that are similar to his ecclesiastical contemporary, Julius II, whose papacy also straddled the secular and ecclesiastical.

Pope Julius II (1443–1513) exemplified the Renaissance papacy. A politician first, he was also a great patron of art. Through his patronage a deliberate program of art associated the cultural and political achievements of ancient Rome with his papacy. Julian inspired a new humanism that was drawn from Rome's classical pagan heritage to justify his secular reign. In private and public architectural projects, Julius immortalized classical antiquity by commissioning the work of great artists like Michelangelo, Raphael, Bernini, Borromini, and Leonardo da Vinci in several magnificent building projects that have come to symbolize a renewed papacy and renewed links with the past.

Erasmus and Julius II, in different ways, both sought to bring the glory of the ancient past back to life. Their scholarly and artistic enterprises involved the collaboration of artists, intellectuals, and patrons in a new civility that helped to create a classical renaissance in a Christian world.

Counter-Reformation

In response to the Reformation, the Catholic Church convened the Council of Trent (1545–1563), the nineteenth ecumenical council. While the council asserted many traditional Catholic doctrines, it also undertook to reform the church through renewed missionary activity and a new spirit of collaboration between the clergy and the laity. The church could boast its venerable antiquity, its centralized organization, and a polished and expressive ceremonial ritual. These were still attractions. The council reaffirmed the traditional doctrines such as the veneration of relics and saints, the concept of faith and good works together as a means to Christian salvation, clerical celibacy, purgatory, transubstantiation, and the seven sacraments; the council also regularized the Mass, now called the Tridentine Mass, from *Tridentum*, the Latin name for the city Trent. Perhaps most importantly, the council insisted that the church's interpretation of the Bible (rather than any individual's interpretation) as well as church dogma and tradition were accepted equally. Protestantism was uncompromisingly rejected. Through the restoration of ecclesiastical discipline and through the widespread reforms in pastoral care that were affirmed by the council, the church was able to regain many reformers and extend its influence into Asia and the Americas.

The Church in the Modern World

Ecumenism

As a result of the reiterative schisms and reform movements we have only touched upon in the discussion above, there are three main branches of Christianity in the modern world: the Roman Catholic Church, Eastern Orthodox churches, and Protestant churches. Fundamentally, the Bible binds all three but there is a wide range of doctrinal differences and ritual distinctions among them. In recent centuries, the Industrial Revolution, fascism, communism, and fundamentalism have further segmented Christian communities, which are for the most part considered denominations of an overarching Christian church.

In contrast to the prevalence of discord that has characterized the Christian church since its inception, the dominant modern trend in intra-Christian dialogue is toward ecumenism, or universality (from the Greek *oikoumene*, "belonging to the whole world"), a movement to establish a unity of Christians. Since the conclusion of the Second Ecumenical Council of the Vatican, or Vatican II (1962–1965), the largest council of Catholic bishops convened in the history of the church, a spirit of ecumenism has called all Christians of all denominations to engage in common efforts to relieve suffering and effect social change. The Catholic Church has been particularly concerned with catholic moral teaching on capital punishment, the right to life, contraception, and homosexuality. The ordination of women and same-sex unions are among the issues that particularly preoccupy Protestant denominations and the Anglican Church. But all Christians have come to new ecumenical understandings of the sacraments, ministry, and the Eucharist. The Roman Catholic Church and the Eastern Orthodox Church remain divided on the question of the celibacy of the clergy but there have been many conciliatory overtures since the pope and the patriarch of Constantinople rescinded their mutual excommunications in 1965. Ecumenism, the most modern movement in the church, seeks what is essential and common to all Christians. For this, the study of the literary and cultural remains of classical antiquity is a profoundly relevant heritage.

STUDY QUESTIONS

1   Create a list detailing the similarities and differences between the eastern (Holy Oriental Orthodox Apostolic) church, and the western (Roman Catholic) church.

2   What are the origins of the schism between east and west?

3   Discuss the inquisitions that arose in Europe during the Medieval and Renaissance periods. What was the impetus behind such persecutions? Are there any parallels between the inquisitions and the persecutions in the early church?

4   What were Martin Luther's main grievances with the Roman Catholic Church? What changes did Protestant reformers suggest to return the church to a "pure" state?

5   Using the bibliographic resources provided at the end of this book as well as other sources, conduct further research into the artistic programs of Julius II. How is it that the identity of the Catholic Church comes to be identified with the ancient (pagan) Roman Empire under which it had been persecuted?

Acta Martyrum: The Latin for the "Acts of the Martyrs," this is the corpus of Christian literature dealing with martyrdom, beginning in the second century. Some of the genuine *Acta* (also called martyrologies) are official accounts of the trial and condemnation of Christians; others are accounts by eyewitnesses or other contemporary sources.

Apocalypse: From the Greek *apokalupsis*, "lifting up," the term refers to the supposed revelation (Apocalypse) of future things made to Saint John on the island of Patmos and preserved in the Revelation to John, the final book in the New Testament.

Apologetics: From the Greek *apologia*, "formal defense," this collection of early Christian Greek and Latin texts attempted to explain and defend the Christian faith, especially against charges levied by Jews and pagans.

Apostle: From the Greek *apostolos*, meaning "sent away," the term usually refers to the twelve Christian apostles who were Jewish men sent away on a mission by Jesus to teach his word.

Apostasy: From the Greek *apostasis*, "stand apart," the term refers to someone who has renounced a religious belief.

Apocrypha: From the Greek *apokrypha*, "hidden things," these are religious texts written between 200 B.C.E. and 100 C.E. and received from the Septuagint rather than the Hebrew scriptures. They have been variously considered canonical, quasi-scriptural, or non-canonical.

Aramaic: A Semitic language with documents dating from the ninth century B.C.E., Aramaic was the *lingua franca*, "common language," of the Near East (Palestine, Syria, parts of Asia, and Egypt) from about the seventh century B.C.E. through the seventh century C.E., although it ceased to be used in a uniform way from the second century B.C.E., when it divided into eastern and western dialects.

Ascension: According to Acts 1:3, the ascension of Jesus into heaven forty days after he was crucified and rose from the tomb. In some accounts (Luke 24:50-53), Jesus ascended on the same day as the Resurrection; by legend, the Ascension occurred in the Mount of Olives and the liturgical celebration of the feast is celebrated with a procession commemorating Jesus' journey there.

Canon: From the Greek *kanon,* "straight rod," the term refers to the authoritative list of books accepted as sacred and constituting the Christian Bible.

Christ: From the Greek *Christos,* "anointed," which in Hebrew is "Messiah," Christ is the savior Christians believe was prophesied in the Hebrew Bible. His sermons and teachings form the basis of Christian doctrine.

Chi-Rho Symbol, also called the *Labarum*: The Christian monogram and military standard adopted by Constantine, comprised of the first two letters (X and R) of the Greek χριστός (*Christos*).

Crucifixion: From the Latin *crux* and *figo,* "to affix to a cross," this extreme punishment in the early Christian period was death by being nailed to a cross. All four gospels record the crucifixion of Jesus between two thieves. According to John 19:19, Pontius Pilate nailed a placard on the top of Jesus' cross with the acronym INRI, *Iesus Nazarenus Rex Iudaeorum,* "Jesus of Nazareth King of the Jews."

Codex Theodosianus: The codification in 438 c.e. of all general laws enacted from the time of the reign of Constantine (306– 337 c.e.) arranged chronologically in sixteen books. Book 16 contains the laws that banned paganism.

Council of Nicea (325 c.e.): The First Ecumenical Council, convened by Constantine to settle the Arian controversy and the date of the celebration of Easter. The Nicene Creed was formulated and included the term *homoousios,* which means "of like substance" or "consubstantial," to describe the essential unity of God the Father and his Son.

Curia: The Latin word for "court," from the time of Julius Caesar it was the name of the senate house in Rome.

Dea Roma: The Latin words for "Goddess Rome," this goddess was the personification of Rome acknowledged with cultic worship.

Dead Sea Scrolls: Composed by a Judaic sect in the desert area of Qumran and discovered in several caves in Wadi Qumran in 1947, these scrolls detail the eschatological movement of this monastic community who believed they were called to prepare the way of the Lord in the wilderness (Isa 40:3-11).

Diaspora: From the Greek *diaspeirein* meaning "to scatter," the word refers to the scattering of the Jews outside the area of Palestine and among the gentiles, after the Babylonian exile.

Disciple: From the Latin word *discipulus,* "learner," the word refers to someone who spreads the word or doctrine of another. From specific reference to the Twelve Apostles, it came to mean a follower of

Jesus who received instructions and then spread the word of God as a teacher.

Docetism: From the Greek *dokein*, which means "to seem," this doctrine was adopted by the Gnostics and claimed that Jesus only existed spiritually and therefore only seemed to die on the cross.

Episcopus: This Latin form shifts from the meaning of the Greek word *episkopos*, "overseer," to mean a spiritual overseer, or bishop.

Eschatology: From the Greek *eschatos* and *logos*, this "doctrine of last things" could be applied to both individuals and humanity. This theme of expectation among Christians anticipated the end of the world and the final judgment and salvation.

Ethnarch: From the Greek *ethnarches*, "leaders of a nation," this term refers to governors or leaders of a province or a people.

Eucharist: From the Greek *eucharistos*, "thanksgiving," this is the central rite in Christian churches in which bread and wine are consecrated and shared, called communion, in memory of the Last Supper of Jesus.

Excommunication: From the Latin *excommunicare*, "to exclude from the community," the term comes to mean "to exclude from the Christian sacraments" and "from the community of the faithful."

Filioque: A Latin word meaning "and [from] the Son," which was attached to the Nicene Creed by the western church in 589 C.E. to assert that the Holy Spirit proceeded from both the Father and the Son. The "*filioque* clause" was not accepted in the eastern church, and the debate over the doctrine contributed to the schism of 1054 C.E.

Gentiles: From the Latin *gens*, "nation," this term refers to people of a non-Jewish faith or nation, especially belonging to the Christians as distinguished from the Jews. Synonyms include "heathen" and "pagan."

Gnosticism: From the Greek *gnosis*, "knowledge," this religious tradition emphasizes knowledge and dualism as interpreted by several religious and philosophical traditions to ensure enlightenment and salvation.

Gospel: From the Old English *god spell*, "good news," the term translates the Greek *euaggelion* and refers to the message of the redemption of the world through Jesus. The term may apply to the four canonical gospels (Matthew, Mark, Luke, and John) of the New Testament, which describe the life, ministry, and resurrection of Jesus, or to the entire New Testament.

Hagiography: From the Greek *hagiographe*, "sacred writing," these biographical texts focus on the lives of saints and martyrs. Usually idealized, they are based upon martyrologies, calendars, poems, studies, and liturgical evidence.

Hebrew: From the Greek word *Hebraios*, which means "one from the other side (of the river)," a member of the ancient people living in what is now Israel. Hebrew is also the Semitic language of the Hebrews in its ancient or modern forms.

Hellenism: From the Greek *Hellenismos*, "imitation of Greek," Hellenism refers to the national Greek culture broadly understood to include their approach to knowledge, an approach that focused upon humanistic and classical ideals including, but not limited to, the pursuit of the arts, moderation, civic responsibility, and body development.

Henotheism: From the Greek *hen-* and *theos*, "one divinity," henotheism refers to the worship of one god without denying the existence of others.

Heresy: From the Greek *hairesis*, which means "choice," heresy came to mean a theological error or belief in an error in matters of faith.

Homily: From later Latin, *homilia*, "speech to the people," a homily is a sermon that offers an elucidation or edifying explanation of scripture.

Hoc signo vinces: The Latin words for "by this sign you will conquer," these words appeared to Constantine in a vision together with the chi-rho symbol and were interpreted as a sign for him to pray to the Christian God for victory against Maxentius at the Battle of the Milvian Bridge in 312 C.E.

Jew: A member of the people whose traditional religion is Judaism, Jews descend from the tribe of Judah whose trace origins are from the ancient Hebrew people of Israel, descendents of Abraham.

Judea: The region occupied by the Jews when they returned from the Babylonian exile in 537 B.C.E., and later, in the time of Jesus, the southern part of Palestine, north of Idumea, west of the Jordan River, and south of Samaria.

Kerygma: From the Greek *kerugma*, which means "to proclaim," kerygma is the preaching of the Christian gospels and refers especially to the original Christian gospel preached by the apostles.

Maccabees: A biblical text named for the second-century B.C.E. family of Jewish patriots who organized a revolt against the Hellenizing Seleucid Antiochus IV Epiphanes. 1 and 2 Maccabees are considered deutero-canonical, that is, from the second canon, because they were not included in the Hebrew Bible but are known from the Greek Septuagint.

Messiah: From Hebrew and Aramaic, often translated as the expected king and deliverer of the world, the Messiah is the promised liberator of the Jewish nation prophesied in the Hebrew Bible. For Christians, the term also refers specifically to Jesus whom they regard as the Messiah who was prophesied.

Mithraism: A widespread Roman mystery cult of the first four centuries C.E. whose followers were exclusively male and usually soldiers, and they worshipped *Sol Invictus Mithras* ("the invincible sun-god Mithras") whose cult-image was represented as a relief on the wall of the meeting place (*mithraeum*) in the act of slaying a bull, a symbol of death and rebirth.

Nag Hammadi Library: A collection of Greek and Coptic papyri codices with mostly Gnostic texts found in 1945 in a jar buried in the Egyptian desert near the city of Nag Hammadi, an area populated in late antiquity by Christian monks.

Oxyrhynchus Papyri: An important collection of papyri discovered in 1897 and dating from the first century B.C.E. to the seventh century C.E., from the late antique monastic center at Oxyrhynchus (modern Behnesa). The collection includes official documents, Greek and Latin literary texts, and a range of early Christian texts, documents, calendars, and hymns.

Pagan: From the later Latin *paganus*, "country dweller," this term refers generally to those who practiced the ancient polytheistic worship of a pantheon of gods. While it cannot be understood as an ancient religion, it was used generally (and, perhaps, erroneously) of anyone who was not a Christian.

Panegyric: A speech or poem of praise delivered on the occasion of an important event. Constantine was the subject of several panegyrics during his reign and his important "pagan vision" is described in a panegyric delivered in 310 C.E. to celebrate his *Quinquennalia*, "five years of rule."

Relic: From the Latin *reliquiae*, "remains," the material remains of a saint and the objects that were in contact with the body are called relics. The veneration of relics was founded in the belief that the special relationship with God enjoyed by martyrs and saints could be extended to believers through worship of their relics.

Resurrection: The bodily resurrection of Jesus on the third day after his crucifixion and burial. This doctrine of belief gave rise to the doctrine of the resurrection of the faithful to eternal life in God's presence.

Sacrament: From the Latin *sacramentum*, "sacred mystery," this series of rituals are believed to have been instituted by Jesus to allow the faithful to symbolically participate in the sacred mysteries. In Christian theology the seven sacraments as codified in the twelfth century and affirmed at the Council of Trent (1545–63) are: baptism, confirmation, holy communion, confession, marriage, holy orders, anointing of the sick.

Sanhedrin: From the Greek *sunedrion*, which means "sitting together," the Sanhedrin was the council of priests who met in the Temple and acted as a legislative body. Jesus and Paul were both condemned before the Sanhedrin.

Schism: From later Latin *schisma*, "separation," the term refers to a division among members of a religious body over a doctrinal or theological issue.

See: From the Latin *sedes*, "seat," the official seat of a bishop, which is usually in the main cathedral (from the Greek *kathedra*, "chair") of a diocese. The ecclesiastical region under the care of a bishop is called his "see."

Septuagint: From Latin *septuaginta* (often abbreviated LXX), this term derives from a legendary account of how the Greek King of Egypt, Ptolemy II Philadelphus, commissioned seventy-two Jewish scholars to translate the Hebrew Bible into Greek so that it could be included in the Library of Alexandria. In a later version of the same legend narrated by Philo of Alexandria, the translators were kept in separate chambers, yet they all produced identical versions of the text.

Sol: The Latin word for "sun," *Sol* is the Sun god, similar to the Greek *Helios* and later equated with Apollo or the Roman Mithras. The feast of *Sol Invictus*, "Invincible Sun," was celebrated on December 25, and Constantine established the same day for the celebration of the birth of Jesus.

Sibylline Books: The collection of prophecies from a number of different Sibyls or prophetic women. According to legend, the last king of Rome bought the books from the Cumean Sibyl. Two collections of these Jewish, Christian, and pagan prophecies survive from antiquity.

Synagogue: From the Greek *sunagoga*, "meeting place," this term describes the meeting place of Jews in the diaspora who could no longer worship at the Temple in Jerusalem. There was no sacrifice; instead, worship consisted of the reading and teaching of the Torah, prayers, and sermons.

Torah: Also called the "Law," the Torah refers to the Pentateuch or the first five books of the Old Testament—Genesis, Exodus, Leviticus, Numbers, Deuteronomy—that contain the teachings of Moses.

Vatican: The modern residence of the Pope, on Vatican Hill (*Mons Vaticanus*) in Rome, the location of Nero's circus in the early Christian period.

Primary Texts in English Translation

The Acts of the Christian Martyrs. Translated by Herbert Musurillo. New York: Oxford University Press, 1972.
> Critical editions of selected early acts of Christian martyrs from Greek and Latin sources with a lengthy introduction, minimal notes, and thorough indices.

Ancient Christian Writers (ACW). New York/Mahwah, N.J., 1946–.
> A multi-volume ongoing series of translations of early Christian writers with introductions, extensive commentaries, notes, and indices, published by the Paulist Press.

Butler's Lives of the Saints. Edited by Herbert J. Thurston, S. J., and Donald Attwater. Westminster, Md.: Christian Classics, 1990. 4 vols.
> In the eighteenth century (1756–1759), Alban Butler adapted the lives of the saints to his own time based upon the *Golden Legend* of Iacobus de Voragine (below). Between 1925 and 1938, Father Herbert Thurston then recast Butler's *Lives* by editing and revising them.

Early Church Fathers. Edited by Alexander Roberts, James Donaldson, Philip Schaff, Henry Wace. Peabody, Mass.: Henrickson, 1994.
> Two multi-volume series of somewhat outdated translations combined: the first is of major early Christian texts from the beginning of the church through the Council of Nicea in 325 C.E., called the Ante-Nicene Fathers (ANF). The second is the Nicene and Post-Nicene Fathers (NPNF) series consisting of the treatises of two seminal post-Nicene theologians, writers, and churchmen—Augustine and John Chrysostom—and a second series of translations of various post-Nicene church fathers and councils. There are thirty-eight volumes with an annotated index of authors and works. The full set is available at the Christian Classics Ethereal Library at http://www.ccel.org/.

The Fathers of the Church (FOTC). Washington, D.C.: The Catholic University of America Press, 1947—.
> A more reliable and modern series of translations of the Greek and Latin early Christian writers than the Early Church Fathers (above), with introductions, commentaries, notes, bibliographies, and indices.

Iacobus de Voragine. *The Golden Legend: Readings on the Saints.* Edited by William Granger Ryan. Princeton, N.J.: Princeton University Press, 1993. 2 vols.

> A thirteenth-century work by Iacobus de Voragine of Varazze (modern) (1230–1298), a Dominican priest and Archbishop of Genoa. Originally it was called the *Readings on the Saints* (*Legenda Sanctorum*), but in time it began to be called *Golden Legend* (*Legenda Aurea*). A compilation of sources including the Greek and Latin Fathers, the work is a collection of saints' lives (traditions, legends, historical and fictive accounts) used to illustrate the Christian belief in salvation history.

Loeb Classical Library (LCL). Cambridge, Mass.: Harvard University Press, 1912–.

> A multi-volume series of Greek and Latin original texts with facing English translations representing the entire classical world—both non-Christian authors and Christian authors who used pagan literature—with introduction, explanatory notes, and bibliographies.

Maas, M. *Readings in Late Antiquity: A Sourcebook.* New York: Routledge, 2000.

> A rich collection of Greek, Latin, Syriac, Coptic, Aramaic early Christian, and late antique texts, some translated here for the first time.

The Peoples' Bible: New Revised Standard Version with the Apocrypha. Minneapolis: Fortress Press, 2008.

> A translation of the Hebrew Bible, the New Testament and Apocrypha with introductory essays highlighting the role of cultures in shaping the Bible, several fine maps, and a gallery of images.

Original Historical Sources in English Translation

Ammianus Marcellinus, *Res Gestae Libri XXXI* (*Thirty-one Books of History*). Translated by John C. Rolfe. London & Cambridge, 1950, rep. 1956–8. 3 vols. Loeb Classical Library.

> Facing Latin and English translation of Roman history from 353–378 C.E., clear, comprehensive, and with an attempt to be impartial.

Codex Theodosianus. Translated by Clyde Pharr. *The Theodosian Code and Novels and the Sirmondian Constitutions.* Princeton, N.J.: Princeton University Press, 1952.

> An English translation of the Latin texts of imperial constitutions from Constantine through the fifth century with commentary, glossary, and bibliography.

Eusebius. *The History of the Church from Christ to Constantine.* Translated by G. A. Williamson, rev. Andrew Louth. New York: Penguin, 1965.

> This seminal ecclesiastical history by Bishop Eusebius of Caesarea (260–339 C.E., bishop from 313 C.E.) includes accounts of doctrinal matters, heresy, the succession of bishops, and persecutions in ten books published in 324–325 C.E. and covering the period from the formation of the church through his own time.

Scriptores Historiae Augustae (*Writers of Augustan History*). Translated by David Magie. London and Cambridge, 1932. 2 vols. Loeb Classical Library.

> Facing Latin and English translation of the biographies of later Roman emperors and usurpers from 117–284 C.E., a mixture of fact and fiction.

Reference Works

Aune, D. E., ed. *The Westminster Dictionary of the New Testament and Early Christian Literature and Rhetoric.* Louisville, Ky.: Westminster John Knox, 2003.

> A comprehensive dictionary covering the literature, texts, authors, and themes of the New Testament and early Christian literature.

Barrington Atlas of the Greek and Roman World. Edited by Richard J. A. Talbert. Princeton, N.J.: Princeton University Press, 2000.

> A comprehensive atlas of the Greek and Roman world from 1000 B.C.E. to 650 C.E. with a CD-ROM version including introduction, bibliography, and lists of modern names and locations, and published with a two-volume directory.

Barton, S. C., ed. *The Cambridge Companion to the Gospels.* Cambridge: Cambridge University Press, 2006.

> An introduction to the history and theology of the gospels.

Bockmuehl, M. N. A., ed. *The Cambridge Companion to Jesus.* Cambridge: Cambridge University Press, 2001.

> A study of Jesus in the context of family, history, Judaism, Christian theology, and doctrine, concluding with a discussion of the future of the study of Jesus Christ.

Bowden, J. ed. *Encyclopedia of Christianity.* New York: Oxford University Press, 2005.

> A comprehensive, single-volume encyclopedia of Christianity in history throughout the world.

The Cambridge Ancient History. Cambridge: Cambridge University Press. *Vol. 11: The High Empire, AD 70–AD 192.* 2nd ed. Edited by Alan K. Bowman, Peter Garnsey, Dominic Rathbone (2000); *Vol. 12: The Crisis of Empire, AD 193–337.* 2nd ed. Edited by Alan Bowman, Averil Cameron, Peter Garnsey (2005); *Vol. 13: The Late Empire, AD 337–AD 425.* Edited by Averil Cameron, Peter Garnsey (1997).

> A scholarly, thorough reference work with text, maps, illustrations, and bibliographies covering the ancient world through 650 C.E.

Cameron, Averil. *The Later Roman Empire: AD 284–430.* Cambridge, Mass.: Harvard University Press, 1993.

> An introductory survey of the late third through early fifth centuries with ample documents, maps, literary sources, English translations, and secondary literature.

Dunn, J. D. G., ed. *The Cambridge Companion to St. Paul.* Cambridge: Cambridge University Press, 2003.

> An overview and assessment of the life, missions, literature, and theology of the apostle Paul.

The Early Christian World. Edited by Philip F. Esler. 2 vols. New York: Routledge, 2000.

> The broad social, cultural, political context of Christianity from 30 to 430 C.E. Many of these articles use a social-scientific methodology to highlight the cultural dimensions of the topics.

Encyclopedia of Early Christianity. Edited by Everett Ferguson. 2nd ed. New York and London: Garland, 1997.

> Concise, accurate summaries and bibliographies on early Christianity through the seventh century.

Encyclopedia of the Early Church. Edited by Angelo Di Berardino and translated by Adrian Walford. 2 vols. New York: Oxford University Press, 1992.

> Archaeological, philosophical, linguistic, theological, historical, and geographical cross-section of Christian traditions and authors through the eighth century with bibliographic amendments by W. H. C. Frend.

Green, Peter. *From Alexander to Actium: The Historical Evolution of the Hellenistic Age.* Berkeley/Los Angeles: University of California Press, 1990.

> A long account of political events from 336–331 B.C.E. against the political, literary, and cultural background of the Near East as it clashed and/or melded with the Mediterranean basin.

Gruen, Eric. *The Hellenistic World and the Coming of Rome.* Berkeley: University of California Press, 1984.

> A study of the melding of Greek and Roman culture in the period of Jesus' birth and ministry from the view that the cultures mutually affected each other in extraordinary ways.

Janz, D. R., ed. *A People's History of Christianity.* 7 vols. Minneapolis: Fortress Press, 2005–2008.

> A series that spans Christian origins (vol. 1) through twentieth-century Christianity (vol. 7), focusing upon the piety, faith, and religious practices of "ordinary Christians."

Millar, Fergus. *The Roman Near East: 31 BC–AD 337.* Cambridge, Mass.: Harvard University Press, 1993.

> A comprehensive study of particular nations and societies (including Judaism and Christianity) in the melting pot of the Near East under Roman rule with literary and archaeological documentation.

Mitchell, M. M. and F. M. Young. *The Cambridge History of Christianity*. 9 vols. Cambridge: Cambridge University Press, 2005–2009.

A complete chronological account of the theological, social, political, regional, global development of Christianity.

Mitchell, S.A. *History of the Later Roman Empire AD 284–641: The Transformation of the Ancient World*. Malden, Mass.: Blackwell, 2007.

A historical survey of the politics, institutions, and military history of the later Roman Empire beginning with the accession of Diocletian.

The Oxford Dictionary of the Christian Church. 3rd ed. Edited by F.L. Cross and E. A. Livingstone. New York: Oxford University Press, 1997.

A concise and handy dictionary of the Christian church from the apostolic through the modern periods.

Quasten, Johannes. *Patrology*. 4 vols. Westminster, Md.: Christian Classics, Inc., 1986.

A comprehensive guide to Christian authors and texts in their political and social context from the beginning of patristic literature to the mid-fifth century.

Stern, M. *Greek and Latin Authors on Jews and Judaism*. Jerusalem: The Israel Academy of Sciences and Humanities, 1984.

A three-volume collection of references to Jews in classical literature with a translation and commentary. *Vol. 1: Herodotus to Plutarch; Vol. 2: Tacitus to Simplicius; Vol. 3: Appendixes, Indices, Addenda and Corrigenda to Volume 2.*

Young, F. M., L. Ayers and A. Louth. *The Cambridge History of Early Christian Literature*. Cambridge: Cambridge University Press, 2004.

A systematic account of the Greek, Latin, and Syriac Christian literature with essays on their social, cultural and doctrinal contexts.

General Bibliography on Early Christianity

Brown, Peter. *The Rise of Western Christendom: Triumph and Diversity, 200–1000 AD*. 2nd ed. Oxford: Blackwell, 2003.

A rich and complex but highly readable overview of the early Christian church as it spread and evolved; illuminated by fascinating and often unexpected details.

Chadwick, Henry. *The Church in Ancient Society: From Galilee to Gregory the Great*. New York: Oxford University Press, 2001.

A standard history of the doctrinal and institutional development of the early church.

Clark, Gillian. *Women in Late Antiquity: Pagan and Christian Lifestyles.* New York: Oxford University Press, 1993.

> The social, domestic, and intellectual arenas of women in the third to sixth centuries based (primarily) upon sources controlled by men.

———. *Christianity and Roman Society.* Cambridge: Cambridge University Press, 2004.

> Six chapters discuss six issues: the early history of the church; Christianity in the ancient sources; martyrdom; asceticism; Christian scripture; and post-Constantinian Christianity, with a concluding annotated bibliographic essay and bibliography.

Ehrman, Bart D. *The New Testament: A Historical Introduction to the Early Christian Writings.* 3rd ed. New York: Oxford University Press, 2004.

> A lucid and accessible introduction to the range of source materials and secondary scholarship available for students beginning a study of early Christianity.

Elsner, Jan. *Art and the Roman Viewer: The Transformation of Art from the Pagan World to Christianity.* New York: Cambridge University Press, 1995.

> A study of the transformation from naturalism toward abstraction in the period when Christianity was transforming the ancient world politically and religiously, with essays comparing sacred pagan and Christian art and useful (black and white) photos.

———. *Imperial Rome and the Christian Triumph; The Art of the Roman Empire AD 100–450.* Oxford History of Art. Oxford: Oxford University Press, 1998.

> A rich study of the effect of the spread of Christianity on the art of the empire, itself transforming and negotiating its pagan past.

Ferguson, Everett. *Backgrounds of Early Christianity.* 3rd ed. Grand Rapids, Mich.: Eerdmans, 2003.

> An overview of the primary sources for all discussions of the cultural and historical context of Christianity, with excellent bibliography.

Freeman, Charles. *A New History of Early Christianity.* New Haven: Yale University Press, 2009.

> An account of the development and spread of early Christianity in broad cultural, political, and religious perspectives with focused considerations of scripture, martyrdom, and Gnosticism.

Frend, W. H. C. *The Rise of Christianity.* Philadelphia: Fortress Press 1984.

> Just over a thousand pages, this is a thorough, scholarly, insightful, brilliantly written account of the first six centuries of Christendom by a rightfully renowned scholar of the early church. With charts, maps, and indices, it is a mini-encyclopedia, a prolegomena for all subsequent medieval and early modern history.

Garcia Martinez, F. *The Dead Sea Scrolls Translated.* Translated by Wilfred G. E. Watson. 2nd ed. Grand Rapids, Mich.: Eerdmans, 1996.

> The standard translation of these vital documents and an excellent source book for all further study.

Gamble, Harry Y. *Books and Readers in the Early Church: A History of Early Christian Texts.* New Haven: Yale University Press, 1995.

> A comprehensive account of the use of books and the extent of literacy among early Christians.

Grant, Robert M. *Augustus to Constantine: The Rise and Triumph of Christianity in the Roman World.* Louisville, Ky.: Westminster John Knox, 2004.

> A selective historical summary of scholarship with discussion of some of the controversies in the first three centuries of the church in the transformation of empire from a principate (Augustus) to a Christian dominate (Constantine).

Jefford, Clayton N. *The Apostolic Fathers: An Essential Guide.* Nashville: Abingdon, 2005.

> An introduction to the texts of the apostolic fathers as they affected the study of the New Testament and the developing doctrines and theology of the early church with discussion of their relationship to later canonical texts.

Klingshirn, William E. and Mark Vessey. *The Limits of Ancient Christianity: Essays on Late Antique Thought and Culture in Honor of R. A. Markus.* Ann Arbor, Mich.: University of Michigan Press, 1999.

> A collection of essays on topics related to early Christian self-definition in honor of R. A. Markus by specialists in the modern field of Late Antiquity.

Kraemer, Ross S. and Mary R. D'Angelo. *Women and Christian Origins.* New York: Oxford University Press, 1999.

> A focused survey of women in Jewish, early Christian, and ancient religious contexts.

Lieu, Judith M. *Christian Identity in the Jewish and Graeco-Roman World.* Oxford: Oxford University Press, 2004.

> A focused theme of identifying how "Jew" and "Christian" were used in the ancient world, and whether "Jew" refers to an ethnic group or a religion.

Logan, Alastair H. B. *The Gnostics: Identifying an Early Christian Cult.* New York: T&T Clark, 2006.

> A short and very useful discussion of the Gnostics as schismatic or sectarian, cult or sect.

Mathews, Thomas F. *The Clash of the Gods: A Reinterpretation of Early Christian Art.* Princeton, N.J.: Princeton University Press, 1993.

> Artistic images and their religious interpretations in the three centuries of change from a predominantly polytheistic to Christian religion.

Metzger, Bruce M. *The Canon of the New Testament: Its Origin, Development and Significance.* New York: Oxford University Press, 1987.

> Historical treatment of the ancient controversies and modern scholarship that shed light upon the somewhat murky process of stabilizing the canon of the New Testament

Newsome, J. D. *Greeks, Romans, and Jews.* Philadelphia: Trinity Press International, 1992.

> The blending and the antagonisms of three cultures in the period of the early church and some of the ways each contributed to its developing doctrines and rituals.

Pearson, Birger. *Ancient Gnosticism: Traditions and Literature.* Minneapolis: Fortress Press, 2007.

> An incisive study of the origin and definition of Gnosticism and its relationship to Judaism and Christianity.

Rousseau, Philip. *The Early Christian Centuries.* London: Longman, 2002.

> An historical approach to the rise of Christianity including portraits of Jesus and Paul in their social contexts.

Sordi, Marta. *The Christians and the Roman Empire.* Tr. Annabel Bedini. Norman, Ok.: University of Oklahoma Press, 1986.

> The relationship between emerging Christianity and the Greco-Roman political structure of the empire in the first three centuries of the early church which argues for a more accurate presentation of persecution and tolerance.

Wilken, Robert. *The Christians as the Romans Saw Them.* 2nd ed. New Haven, Conn.: Yale University Press, 2003.

> A depiction of how Christianity appeared to non-Christian Greek and Latin writers through close readings of select texts from the second through fourth centuries.

Further Readings by Chapter

Chapter I

Ando, Clifford (ed.), *Roman Religion.* Edinburgh: Edinburgh University Press, 2003.

Beard, Mary, John North and S. R. F. Price, *Religions of Rome* (2 vols.). Cambridge: Cambridge University Press, 1998.

Benko, Stephen. *Pagan Rome and the Early Christians.* Bloomington: Indiana University Press, 1984.

Bowes, Kim. *Private Worship, Public Values, and Religious Change in Late Antiquity.* Cambridge; New York: Cambridge University Press, 2008.

Davies, Jason P. *Rome's Religious History: Livy, Tacitus and Ammianus on Their Gods.* Cambridge: Cambridge University Press, 2004.

Fishwick, Duncan. *The Imperial Cult in the Latin West.* New York: Brill, 1987.

Gradel, Ittai. *Emperor Worship and Roman Religion.* Oxford: Oxford University Press, 2002.

Klauck, Hans-Joseph. *The Religious Context of Early Christianity: A Guide to Graeco-Roman Religions.* Tr. Brian McNeil. Minneapolis: Fortress Press, 2003.

Lampe, Peter, *From Paul to Valentinus: Christians at Rome in the First Two Centuries.* Translated by M. Steinhauser. Minneapolis: Fortress Press, 2003.

Mikalson, Jon D. *Ancient Greek Religion.* Oxford: Blackwell Publishing, 2005.

Petropolou, Maria-Zoe. *Animal Sacrifice in Ancient Greek Religion, Judaism, and Christianity, 100 BC to AD 200.* Oxford: Oxford University Press, 2008.

Rehak, Paul. *Imperium and Cosmos.* Madison: University of Wisconsin Press, 2006.

Revell, Louise. *Roman Imperialism and Local Identities.* New York: Cambridge University Press, 2009.

Rives, James B. *Religion in the Roman Empire.* Blackwell Ancient Religions, 2. Oxford: Blackwell, 2007.

Rose, Charles Brian. *Dynastic Commemoration and Imperial Portraiture in the Julio-Claudian Period.* Cambridge: Cambridge University Press, 1997.

Ross-Taylor, Lily. *The Divinity of the Roman Emperor.* Middletown: APA, 1931.

Scheid, John. *An Introduction to Roman Religion.* Edinburgh: Edinburgh University Press, 2003.

Stroumsa, Guy G. *The End of Sacrifice: Religious Transformations in Late Antiquity.* Translated by Susan Emanuel. Chicago: University of Chicago Press, 2009.

Thomassen, Einar, ed. *Canon and Canonicity: The Formation and Use of Scripture.* Copenhagen: Museum Tusculanum Press, University of Copenhagen, 2010.

Wilken, Robert L. *The Christians as the Romans Saw Them.* 2nd ed. New Haven, Conn.: Yale University Press, 2003.

Chapter 2

Avidov, Avi. *Not Reckoned among Nations: The Origins of the So-Called "Jewish Question" in Roman Antiquity.* Texts and Studies in Ancient Judaism 128. Tübingen: Mohr Siebeck, 2009.

Barclay, John M. G., ed. *Negotiating Diaspora: Jewish Strategies in the Roman Empire.* New York: T&T Clark, 2004.

Bartlett, John R., ed. *Jews in the Hellenistic and Roman Cities.* London: Routledge, 2002.

Bremmer, Jan N. *Greek Religion and Culture, the Bible, and the Ancient Near East.* Jerusalem Studies in Religion and Culture, Vol. 8. Leiden/Boston: Brill, 2008.

Collins, John J. *Between Athens and Jerusalem: Jewish Identity in the Hellenistic Diaspora.* 2nd ed. Grand Rapids, Mich.: Eerdmans, 2000.

Dunn, James D. G., ed. *Jews and Christians: The Parting of the Ways, A.D. 70–135.* Grand Rapids, Mich.: Eerdmans, 1999.

Edmondson, Jonathan C., Steve Mason, and James B. Rives, eds. *Flavius Josephus in Flavian Rome*. Oxford: Oxford University Press, 2005.

Fiensy, David A. *The Social History of Palestine in the Herodian Period*. Lewiston, Me.: Mellen, 1991.

Fine, Steven. *Jews, Christians and Polytheists in the Ancient Synagogue: Cultural Interaction during the Greco-Roman Period*. London: Routledge, 1999.

Fredriksen, Paula. *Augustine and the Jews: a Christian Defense of Jews and Judaism*. New York: Doubleday, 2008.

Gardner, Gregg, and Kevin L. Osterloh. *Antiquity in Antiquity: Jewish and Christian Pasts in the Greco-Roman World*. Texte und Studienzumantiken Judentum, 123. Tübingen: Mohr Siebeck, 2008.

Grabbe, Lester. *Judaism from Cyrus to Hadrian*. 2 vols. Minneapolis: Fortress Press, 1992.

Gruen, Eric. *Jews Amidst Greeks and Romans*. Cambridge, Mass.: Harvard University Press, 2002.

Hayes, John H., and Sara R. Mandell. *The Jewish People in Classical Antiquity from Alexander to Bar Kochba*. Louisville, Ky.: Westminster John Knox, 1998.

Hoehner, Harold W. *Herod Antipas*. Cambridge: Cambridge University Press, 1972.

Lieu, Judith, John North and Tessa Rajak. *The Jews Among Pagans and Christians*. London: Routledge, 1992.

Luijendijk, AnneMarie. *Greetings in the Lord: Early Christians and the Oxyrhynchus Papyri*. Harvard Theological Studies 60. Cambridge, Mass.: Harvard Divinity School, 2008.

Rajak, Tessa. *Jewish Dialogue with Greece and Rome: Studies in Cultural and Social Interaction*. Leiden: Brill, 2002.

Richardson, Peter. *Herod: King of the Jews and Friend of the Romans*. Columbia, S.C.: University of South Carolina Press, 1996.

Rutgers, Leonard V. *Making Myths: Jews in Early Christian Identity Formation*. Leuven: Peeters, 2009.

Schäfer, Peter. *The History of the Jews in the Greco-Roman World*. New York: Routledge, 2003.

Schürer, Emil. *A History of the Jewish People in the Age of Jesus Christ (175 B.C.–A.D.135)*. Edited by and revised by G. Vermes, F. Millar, M. Goodman, P. Vermes. 4 vols. Edinburgh: T & T Clark, 1987.

Schwartz, Daniel R. *Agrippa I: The Last King of Judaea*. Tübingen: J.C.B. Mohr, 1990.

Schwartz, Seth. *Imperialism and Jewish Society: 200 B.C.E. to 640 C.E.* Princeton: Princeton University Press, 2001.

———. *Were the Jews a Mediterranean Society? Reciprocity and Solidarity in Ancient Judaism*. Princeton, N.J.: Princeton University Press, 2009.

Seyoon, Kim. *Christ and Caesar: The Gospel and the Roman Empire in the Writings of Paul and Luke.* Grand Rapids, Mich.: Eerdmans, 2008.

Smallwood, E. M. *The Jews under Roman Rule from Pompey to Diocletian.* Leiden: Brill, 1976.

Williams, Margaret H. *The Jews among the Greeks and Romans. A Diasporan Sourcebook.* London: Duckworth, 1998.

Chapter 3

Ando, Clifford. *Imperial Ideology and Provincial Loyalty in the Roman Empire.* Berkeley: University of California Press, 2000.

Athanassiadi, P. and Michael Frede, eds. *Pagan Monotheism in Late Antiquity.* Oxford: Clarendon, 1999.

Barnes, Timothy D. *Constantine and Eusebius.* Cambridge, Mass.: Harvard University Press, 1981.

Beck, Roger. *The Religion of the Mithras Cult in the Roman Empire: Mysteries of the Unconquered Sun.* Oxford: Oxford University Press, 2006.

Burckhardt, Jacob. *The Age of Constantine the Great.* Translated by Moses Hadas. New York: Doubleday, 1956.

Clauss, Manfred. *The Roman Cult of Mithras: The God and His Mysteries.* Edinburgh: Edinburgh University Press, 2000.

Drake, H. A. *Constantine and the Bishops: The Politics of Intolerance.* Baltimore: Johns Hopkins University Press, 2000.

Drijvers, J.W. *Helena Augusta: The Mother of Constantine the Great and the Legend of her Finding of the True Cross.* Leiden: Brill, 1992.

Edwards, Mark. *Constantine and Christendom: The Oration to the Saints, The Greek and Latin Accounts of the Discovery of the Cross, The Edict of Constantine to Pope Silvester.* Liverpool: Liverpool University Press, 2003.

Eusebius. *Life of Constantine.* Translated by Averil Cameron and Stuart G. Hall. Oxford: Oxford University Press, 1999.

Hall, Linda Jones. "Cicero's *instinctu divino* and Constantine's *instinctu divinitatis*: The Evidence of the Arch of Constantine for the Senatorial View of the Vision of Constantine." *Journal of Early Christian Studies* 6.4 (1998) 647–71.

Hekster, Olivier. *Rome and Its Empire, AD 193–284: Debates and Documents in Ancient History.* Edinburgh: Edinburgh University Press, 2008.

Nabarz, Payam, and Caitlin Matthews. *The Mysteries of Mithras: The Pagan Belief that Shaped the Christian World.* Rochester, Vt.: Inner Traditions, 2005.

Lenski, Noel. *The Cambridge Companion to the Age of Constantine.* New York: Cambridge University Press, 2006.

Nixon, C. E. V., and Barbara Saylor Rodgers. *In Praise of Later Roman Emperors: The Panegyrici Latini.* Berkeley: University of California Press, 1994.

Selinger, Reinhard. *The Mid-Third Century Persecutions of Decius and Valerian.* New York: Peter Lang, 2004.

Southern, P. *The Roman Empire from Severus to Constantine.* New York: Routledge, 2001.

Twomey, Vincent, and Mark Humphries, eds. *The Great Persecution: The Proceedings of the Fifth Patristic Conference, Maynooth, 2003.* Irish Theological Quarterly Monograph Series. Dublin; Portland, Ore.: Four Courts, 2009.

Van Dam, Raymond. *The Roman Revolution of Constantine.* Cambridge: Cambridge University Press, 2007.

Watson, Alaric. *Aurelian and the Third Century.* New York: Routledge, 1999.

Chapter 4

Bowersock, G. W. *Martyrdom and Rome.* Cambridge: Cambridge University Press, 1995.

Bowes, Kim. *Private Worship, Public Values, and Religious Change in Late Antiquity.* Cambridge: Cambridge University Press, 2008.

Boyarin, Daniel. *Dying for God: Martyrdom and the Making of Christianity and Judaism.* Palo Alto: Stanford University Press, 1999.

Cain, Andrew, and Noel Lenski. *The Power of Religion in Late Antiquity.* Burlington, Vt.: Ashgate, 2010.

Clark, Gillian. *Women in Late Antiquity: Pagan and Christian Lifestyles*: Oxford University Press, 1993.

Curran, John R. *Pagan City and Christian Capital: Rome in the Fourth Century.* New York: Oxford University Press, 2000.

Denzey, Nicola. *The Bone Gatherers: The Lost Worlds of Early Christian Women.* Boston: Beacon Press, 2007.

Elsner, Jan, and Ian Rutherford, eds. *Pilgrimage in Graeco-Roman and Early Christian Antiquity: Seeing the Gods.* New York: Oxford University Press, 2008.

Grig, Lucy. *Making Martyrs in Late Antiquity.* London: Duckworth, 2004.

Harris, W. V. *The Transformations of* Urbs Roma *in Late Antiquity.* Journal of Roman Archaeology, supplementary series 33, Portsmouth, R.I.: Journal of Roman Archaeology, 1999.

Horsley, Richard A. *Paul and the Roman Imperial Order.* Harrisburg, Pa.: Trinity Press International, 2004.

Huskinson, J. M. Concordia Apostolorum: *Christian Propaganda at Rome in the Fourth and Fifth Centuries.* Oxford: BAR, 1982.

MacMullen, Ramsay. *The Second Church: Popular Christianity A.D. 200–400.* Writings from the Greco-Roman World Supplements 1. Atlanta: Society of Biblical Literature, 2009.

Markus, R. A. *The End of Ancient Christianity.* Cambridge: Cambridge University Press, 1990.

Mosshammer, Alden A. *The Easter Computus and the Origins of the Christian Era.* Oxford Early Christian Studies. Oxford/New York: Oxford University Press, 2008.

Nicolai, V. F., Fabrizio Bisconti and Danilo Mazzoleni. *The Christian Catacombs of Rome: History, Decoration, Inscriptions.* Regensburg: Schnell & Steiner, 1999.

Portella, Ivannadella. *Subterranean Rome.* Cologne: Könemann, 2000.

Rutgers, L. V. *Subterranean Rome: In Search of the Roots of Christianity in the Catacombs of the Eternal City.* Leuven: Peeters, 2000.

Salzman, Michele. *On Roman Time: The Codex Calendar of 354.* Berkeley: University of California Press, 1990.

Sampley, J. Paul, ed. *Paul in the Greco-Roman World: A Handbook.* Harrisburg, Pa.: Trinity Press International, 2003.

Schott, Jeremy M. *Christianity, Empire, and the Making of Religion in Late Antiquity.* Divinations. Philadelphia: University of Pennsylvania Press, 2008.

Scodel, Ruth, and Anja Bettenworth. *Whither* Quo vadis?:*Sienkiewicz's Novel in Film and Television.* Chichester; Malden, Mass.: Wiley-Blackwell, 2008.

Traina, Giusto. *428 AD: An Ordinary Year at the End of the Roman Empire* (1st ed. in Italian, 2007). Princeton, N.J.: Princeton University Press, 2009.

Tronzo, William. *St. Peter's in the Vatican.* Cambridge: Cambridge University Press, 2005.

Wright, N.T. *Paul: In Fresh Perspective.* Minneapolis: Fortress Press, 2009.

Chapter 5

Brown, Peter. *Authority and the Sacred: Aspects of the Christianization of the Roman World.* New York: Cambridge University Press, 1995.

Cameron, Averil. *Christianity and the Rhetoric of Empire: The Development of Christian Discourse.* Berkeley: University of California Press, 1991.

Chuvin, Pierre. *A Chronicle of the Last Pagans.* Translated by B.A. Archer. Cambridge, Mass.: Harvard University Press, 1990.

Cooper, Kate. *The Fall of the Roman Household.* Cambridge: Cambridge University Press, 2007.

Croke, Brian, and Jill D. Harries, eds. *Religious Conflict in Fourth-Century Rome.* Sydney: University of Sydney Press, 1982.

Drijvers, Jan W. and David Hunt, eds. *The Late Roman World and Its Historian: Interpreting Ammianus Marcellinus.* New York: Routledge, 1999.

Heather, Peter. *The Fall of the Roman Empire: A New History.* New York: Oxford University Press, 2005.

Hopkins, Keith. *A World Full of Gods: The Strange Triumph of Christianity.* New York: Free, 2000.

Lançon, Bertrand. *Rome in Late Antiquity*. Translated by A. Nevill. Edinburgh: Edinburgh University Press, 2000.

Lee, A. D. *Pagans and Christians in Late Antiquity: A Sourcebook*. New York: Routledge, 2000.

MacMullen, Ramsey, and Eugene N. Lane. *Paganism and Christianity 100–425 CE*. Minneapolis: Fortress, 1992.

Matthews, John. *Western Aristocracies and Imperial Court, AD 364–425*. New York: Oxford University Press, 1975, reprint 1990.

McLynn, Neil B. *Ambrose of Milan: Church and Court in a Christian Capital*. Berkeley: University of California Press, 1994.

Millar, Fergus. *A Greek Roman Empire: Power and Belief under Theodosius II (408–450)*. Berkeley: University of California Press, 2006.

Potter, D. S. *The Roman Empire at Bay, AD 180–395*. New York: Routledge, 2004.

Salzman, Michele Renee. *The Making of a Christian Aristocracy: Social and Religious Change in the Western Roman Empire*. Cambridge, Mass.: Harvard University Press, 2002.

Sogno, Cristiana. *Q. Aurelius Symmachus: A Political Biography*. Ann Arbor, Mich.: University of Michigan Press, 2006.

Tougher, Shaun. *Julian the Apostate*. Debates and Documents in Ancient History Series. Edinburgh: Edinburgh University Press, 2007.

Ward-Perkins, Brian. *The Fall of Rome and the End of Civilization*. Oxford, 2005.

Williams, Stephen and J. G. P. Friell. *Theodosius: The Empire at Bay*. New Haven, Conn.: Yale University Press, 1994.

Further Readings by Chapter Topics

Greco-Roman Religions as Background for Christianity

Davies, Jason P. *Rome's Religious History: Livy, Tacitus and Ammianus on Their Gods*. Cambridge: Cambridge University Press, 2004.

> A scholarly discussion on the theme of religion in historiography on the premise that whatever else it was to the ancients, religion (if practiced correctly) was a means of ensuring a good outcome in human affairs.

Gradel, Ittai. *Emperor Worship and Roman Religion*. Oxford: Oxford University Press, 2002.

> An important book for understanding the development of the imperial cult as religion and politics, with implications for the study of Roman religion and culture more generally.

Klauck, Hans-Joseph. *The Religious Context of Early Christianity: A Guide to Graeco-Roman Religions*. Translated by Brian McNeil. Minneapolis: Fortress Press, 2003.

> A reference tool for the study of Greek and Roman religions (not Judaism), including mystery cults, emperor worship, miracles, magic, et al. from primary texts with a bibliography of secondary sources.

Mikalson, Jon D. *Ancient Greek Religion.* Oxford: Blackwell, 2005.

> A comprehensive introductory study of Greek worship through archaeological remains and literary studies including myths and elements of domestic, communal, and state worship.

Judaism as Background for Christianity

Grabbe, L. *Judaism from Cyrus to Hadrian.* 2 vols. Minneapolis: Fortress Press, 1992.

> A basic textbook of historic events and personalities in Jewish history.

Hayes, John H., and Sara R. Mandell. *The Jewish People in Classical Antiquity from Alexander to Bar Kochba.* Louisville, Ky.: Westminster John Knox, 1998.

> A readable and useful compendium of important events in Jewish history from 333 B.C.E. to 135 C.E., the Second Jewish War.

Hengel, Martin. *Acts and the History of Earliest Christianity.* Translated by John Bowden. Philadelphia: Fortress Press, 1979.

> Nuanced study of the complicated reactions of early Christians to Jewish Law and a good account of the differences between Paul and Peter on the one hand and the more traditional Jewish Christians on the other.

Rajak, Tessa. *Jewish Dialogue with Greece and Rome: Studies in Cultural and Social Interaction.* Leiden: Brill, 2002.

> A collection of essays on Judaism spanning the Second Temple to the late antique periods with a concentration upon encounters with Hellenism and Roman authority.

Schäfer, P. *The History of the Jews in the Greco-Roman World.* New York: Routledge, 2003.

> An investigation of the political, religious, social, and economic conditions of Hellenized Palestine under Roman rule and the tensions those cultural exchanges engendered.

Schürer, E. *A History of the Jewish People in the Age of Jesus Christ (175 B.C.–A.D.135).* Edited by and revised by G. Vermes, F. Millar, M. Goodman, P. Vermes. 4 vols. Edinburgh: T & T Clark, 1987.

> Generally considered the most important scholarly historical text on Judaism, Jesus and Christianity, and Jewish literature.

Smallwood, E. M. *The Jews under Roman Rule from Pompey to Diocletian.* Leiden: Brill, 1976.

> A focused study of Jewish-Roman relations with good source materials including laws concerning the Jews and their (im-)practical applications.

Williams, Margaret H. *The Jews among the Greeks and Romans. A Diasporan Sourcebook.* London: Duckworth, 1998.

> A wide range of sources for Jewish history on stone, papyrus, literature, and law all translated into English and collected in a single volume.

The Herods

Hoehner, Harold W. *Herod Antipas.* Cambridge: Cambridge University Press, 1972.

> A detailed discussion of Herod Antipas as he appears in the gospels with some (at times) unreliable historical and theological background.

Richardson, Peter. *Herod: King of the Jews and Friend of the Romans.* Columbia, S.C.: University of South Carolina Press, 1996.

> An analysis of the presentations of Herod in Josephus with no discussion of the discrepancies, which amounts to fictionalized history rather than history. Still, useful for understanding some of the conflicting accounts and complexities of the political and cultural drama of this period in Jewish and Roman history.

Schwartz, Daniel R. *Agrippa I: The Last King of Judaea.* Tübingen: J.C.B. Mohr, 1990.

> A scholarly analysis of the sources (especially Josephus as historiographer) and the importance of Agrippa's persecution of the Jewish Christians in Jerusalem at a pivotal point in the development of the *new* religion.

Diocletian and Constantine

Athanassiadi, P., and Michael Frede, eds. *Pagan Monotheism in Late Antiquity.* Oxford: Oxford University Press, 1999.

> A collection of studies reviewing the concept of monotheism apart from Judaism and Christianity, from the Greek archaic period through the fifth century C.E.

Barnes, T. D. *Constantine and Eusebius.* Cambridge, Mass.: Harvard University Press, reprint, 2006.

> The standard most comprehensive account of the reigns of Diocletian and Constantine including a full analysis of Eusebius's writing.

Beck, Roger. *The Religion of the Mithras Cult in the Roman Empire: Mysteries of the Unconquered Sun.* Oxford: Oxford University Press, 2006.

> A detailed study of the archaeological evidence to propose, among other things, an astrological and astronomical interpretation of the symbols surrounding the Mithras cult.

Burckhardt, Jacob. *The Age of Constantine the Great.* Translated by Moses Hadas. New York: Doubleday, 1956.

> A classic, well-written, subjective interpretation of the life, times, and motivations of Constantine by the famed Swiss historian.

Drake, H. A. *In Praise of Constantine: A Historical Study and New Translation of Eusebius's Tricennial Orations.* Berkeley: University of California Press, 1976.

> A translation of the orations connected with the thirtieth jubilee of Constantine in 335–336 C.E. as a reflection of his religious policy.

Edwards, Mark. *Constantine and Christendom: The Oration to the Saints, The Greek and Latin Accounts of the Discovery of the Cross, The Edict of Constantine to Pope Silvester.* Liverpool: Liverpool University Press, 2003.

> Translations of three Constantinian texts: the first is his own oration delivered on Good Friday in Serdica, April 12, 317 C.E., and the others spurious legends of the cross and the Donation of Constantine.

Eusebius. *Life of Constantine.* Translated by Averil Cameron and Stuart G. Hall. Oxford: Oxford University Press, 1999.

> Most important source for Constantine's reign and his support of Christianity, written just after his death by Eusebius, who was over zealous in his promotion of Christianity.

Frend, W. H. C. *Martyrdom and Persecution in the Early Church: A Study of a Conflict from the Maccabees to Donatus.* Oxford: Blackwell, 1965.

> A vast and wide-ranging study of Christian conflicts with the state beginning with the Maccabean revolution and continuing through the Donatist controversy in North Africa as subtext for the division between the eastern and western churches and the development of martyrdom as a means to personal salvation.

Lenski, Noel. *The Cambridge Companion to the Age of Constantine.* New York: Cambridge University Press, 2006.

> A comprehensive one-volume survey of Constantine and his times, scholarly and accessible, with excellent illustrations.

Nixon, C. E. V., and Barbara Saylor Rodgers. *In Praise of Later Roman Emperors: The Panegyrici Latini.* Berkeley: University of California Press, 1994.

> A translation of, and historical commentary on, the twelve Latin panegyrics of anonymous Gallic orators. Of particular interest are those on Constantine since they allow us to trace his public religious "conversion."

Christians and Pagans

Brown, P. *The Making of Late Antiquity.* The 1976 Carl Newell Jackson Lectures. Cambridge, Mass.: Harvard University Press, 1978.

> A short but piercingly insightful discussion of the profound changes in Roman society in the second through fourth centuries.

———. *The World of Late Antiquity: AD 150–750.* 2nd ed. New York: W.W. Norton, 1989.

> A good overview of late antiquity with emphasis upon the cultural and religious changes that anticipate, accompany, and may be considered consequences of, the fall of Rome.

Chandlery, P. J. *Pilgrim-Walks in Rome: A Guide to its Holy Places.* 3rd ed. London: Manresa Press, 1908.

> An old but still informative account of early Christian archaeological remains and the fourth-century marketing of shrines, relics, and the papacy.

Chuvin, P. *A Chronicle of the Last Pagans*. Translated by B. A. Archer. Cambridge, Mass.: Harvard University Press, 1990.
> A positive view of pagans and paganism from Diocletian to Justinian organized around the edicts restricting pagan religious practices.

Croke, Brian, and Jill D. Harries, eds. *Religious Conflict in Fourth-Century Rome*. Sydney: University of Sydney Press, 1982.
> A sourcebook for documents concerned with the fourth-century conflict between Christianity and paganism in Rome with a good index and bibliography.

Curran, John R. *Pagan City and Christian Capital: Rome in the Fourth Century*. New York: Oxford University Press, 2000.
> Ostensibly about the effect of Christianity on the topography and society of Rome in the fourth century, this book also offers keen observations on the buzz words of late antique scholarship: paganism, conversion, Christianity, and religion.

Huskinson, J. M. *Concordia Apostolorum: Christian Propaganda at Rome in the Fourth and Fifth Centuries*. Oxford: BAR, 1982.
> A study of the iconography of the apostles Peter and Paul especially the embrace (*concordia Apostolorum*) that indicates their joint rule in Rome and confirms the apostolic succession and Rome's primacy. Filled with interesting arguments and studies of a wide variety of visual representations.

Lee, A. D. *Pagans and Christians in Late Antiquity: A Sourcebook*. New York: Routledge, 2000.
> An excellent collection of sources for Christianity in the late antique period as well as other religions, e.g., Zoroastrianism.

MacMullen, R., and E. N. Lane. *Paganism and Christianity 100–425 CE*. Minneapolis: Fortress Press, 1992.
> A sourcebook for ancient texts that shed light upon the experience and attitudes of Christians and varied aspects of paganism in the early centuries of Christianity.

MacCormack, S. *Art and Ceremony in Late Antiquity*. Berkeley: University of California Press, 1981.
> A study of particular ceremonies as they pertain to the role of the emperor as divine monarch in the struggle between paganism and Christianity.

Matthews, John. *Western Aristocracies and Imperial Court, AD 364–425*. New York: Oxford University Press, 1975, reprint 1990.
> Excellent discussion of the history of the period with astute observations on political motivations and interactions between western aristocracies and imperial (east and west) courts from Valentinian I to Valentinian III.

McLynn, Neil B. *Ambrose of Milan: Church and Court in a Christian Capital.* Berkeley: University of California Press, 1994.

> A fresh consideration of the confrontations between ecclesiastical and imperial power when Ambrose was Bishop in Milan (374–397 C.E.), the center of the Western imperial court.

Mitchell, Stephen. *A History of the Later Roman Empire, AD 284–641: The Transformation of the Ancient World.* Malden, Mass.: Blackwell, 2007.

> An excellent bibliography by geographic regions of the entire late antique world.

Salzman, M. *On Roman Time: The Codex Calendar of 354.* Berkeley: University of California Press, 1990.

> A complete study of the *Codex Calendar of 354* and its implications for the transformation of Rome from pagan capital to Christian capital emphasizing the essential appropriation of sacred time.

Sogno, Cristiana. *Q. Aurelius Symmachus: A Political Biography.* Ann Arbor, Mich.: University of Michigan Press, 2006.

> A close study of the writings and political career of the Roman pagan senator Symmachus, which demonstrates the importance of politics over religion in the transformation of Rome from pagan imperial to Christian capital.

Williams, Stephen, and J. G. P. Friell. *Theodosius: The Empire at Bay.* New Haven, Conn.: Yale University Press, 1994.

> The military achievements of Theodosius against the background of church history, and his role in repressing paganism and promoting orthodoxy.

Websites
Early Christian Art
http://www.angelfire.com/art2/roberto/giotto.htm

> A fine collection of images with commentary on major art works and painting cycles *From Greece to Giotto.* Especially relevant are the discussions of the sarcophagus of Junius Bassus, the mosaics, and fresco cycles in early Christian churches in Rome.

Early Christian Catacombs
http://dlibrary.acu.edu.au/research/theology/ejournal/Issue2/Damien_Casey.htm

> Called *Fractio Panis, Breaking Bread,* this site includes a wide collection of images from Roman catacombs with interesting commentary on, for example, the ministry of women in the early church.

Constantine's "Conversion"
http://www.wga.hu/frames-e.html?/html/p/piero/francesc/index.html

> The complete cycle of Piero della Francesca's paintings in Arezzo that illustrate the life of Jesus and the dream of Constantine and his victory over Maxentius at the Milvian Bridge.

Roman Art and Architecture

http://www.romeartlover.it/Romeartlover.html

> Excellent site for Roman art and architecture with eighteenth-century drawings, maps, and a comprehensive list of Roman churches built before 1800.

Churches of Rome

http://penelope.uchicago.edu/Thayer/E/Roman/Texts/secondary/journals/AJA/10/3/Roman_
Church_Mosaics*.html

> An exhaustive list of early church mosaics of the first nine centuries with black and white photos to illustrate that the mosaics followed traditional subjects and placement in the churches. Latin inscriptions where they occur are included.

http://www.initaly.com/regions/latium/church/church.htm

> Articles and photographs of the churches of Rome reproduced from the Rome-based monthly magazine called *Inside the Vatican*.

http://en.wikipedia.org/wiki/Churches_of_Rome

> Comprehensive site with lists of early churches and links to all churches listed, from the fourth through the twenty-first centuries.

The Cathedral at Orvieto

http://www.bluffton.edu/~sullivanm/italy/orvieto/cathedral/duomo.html

> An exquisite example of Old and New Testament stories interwoven in mosaics and sculptures on the façade of this medieval cathedral.

Christianity: General

http://www.religionfacts.com/christianity/index.htm

> An entire history of Christianity with links to articles and discussions of major doctrines, texts, and practices.

http://biblia.com/jesusart/

> More than 300 images of various depictions of Jesus through centuries of church development with biblical quotations accompanying many illustrations.

A

Acts of Peter, 59, 60, 68, 69, 119, 131

Agnes, patron saint of Rome, 121–40

Alexander the Great, 1, 4, 8, 145

Alhambra decree, 180

altar of Victory, 29, 114, 123, 142–73

Ambrose (Aurelius Ambrosius), *Agnes beatae virginis*, 123, 124, 125, 126

    Bishop of Milan, 114, 123, 151

    Council of Constantinople, 156

    De fide, 152

    De officiis ministrorum, 123

    De viriginibus ad Marcellinam sororem, 122–23, 125

    Epistulae 17 and 18, 143, 156, 159, 161

    Epistulae 40 and 41, 167

    incident in Callinicum, 167

    massacre at Thessalonica, 67, 168–69

    Saint Agnes, 122–39

Ammianus Marcellinus, 108, 172

    Res gestae, 141

Anglican Church/Church of England, 181, 183

Antipater (Herod's father), 9, 38, 40

    and Julius Caesar, 10, 38

    Herod's son, 43

Apostles, 50, 65, 69

Apostolic Council in Jerusalem, 12, 59, 115

Arcadius (Flavius Arcadius), emperor, 77, 114, 154

Arch of Constantine, 99, 102, 103, 104

Arianism, 108, 109, 110, 123, 149–50, 151, 176

Arius, priest in Alexandria, 32, 110, 149, 151, 176

Athanasius, Bishop of Alexandria, 150, 151

Augustus. *See* Octavian

Aurelian (Lucius Domitius Aurelianus), emperor, 24, 74, 75, 77, 78, 80, 82, 84, 102, 105

Ausonius, Decimus Magnus, 142, 146–48

    consul, 148

    Mosella, 147

B

Basilica of the Apostles at the Catacombs, 119

Basilica of the Apostles on the Appian Way, 119, 120

Basilica of Sant' Agnese, 122, 126, 137

Basilica of San Clemente, 7

Basilica of San Giovanni in Laterano, 75, 96

Basilica of San Paolo fuori le Mura, 102, 109, 119

Basilica of San Pietro, 60, 96, 109, 119, 180

Basilica of San Lorenzo in Lucina, 108

Basilica of San Sebastiano, 119

Basilica of Sant' Ambrogio, 123

Basilica of Santa Croce in Gerusalemme, 105

Basilica of Santa Maria del Populo, 12

Basilica of Santa Maria in Trastevere, 108

Basilica of Santa Maria Maggiore, 113

Basilica of Santa Maria Novella, 47

Basilica of Maxentius and Constantine, 76

Basilica of Santa Pudenziana, 116, 117

Basilica of Santa Sofia, 105

Battle of Actium, 1, 4, 10, 39, 41

Battle of Hadrianople, 148